W9-ADO-649

The **Little Big Book** Series

CLOSING THE COMMUNICATION GAP

AN EFFECTIVE METHOD FOR ACHIEVING DESIRED RESULTS

The **LITTLE BIG BOOK** Series

The **Little Big Book** Series

CLOSING THE COMMUNICATION GAP

AN EFFECTIVE METHOD FOR ACHIEVING DESIRED RESULTS

H. James Harrington • Robert Lewis

CRC Press
Taylor & Francis Group
Boca Raton   London   New York

CRC Press is an imprint of the
Taylor & Francis Group, an **informa** business

A PRODUCTIVITY PRESS BOOK

CRC Press
Taylor & Francis Group
6000 Broken Sound Parkway NW, Suite 300
Boca Raton, FL 33487-2742

© 2014 by Taylor & Francis Group, LLC
CRC Press is an imprint of Taylor & Francis Group, an Informa business

No claim to original U.S. Government works

Printed on acid-free paper
Version Date: 20130729

International Standard Book Number-13: 978-1-4665-7488-5 (Paperback)

Library of Congress Cataloging-in-Publication Data

Harrington, H. J. (H. James)
    Closing the communication gap : an effective method for achieving desired results/ H. James Harrington, Robert Lewis.
        pages cm. -- (The little big book series)
    Includes bibliographical references and index.
    ISBN 978-1-4665-7488-5 (pbk.)
    1. Communicative competence. 2. Interpersonal communication. 3. Communication. I. Lewis, Robert, 1949- II. Title.

P37.5.C64.H37 2014
302.2--dc23   2013018310

Visit the Taylor & Francis Web site at
http://www.taylorandfrancis.com

and the CRC Press Web site at
http://www.crcpress.com

Dedication

I dedicate this book to my son James S. Harrington, who has made me very proud of what he is been able to accomplish professionally and even more proud of his personal characteristics. He has developed into a loving, caring, thoughtful individual who has helped me to get through some very difficult times, and he has provided me with a granddaughter who brings the sunshine into my life.

I also dedicate this book to Candy Rogers, my longtime business associate and dedicated friend. Without her help over the years, I would have been able to accomplish only a small part of what I actually have accomplished. She stood in the shadows as I received many recognition awards, most of which I would not been able to receive without her help. No man stands alone—it is the people who walk down the path alongside him that make the difference.

H. James Harrington

I dedicate this book to my wife, Debbie Lewis, and to our children, Rob, Kim, and Tiffany. They taught me the importance of communication.

Robert D. Lewis

Contents

Preface

Improving communication in business means higher profits. Improving communication in our personal lives means happier, longer, and more prosperous years. Improving communication in government means shorter lines, less paperwork, and happier citizens. Improving communication in church or in school means bigger offerings and higher grades. Improving communication in the healthcare industry means quicker recoveries, fewer lawsuits, and happier nurses and patients. Communication is important.

Communication seems easy, but it is not. Communication takes years to learn, yet when learned, must always be improved. Communication happens in so many different ways. It can be spoken, pantomimed, written, sung, or drawn. And, it can be done well or poorly using any of these methods.

Some of the topics covered in this book are how to listen, how to use social media in marketing, basic tips about public speaking, and dealing with difficult people. Topics of interest to people in the workplace also include how to talk to your employees, how to talk to your boss, and how to talk to a corporation. Both the formal and the informal communication systems of an organization are defined and discussed.

This book is designed as a comprehensive overview of the many dimensions to communication available in the early twenty-first century. It can be read by an individual for personal growth, or it can be used by a company to teach employees the importance of quality communication. A quality assurance department can use it to assist in lowering errors and waste in the workplace. Those involved in postsecondary education can use it as a communication textbook or supplemental textbook on the 101 level. However it is used, we trust that it will help improve communication by closing the communication gap: the gap between what the communicator means and what the listener actually understands.

Here's to quality communication.

To communicate well is a challenge. When it's done well, it's a joy.

H. James Harrington

About the Authors

H. JAMES HARRINGTON

In the book, *Tech Trending* (Amy Zuckerman, Capstone, 2001), **Dr. H. James Harrington** was cited as "the quintessential tech trender." The *New York Times* referred to him as having a "knack for synthesis and an open mind about packaging his knowledge and experience in new ways—characteristics that may matter more as prerequisites for new-economy success than technical wizardry." The author Tom Peters stated, "I fervently hope that Harrington's readers will not only benefit from the thoroughness of his effort but will also 'smell' the fundamental nature of the challenge for change that he mounts." William Clinton, past president of the United States, appointed Dr. Harrington to serve as an ambassador of goodwill. It has been said about him, "He writes the books that other consultants use."

Harrington Institute was featured on a half-hour TV program, *Heartbeat of America*, which focuses on outstanding small businesses that make America strong. The host William Shatner stated, "You [Dr. Harrington] manage an entrepreneurial company that moves America forward. You are obviously successful."

Dr. Harrington now serves as the chief executive officer for the Harrington Institute. He also serves as the chairman of the board for a number of businesses. Dr. Harrington is recognized as a world leader in applying performance improvement methodologies to business processes. He has an excellent record of coming into an organization, working as its chief executive officer (CEO) or chief operating officer (COO), resulting in a major improvement in its financial and quality performance.

In February 2002, Dr. Harrington retired as the COO of Systemcorp A.L.G., the leading supplier of knowledge management and project management software solutions when Systemcorp was purchased by IBM. Prior to that, he had served as a principal and one of the leaders in the Process Innovation Group at Ernst & Young; he retired from Ernst & Young when the company was purchased by Cap Gemini. Dr. Harrington had initially joined Ernst & Young when it purchased Harrington, Hurd & Rieker, a consulting firm that Dr. Harrington started. Before that, Dr. Harrington was with IBM for more than 40 years as a senior engineer and project manager.

Dr. Harrington is past chairman and past president of the prestigious International Academy for Quality (IAQ) and of the American Society for Quality Control (ASQC). He is also an active member of the Global Knowledge Economics Council.

H. James Harrington was elected to the honorary level of the IAQ, the highest level of recognition in the quality profession. He is a government-registered quality engineer, an ASQC-Certified Quality and Reliability Engineer, and a Permanent Certified Professional Manager by the Institute of Certified Professional Managers. He is also a certified Master Six Sigma Black Belt and has achieved the title of Six Sigma Grand Master. H. James Harrington has an MBA and PhD in engineering management and a BS in electrical engineering.

Dr. Harrington's contributions to performance improvement around the world have brought him many honors. He was appointed the honorary advisor to the China Quality Control Association and was elected to the Singapore Productivity Hall of Fame in 1990. He has been named lifetime honorary president of the Asia-Pacific Quality Control Organization and honorary director of the Association Chilean de Control de Calidad. In 2006, he accepted the honorary chairman position of Quality Technology Park of Iran.

Dr. Harrington has been elected a Fellow of the British Quality Control Organization and the American Society for Quality Control. In 2008, he was elected to be an Honorary Fellow of the Iran Quality Association and Azerbaijan Quality Association. He was also elected an honorary member of the quality societies in Taiwan, Argentina, Brazil, Colombia, and Singapore. He is also listed in the *Who's Who Worldwide* and *Men of Distinction Worldwide*. He has presented hundreds of papers on performance improvement and organizational management structure at the local, state, national, and international levels.

- The Harrington/Ishikawa Medal, presented yearly by the Asian Pacific Quality Organization (APQO), was named after H. James Harrington to recognize his many contributions to the region.
- The Harrington/Neron Medal was named after H. James Harrington in 1997 for his many contributions to the quality movement in Canada.
- Harrington Best TQM Thesis Award was established in 2004 and named after H. James Harrington by the European Universities Network and e-TQM College.
- The Harrington Chair in Performance Excellence was established in 2005 at the Sudan University.
- The Harrington Excellence Medal was established in 2007 to recognize an individual who uses the quality tools in a superior manner.
- The H. James Harrington Scholarship was established in 2011 by the American Society for Quality (ASQ) Inspection Division.

H. James Harrington has received many awards, among them the Benjamin L. Lubelsky Award, the John Delbert Award, the Administrative Applications Division Silver Anniversary Award, and the Inspection Division Gold Medal Award. In 1996, he received the Lancaster Award of the American Society of Quality Control in recognition of his international activities. In 2001, he received the Magnolia Award in recognition for the many contributions he has made in improving quality in China. In 2002, H. James Harrington was selected by the European Literati Club to receive a lifetime achievement award at the Literati Award for Excellence ceremony in London. The award was given to honor his excellent literature contributions to the advancement of quality and organizational performance. Also in 2002, H. James Harrington was awarded the International Academy of Quality President's Award in recognition for outstanding global leadership in quality and competitiveness and contributions to IAQ as Nominations Committee chair, vice president, and chairman.

In 2003, H. James Harrington received the Edwards Medal from the ASQ. The Edwards Medal is presented to the individual who has demonstrated the most outstanding leadership in the application of modern quality control methods, especially through the organization and administration of such work. In 2004, he received the Distinguished Service Award, which is ASQ's highest award for service granted by the society. In 2008, Dr. Harrington was awarded the Sheikh Khalifa Excellence Award (UAE) in recognition of his superior performance as an original quality and excellence guru who helped shape modern quality thinking. In 2009, Dr. Harrington was selected as the Professional of the Year (2009). Also in 2009, he received the Hamdan Bin Mohammed e-University Medal. In 2010, the Asian Pacific Quality Organization awarded Dr. Harrington the APQO President's Award for his "exemplary leadership." The Australian Organization of Quality NSW's board recognized him as the "Global Leader in Performance Improvement Initiatives" in 2010.

In 2011, he was honored to receive the Shanghai Magnolia Special Contributions Award from the Shanghai Association for Quality in recognition of his 25 years of contributing to the advancement of quality in China. This was the first time that this award was given. In 2012, Dr. Harrington received the ASQ Ishikawa Medal for his many contributions in promoting the understanding of process improvement and employee involvement on the human aspects of quality at the local, national, and international levels. Also in 2012, he was awarded the Jack Grayson Award. This award recognizes individuals who have demonstrated outstanding leadership in the application of quality philosophy, methods and tools in education, healthcare, public service, and not-for-profit organizations. Harrington also received the A. C. Rosander Award in 2012. This is ASQ Service Quality Division's highest honor. It is given in recognition of outstanding long-term service and leadership resulting in substantial progress toward the fulfillment of the division's programs and goals. In addition, in 2012 Dr. Harrington was honored by the APQO by being awarded the Armand V. Feigenbaum Lifetime Achievement Medal. This award is given annually to an individual whose relentless pursuit of performance improvement over a minimum of 25 years has distinguished himself or herself with work in promoting the use of quality methodologies and principles within and outside the organization of which he or she is part.

Dr. Harrington is a prolific author, publishing hundreds of technical reports and magazine articles. For the past 8 years, he has published a monthly column in *Quality Digest Magazine* and is syndicated in five other publications. He has authored 37 books and 10 software packages. His e-mail address is hjh@harrington-institute.com.

ROBERT D. LEWIS

Robert D. Lewis (Bob) spent his early years in the civic and religious nonprofit world, where the importance of communication carried an enhanced role. It was there that his study and practice of communication took on serious and academic dimensions. One of his most helpful experiences in communication training was with Dr. John S. Savage, the founder and president of L.E.A.D. Consultants, Incorporated, for 25 years, and currently a senior consultant/trainer for the Kilgore Group. Lewis spent 200 hours in workshops with Dr. Savage and his associates studying listening skills, such as story listening, body language, and neurolinguistic programming theory and techniques. As an ordained minister, Lewis learned the importance of listening, the power of a question, and the importance of effective public speaking.

Currently, Lewis serves on two nonprofit boards of directors and is a trainer, consultant, and financial coach for the APM Foundation for Financial Education (http://www.theAPMfoundation.org). He also serves as a consultant and the director of financial services for Continuous Improvement Ministries (CIM) of Roseville, California (http://www.ciministries.net). He is the vice president for mission support development for Marketplace Missions, Incorporated (MPM), of Auburn, California (http://www.marketplacemissions.net), and volunteers his time to help with the children's home Sonshine Hacienda (http://www.sonshinehacienda.org), operated by MPM in Mexico.

Lewis has served as the senior pastor for three different churches and as the associate director of evangelism for the California Southern Baptist

Convention. He retired from the position of executive director of the Sacramento Association of Southern Baptist Churches in 2006.

In addition, Lewis has directed regional training schools and seminars and has served on boards from credit unions to private organizations. Lewis also served Golden Gate Seminary, Mill Valley, California, as a part-time adjunct professor of supervised ministry and served on the committee that reviewed doctor of ministry candidates' project proposals, project dissertation/reports, and orals. Other teaching experience includes work as an adjunct professor for the Degree Completion Program at William Jessup University, Rocklin, California.

In 1998, Lewis joined the Performance Improvement Network, doing consulting with Dr. H. James Harrington and Dr. Kenneth Lomax. He continues to do contract work with these men.

Lewis holds an AA from Missouri Baptist College, Hannibal-LaGrange Campus, in Hannibal; a BA degree from Oklahoma Baptist University in Shawnee; and the master of divinity and doctor of ministry degrees from Golden Gate Baptist Theological Seminary in Mill Valley, California. His e-mail address is boblewis.california@gmail.com.

Acknowledgment

We want to acknowledge Candy Rogers, who has dedicated many hours of her time to editing and formatting the book into final product format. We could not have done it without her dedication, help, and encouragement.

In addition, we would like to acknowledge all of the help and insight we have received from the professionals who we have come in contact with over the years. This book contains the accumulated knowledge and experience that we have had over the past 50 years. We thank those individuals who have taken the time to stop and share their thoughts and refine our thinking. The concepts that we discuss throughout this book are not the brainchild of just the two authors. This book is the result of all the information and personal experiences we have encountered in this long pass through life.

1

Good Talk, More Money

Our ability to communicate has made mankind the dominant force on the earth.

—H. James Harrington

If a corporation were a person, communication would be the bloodstream.

—Lee Iacocca, former CEO of Chrysler Corporation

INTRODUCTION

What does good talk have to do with making money? Everything. And good talk also affects every relationship in life for the better. Good talk is foundational to success, and that includes business success, government success, not-for-profit organization success, as well as family success. It also affects personal friendships. An ancient proverb says, "A word fitly spoken is like apples of gold in settings of silver." The American author, Mark Twain, said: "The difference between the right word and the almost right word is the difference between lightning and a lightning bug."

By *good talk* we mean the much broader, inclusive term *total quality communication*. By *communication*, we mean an exchange of information and ideas between two parties. It can be exchanged verbally, nonverbally through body language or signage, or by written and electronic means.

By *not-for-profit success*, we mean raising more funds and accomplishing the mission more effectively and efficiently. We mean happier volunteers and more volunteers. We mean getting the message out to more people and having better strategic alliances with other not-for-profit groups.

By *family success*, we mean staying together and providing a healthy environment for personal growth and development. We mean the producers of income for the family getting better-paying jobs or selling more goods or services. We think about the children getting more out of their education and extracurricular activities.

By *government success*, we mean better relationships with the citizens of the country being governed. We mean openness and honesty and increased sharing of information between the various departments and agencies of the government. And, we certainly mean more honesty and transparency to the citizens and to other governments. This kind of communication would increase the wealth, strength, and popularity of a government by helping it become more efficient, effective, and adaptable. The workers of the government would also become happier and more productive.

By *business success*, we mean increased profits, but we do not mean just the profits of your company; we also mean your personal success and profit, whether you are an employee, a business associate, or a C-level manager (meaning a top corporation executive who has a title starting with the word *chief*, like chief executive officer [CEO], chief information officer, chief financial officer, etc.). After all, a business represents money to people, yet it definitely represents more than money for people. It can be a channel to express one's talent and giftedness, a way to provide for one's family, or a tool to create one's identity in society. It is clear, however, that if the business is not profitable, it cannot stay. It has to go. This book argues that improvement in the communication channels of a business can provide more profit for the business and explains why and how. One of the most powerful results for a business experiencing total quality communication is the emergence of a pool of high-performance individuals.

To us, it seems a no brainer that a business, government, or a not-for-profit organization should possess good internal and external communication skills. To us, it seems vital to be skilled and accurate when talking in house to one another in a business enterprise when the parties share a common mission and are working toward common goals. It seems equally as vital to be able to communicate in a clear manner with the marketplace, with strategic partners, and with the community in which the business is located.

Here are a few reasons poor-quality communication should be eliminated:

- Poor-quality communication causes mistakes, which result in having to do over again the work that has already been done (called *rework*) and in waste (wasted employee time that the company paid for, wasted materials used in the first effort, and all the side effects from these things).
- Poor quality communication causes bad feelings, which result in poor morale and more poor-quality communication.
- Bad morale and unhappy work conditions can lead to illness, absenteeism, and high turnover rates.
- The lack of a common, well-understood objective for the organization results in disjointed work effort that is not focused on the organization's real objectives.

The results of poor-quality communication are not pleasant. Nevertheless, businesses must study them to understand the universal critical success factor in business: total quality communication.

Quality communication holds the enterprise together like glue. It connects the business to the customer. It can make employees love and respect one another or hate one another. It can endear the CEO to the business and board or frustrate them with his or her very presence. And, its root word gives a clue to the reasons for these facts. The root word of communication is *common,* from which we derive the word *commune.* To have true communion, a group must respect, trust, and in the best-case scenario, care for one another. People must have virtue and be trustworthy people who keep their word. Good people make good communication, and good people commune with one another in a lasting way.

Jim Collins's best-selling book, *Good to Great,*[1] teaches about companies that have gone beyond the level of being a good to becoming a great enterprise. The leaders of these great companies possessed and modeled the virtues of which we speak. These leaders were not noted for being spellbinding orators. Their lives, over time, said so much more than words that when they spoke, it gave greater power to their words. They produced in their company, over time, an environment of greatness. People respect and trust one another in such an environment. They become a team rather than a group of individuals. Quality communication exists in this kind of setting.

Quality communication is more than well-written e-mails and clear and accurate reports. These may be a result of total quality communication, yet we mean more than this kind of technical expertise when we speak of quality communication. When all the aspects of a company's communication converge into an integrated system that continually improves, we are experiencing quality communication.

A world-renowned psychologist, Abraham Maslow,[2] who wrote about the hierarchy of needs and self-actualization, said, "Secrecy, censorship, dishonesty, and blocking of communications threatens all the basic needs" p. 25. If maladjusted and suboptimal individuals, whose lives are not worthwhile, run the company, how excellent can the company become? And, if a company environment prevents self-actualization, how can it produce high-performance individuals? Maslow's research and study shows that an environment that has poor-quality communication cannot produce high-performance individuals. How does poor-quality communication manifest itself? Let us look at a few major categories of poor-quality communication that rob an organization of any kind of its "bottom line."

POOR-QUALITY COMMUNICATION

Poor-quality communication adversely affects the bottom line. Do you remember the Paul Simon song, "Fifty Ways to Leave Your Lover"? Well, there must be at least that many ways to cut a company's profits through poor-quality communication.

Four basic categories of poor-quality communication are discussed in this chapter:

- Miscommunication,
- Noncommunication,
- Misunderstanding, and
- Withholding information.

These categories are familiar to most people, yet taking time to look at them anew will focus on the everyday look and feel of poor-quality communication.

Miscommunication

The word *miscommunicate* means a person *fails* to adequately, say, write or signal the information to the intended target. Simply put, miscommunication is like a bad throw in baseball. And like a bad throw can cost the baseball team a run, or even the game, miscommunication can result in honest mistakes that cost money to fix.

Any thoughtful and observant employee or organizational leader has recognized the destructiveness created in an organization by miscommunication. When a person receives information in a business and takes action based on that information, resources are used. Human resources are used. Material resources are used. Time and work-hours are used on the assembly line, in the kitchen, or on the shop floor.

Miscommunicating can strain relationships and cause competition that will undermine morale and lower production. Take Fred, a manager of a popular, well-located grocery store:

> Fred's store was low on his inventory of organic fruit juices. Two conventions were booked for the weekend at the hotel down the street. One convention was the Healthful Living Symposium, and the other was a convention of vegans. Fred remembered the Healthful Living Symposium from last year. Attendees had bought all his organic fruit juices the first morning they were there, and he spent the rest of the weekend apologizing. He sent a fax to his supplier and ordered 12 dozen bottles of assorted organic fruit juices. The supplier's truck arrived on Thursday afternoon and unloaded the order. The driver wheeled in 1 case with 12 bottles. When the driver handed Fred the clipboard to sign, Fred was aghast. He stammered and finally asked, "Where are the other cases? I ordered a gross!" The driver revealed the second page on the clipboard with Fred's fax. In Fred's rush, he forgot to write the word *dozen* after the number *12*. Fred spent the weekend apologizing again, and it cost his grocery store a cruise-winning month of sales. An improved order process could prevent this miscommunication issue in the future.

Noncommunication

Noncommunication means the failure to share information with others. In the business setting, it could be the lack of awareness that information has value to other departments, so it is not shared. Often, employees and management fail to see the connection between information that they possess and its pertinence and value to the other departments and offices in the company. A business is a system in which each part is connected. Each part is a contributing part of the whole. Because a business is a holistic system, "what happens in Vegas doesn't stay in Vegas," to borrow a famous television ad line. In business, everyone on the team needs to know what is happening in order to cooperate and make value-added decisions.

Businesses have mechanisms and formal channels for sharing certain information. These channels and mechanisms do not include all types of information. In this case, the business would have to revamp its structure to include more types of information sharing to solve the problem of noncommunication.

> John was a line manager, and Timothy was his supervisor. Recently, top management had become concerned about the inefficiency on John's line. It was the bottleneck slowing production of the whole plant, and the chart showed special cause. The company CEO had personally put pressure on Timothy to fix it—now.
>
> Timothy conducted interviews. He interviewed John and several of the employees. He observed the line in action. Soon, he found the problem. Carol was not only making a lot of mistakes but also was talking too much and distracting the other employees. He decided that she had to be fired. He called John and told him to take care of Carol. A week later, Carol was still on the job. The supervisor stepped in and fired Carol and demoted John. John's plans to move up the ladder in his company were permanently thwarted. Timothy had not communicated well to John. John thought that "take care of Carol" had meant to give her training and help her improve, not fire her. Besides, no one had told John about his line being the focus of upper management. He was aware of the problem Carol was causing and had a plan to deal with it. Carol had a skill no one else had on his line, so she was valuable, yet she had just lost a child in a tragic accident and was not able to focus on work the way she normally did. John also did not understand the pressure that was being placed on his supervisor, Timothy, by top management. A well-educated and good manager was lost to the company, as was a good employee. This happened because of an issue with a type of poor-quality communication known as *noncommunication*.

Misunderstanding

Misunderstanding means neither to read nor to hear correctly that which was said or written. Staying with our sports analogy, it is like not catching a pass in football. Misunderstanding can happen for a number of reasons. Several types of human error could cause it to occur. It could be the malfunction of a telephone. It could be an inner ear issue. It could be the handsome, single man in cubicle 18 walking by and winking at you. Or, it could be that your brain interprets key words of the message to mean something different from what the speaker's brain takes them to mean.

Misunderstanding and *miscommunication* have a linked, technical meaning in the theory of communication. Words, according to this theory of communication, are encoded thoughts. We cannot read the mind or thoughts of another person, so the thoughts of that person have to be put into *words*. The speaker sends the message in words. The hearer must decode the words into his or her thoughts. The word *gap* is used as a technical word in the study of human communication. It means the gap between what the speakers (senders of information) *mean* by their words and what the hearers (receivers of information) *understand* the speakers to be saying with their words. The greater the level of error and misunderstanding in communication, the larger the communication gap will be.

If a customer has ordered 500 loaves of wheat bread and the bakery produces 500 loaves of rye bread, you do not have to be Ben Bernanke to know that a lot of loaves of rye bread are likely going to be donated to the local homeless shelter. The bakery owner is going to be in a bad mood. The people who wrote up the order will be on the hot seat, so they will put the blame on the poor reading ability of the baker. The baker will blame the poor writing ability of the salespeople. The customer will have a big surprise when he receives the bakery goods and opens up the 500 loaves of rye bread. And, the bakery's profits will suffer. Employee morale and relationships will suffer. You can substitute the *bread* in this illustration for cloud storage space, telephones, high school textbooks, automobiles, church hymnals, smartphones, or any kind of product that is produced or used by a business or nonprofit organization. Somewhere between the 500 loaves of wheat bread and the making of 500 loaves of rye bread, misunderstanding took place.

Withholding Information

Withholding information can limit an employee's or a first-line manager's capacity to make the right decisions and can lower trust in the organization. Why would information be withheld? Most managers and team leaders do not realize that their information is valuable to others in the company. Some people do it to control others around them. They dole out information as they think those under them, or over them, need to know. Others actually want to sabotage a fellow employee that threatens them.

That is exactly what happened to Sandra, who was sent to Japan by her division vice president (VP). Her VP was threatened by Sandra and a little worried about being passed up by her in the hierarchy. Yet, she was the one with the expertise in the specialized product line that had brought the call from Japan.

Sandra was excited by the fact that her company was invited by this particular large Japanese corporation to come to Japan to bid on a contract for a multimillion-dollar project. Sandra knew that her company was one of three being considered. This would be the big break her young company needed, not to mention a big commission for her and a feather in her cap with the CEO. Everything seemed to be going exceptionally well. On the last day, Sandra was feeling confident. She found herself alone with the top decision maker for the first time and saw it as a window of opportunity. She began to use her skills as the best closer at her company to wrap up this deal before the other two companies could beat her to it. She, at one point, had the contract on the table and had offered her pen to the Japanese executive so he could sign it. She was met with icy resistance. Another company got the contract.

When Sandra contacted the sales representative from the competitor to ask how she got the contract, an amazing thing was discovered. The competing sales representative never talked about the deal the whole weekend. She never asked for the business. She basically sat quietly and talked about the beautiful decorations or some other topic totally unrelated to the issue at hand. That is when Sandra first learned the term *cross-cultural communication*, and that is also when her manager smiled to himself.

Withholding information sometimes is related to not understanding how the smallest details can affect someone in the company in ways unknown to the possessor of the information. Deliberately sabotaging another employee relates totally to our human condition with its insecurities and individual moral values. Whatever the motive or reason, training and awareness will lower the incident rate of withholding information and increase good decision making and trust.

One of the biggest problems we have today in many organizations is a cultural shift from a knowledge-hoarding culture to a knowledge-sharing culture. Today, in most organizations people are promoted and receive increased remuneration based on the knowledge they have compared to other individuals in the group. Our measure of an individual's worth is based on the knowledge the individual has accumulated compared to other people in the organization. In reality, the most valuable people are the ones who readily share their knowledge with their coworkers so that the organization can make maximum use of this information. The measure of an individual's worth should not be based on the knowledge the individual has but on the knowledge the individual shares. The heavy emphasis in the progressive organizations today on knowledge management systems is driven by this needed change from a knowledge-hoarding environment to a knowledge-sharing environment.

QUALITY COMMUNICATION

The ability to communicate is everything.

—Lee Iacocca, former CEO of Chrysler Corporation

What is quality communication? It is the antithesis of poor-quality communication. It is the opposite of miscommunication, of noncommunication, of misunderstanding, and of withholding or deleting information. Quality communication is a near-perfect transfer of information and meaning from one person to another.

Why is quality communication important? It is important because it changes the culture of an organization to be conducive to high-performance individuals and high-performance teams. It creates an environment that is capable of high-quality output and lower waste. If ever there was a time in history when quality communication was scientifically understood and an operational imperative, we have arrived at that time.

In the last two decades of the twentieth century, we saw incredible historical, political, economic, and technological changes that have continued into the twenty-first century. All this has had an impact on communication in business. In the old days, employee communication was relegated to a person with a camera covering company picnics and softball tournaments. The purpose was to use the company newsletter to bolster employee morale. Currently, communication in a company serves to align employee objectives and organizational goals.

In the future, however, communication will be understood as the basic force in creating organizational reality. Without language, the world of culture could not exist. *Meaning* would not exist without human language according to some academics who study communication. Current academic studies point to the conclusion that communication creates culture. Cultures are a natural result of human interaction and communication. Communication creates cultures, and high-quality communication transforms existing cultures for the better.

COMMUNICATION AND LANGUAGE

Communication and language are the seedbed of organizational formation. Communication is bigger than good grammar or an occasional employee meeting. It encompasses the very nature and structure of the organization. It is the seedbed of organizational life. It influences and creates the personality and culture of the organization. Language and communication are that powerful. For people to truly communicate means they share life in common, and that changes people and businesses. If communication creates the climate of an organization, then changing the existing communication system could change a toxic climate that holds people back into a healthy, open climate that allows the talents of people to flourish. This allows teams and individuals to function at a very high level because they have an environment that encourages community and sharing.

How many companies have employed you over your lifetime? Did they all have the same customs, written laws, unwritten laws, ceremonies, practices, and hero stories? No, they did not. Every company has a unique culture. While every corporate culture is unique, each of these different, unique cultures is able to produce the required ingredient conducive to high-performance teams. And, even though the same ingredient is necessary in all cultures for high-performance teams to flourish, this ingredient removes the harmful features of that culture while enhancing the unique cultural distinctions of each organization. It does not eliminate the good things. After all, you know the key ingredient for high-performance teams: an environment of quality communication.

Your company may have a friendly culture yet not have a place that is safe for sharing candid feelings and views. A setting like this would not be one of quality communication. In most corporate cultures, saying that you cannot see any clothes on the emperor, in contradiction of official statements to the contrary, will get you demoted, left behind, or fired. These cultures would ensure that any high-performance team brought into existence would be dead on arrival. Providing quality communication in a business or a nonprofit organization will eliminate this effect.

High-performance teams are no longer luxuries in the global marketplace. A global corporation has no choice but to provide an environment of high-quality communication. To do this, the barriers to communication must be addressed as a whole and not as a part. That is to say, quality communication must be understood from a systems perspective. When this takes place, the correct strategy can be devised for producing high-performance teams, which means higher profits for the company and the shareholders.

Systems theory teaches that it is difficult to change a system. Therefore, it would be difficult to change a corporate environment from one that is anathema to high-performance teams into one that fosters them. Yet, systems theory also postulates that a seemingly small change in the right place yields big results for the whole corporate system. Changing the communication of a corporate system to one of quality would be the place to start to change corporate culture and therefore the whole corporate system. Changing the communication of a company might seem like an unimportant thing to a CEO and the company's employees. It might seem like a little thing. Yet, this "little leverage point" will yield fantastic results that will be conducive to high-performance teams.

The International Association of Business Communicators conducted a poll that revealed the following as the top five barriers to effective organizational internal communication:[3]

- Excluding communication in the organization's strategy plan
- Avoiding frank discussions of hard issues
- Distrust of employees' managers
- The belief that hording information brings pain
- A simplistic and narrow view of communication

The other way of saying this is that a company or nonprofit organization should proactively create a culture of contribution, input, and involvement as opposed to a culture of separation and fear. A culture of contribution, input, and involvement means that self-interests and personal missions of the employees are acknowledged and allowed to operate at the point they intersect the mission of the company. The employee's personal mission and the company's corporate mission would help move one another along in this preferred culture.

James R. Fisher, Jr., makes the following suggestions to a company that wishes to develop a culture of openness and contribution:[4]

- Revitalize workers to be students and to learn from what they do.
- See that management practices what it preaches so that workers will preach what it practices.
- Treat workers with respect and as first customers.

- Manage conflict and confrontation rather than sweeping them under the rug.
- Be consistent with the message, fair in its regulation, and firm in its variances with the norm.
- Treat workers as owners and they will not behave as renters.
- Pay attention to skill deficits and implement appropriate training; then, workers will feel useful rather than used.
- Do not allow gender, race, religion, or politics to distract the focus from the mission.
- Make workers part of the problem so they will own the solution.
- Do not judge worker motivation by assuming preconceived biases.
- Encourage workers to be performers, not personalities—to take pride in making a difference, not to be obsessed with making an impression.

QUALITY RELATIONSHIPS

Quality communication cannot take place unless quality relationships are developed. Some may be saying, "Here comes the touchy-feely stuff again. We don't need that unrealistic stuff. All we need to do is get to work and do what we know how to do." Let me try to help you reframe the message of this book. What this book is addressing and what you are concerned about are not different things but the same. Hard data from interviews and case studies verify that corporate pain and toxic organizations exist. These terms describe the results of poor-quality relationships in a business setting. Having these things within your employees and managers prevents you getting the work done.

Why does an environment become toxic? In our experiences, it is usually because of one of two reasons. One is that management does not care about the human side of their employees. This leads to bad corporate design, bad personnel policies, and unfriendly facilities that fail to take the human side into account. Another is because of the lack of virtue on the part of the people working within the corporate structure. When a group of people lack skills to relate kindly to other people, respecting the humanity of others, and forgiving the shortcomings, the ingredients for a toxic corporate culture exist. Other influences exist that also spill into the workplace, but these two are the major things over which the company has some control. In other words, the relationships between the people in a company have to be of the highest quality to make possible the highest quality of communication. The relationship of the boss to the employees must be one of servanthood and stewardship. The relationship of the employees to one another must be based in human kindness and love. Without these basic virtues, high-quality work cannot be attained and maintained.

This topic is of strategic importance to your business and should be recognized for your company to enjoy a high level of success. The fantastic rate of change in the life of workers—with layoffs, restructuring, mergers and acquisition, and currently the global economic downturn—has brought to your business a permanent climate of stress and *dis*-ease. If you mistake this for touchy-feely stuff or warm fuzzies, you will miss the cry for help from your business organization. A good start to a good relationship between management and employees would be for management to acknowledge stress and take it into account.

Here is an interesting fact to back up this line of thought. In addition to the data from the business community, a body of common knowledge exists. Medical research has demonstrated the physical and psychological effects of stress on a person. Just remembering for 5 minutes a stressful event that took place at work lowers the body's immune system for the next 5 hours. We already knew it could make us sick to our stomachs. Your employees—and you—really are getting sick more often because of the stress at work, and that affects your bottom line. Work can make one sick. Lowering the stress at work in the areas over which we have control will go a long way to you "getting the work done" and improving communication and profits.

Poor-quality communication, which is another way of saying poor-quality relationships, causes corporate pain. Corporate pain is a technical term that describes emotional pain in the lives of the individuals working within the same business group relationship. The pain always exists in the individual, group, and overall system unless it is dealt with specifically, directly, and openly. This pain within the corporate body is linked throughout the organization by a web of relationships, both social and organizational. The pain that comes from poor relationships between the corporation and its employees and managers, as well as between the employees themselves, makes the organization less adaptable, less effective, and less efficient. It becomes more entrenched in the status quo. To change this, quality relationships of every kind must be developed for communication in the larger, more complete, sense of the term dealing with human relationships.

Think of your corporation as a person. If your company were a person, how would you describe its personality? If your employees were in a safe environment and would honestly tell you, wouldn't you like to know how they would answer that question? Much would be revealed about how much corporate pain and how much individual pain were in your system by those answers. Just like a real person, your corporation has only so much capacity for unresolved emotional pain. Like a person, unless the emotional pain is handled, it leads to health disorders and mental disorders.

How much energy does your business have to carry out its mission? The maximum amount of energy a healthy corporation can expend on carrying out its mission is about 80%. That would leave about 20% of the corporate energy in a healthy corporation to do the back-office work of the organization with an energy reserve for emergencies.

If a corporation carries unresolved emotional pain, and that corporation is pretending this pain does not exist, it takes energy to keep a lid on this emotional pain. Where does the energy come from to keep the emotional pain in check? It comes from the only place available: the energy that is used to carry out the mission of the corporation. How is this tied to communication? People who are hurting (and the last time I checked, employees and managers were people) need to talk it out and obtain resolution—or at least be heard fairly. This simple, although scary, step eliminates the emotional pain. This act of talking to an interested and relevant person relieves the pressure like the valve on a pressure cooker releases steam and prevents an explosion of the pressure cooker. If honest communication is not allowed, it is stuffed. When it cannot be held anymore, it manifests itself in illness or in crazy behavior—like "going postal."

It is so interesting to listen to the words academics and consultants use to describe the results of poor-quality communication in an organization. Words like *dysfunctional* and *toxic* are used. Unless someone in the organization steps up to the plate and deals with the emotional pain and misunderstandings in the organization, the organization moves into bureaucracy and toward death. Little work is done. No one gets paid.

Actually, someone spends a lot of time dealing with the corporate pain. These people are often in management and are usually very productive themselves. They can produce enough in half the time to keep the organization happy. They use the rest of the time to be a counselor, priest, diplomat, and translator. Sometimes, a company uses the human resources department when the situation becomes impossible for the manager to handle. This position of counselor and referee does not appear on the organizational chart, has no written position description, and receives no remuneration. It only costs the organization money indirectly.

In addition to this person, a company also pays medical doctors, hospitals, and mental health professionals. These are the people your employees see more of than normal when they must work in a company that has poor-quality communication or, more bluntly, a toxic environment. This also costs the company money.

What do the part-time counselors in your company do to keep the organization going? According to Peter Frost and Sandra Robinson,[5] toxic handlers, as they call them, do five things to reduce corporate pain:

- Toxic handlers listen caringly
- Toxic handlers talk it out with upset people
- Toxic handlers head off problems before they happen
- Toxic handlers keep confidences and are trustworthy
- Toxic handlers edit angry memos into less inflammatory language

When a company proactively provides the environment in which good relationships can grow, this lowers the costs to the company and increases the profits. Training in communication for employees and management is a key component of this type of environment that lowers the possibility of toxicity.

VIRTUES, INTEGRITY, AND TRUST

Quality relationships require virtues and a friendly environment of integrity and trust. Business is relationships. Business has relationships between manufacturer and suppliers; between CEO and board of directors; between managers and employees; between corporation and community; between corporation and governments; and between the sales force and the customers. Then, we could talk about all the relationships between divisions and departments. Next, there are employee-to-employee relationships. The list goes on and on and on. What if all these relationships were built on integrity and trust? What a powerful workplace and company that would be.

It seems that in a business setting, a decision maker more easily justifies violating universal human virtues by distancing himself or herself from the act of making the decision. The term *business decision* is used as a sterile term that tricks the conscience into distancing the decision maker from his or her own personal ethics in making the business decision. Many business decisions are devoid of virtue for this reason. Many acts of hatefulness, duplicity, greed, and falsehoods have been condoned by the statement, "This is business."

Business ethics boil down to the ethics of the people who make the decisions. If we would think of business decisions as being made by those who conduct business rather than the idea that the impersonal business itself makes the decision, then it might be easier to see the relevance of virtue in business. If the people who run the business are bad, it is unlikely that the business can be good. If the employees steal from the employer and each other, how can the business prosper over the long term? What does stealing from an employer say about the virtue of the thief?

What does this discussion of virtue have to do with communication? Quality communication is based on human relationships. Human relationships are based on *communion* or finding common ground. Language is the key in developing relationships, and relationships can only exist in an environment of virtue, where integrity and trust are a way of life. One does not share information or material goods with another thought to be a thief or robber. One does not have communion with another whose aim is to harm and take advantage. One does not share critical information with a manager who will fire him for being a bearer of bad news.

Virtue is a term that describes a quality of human relationship. Quality relationships are not possible in a setting devoid of virtue. Integrity and trust must be practiced on every level and in every situation. When this is done, people, countries, and businesses prosper. In a historical sense, the United States of America exemplified for many years the results possible if a group of people had a critical mass of virtue and practiced integrity and trust. How did the United States become the richest nation? Many other nations have had the natural resources and a workforce that matched what the United States has had. Why not one of them? Could the moral values of the United States have contributed to its prosperity? Could it be that, for years, a man's word was his bond, and that people on the whole helped one another succeed? People paid off their debts. Enough people and institutions possessed a practical virtue that produced relationships of integrity and trust that creation of enormous wealth that lifted the style of living of the whole population was possible. Just read the original writings of the founding fathers. Read the original writings of Abraham Lincoln. Look at the early motion picture industry and the classic movies and what values they reflected. Now that those virtues are disappearing in the United States, we are saying for the first time that our children and grandchildren will be worse off than we are.

Improving communication in a company is more than improving grammar or putting together a more effective PowerPoint presentation. It goes to the character of the company. The character of an organization is reflected in the action and communications of everyone from the board room to the boiler room. Quality communication, by definition, will change the culture of the organization.

LIFELONG LEARNING

Lifelong learning is required in growing relationships as well as in companies that are efficient, effective, and adaptable. Lifelong learning has always been the way of excellence. In history, persons who were dedicated to lifelong learning contributed much to the world. They themselves are known and studied today. Leonardo da Vinci and Benjamin Franklin are among the most famous. In the fast-paced world today, with knowledge reportedly doubling every 5 years, one has to study continuously to stay current with the marketplace. And, we do live in a fast-paced world. A state-of-the-art product in the marketplace has a short life span. Knowledge is increasing at a rapid pace.

Learning throughout one's life is no longer an option. It is a requirement. What is a lifelong learner? A natural lifelong learner is a curious person. This person enjoys learning about areas in which they are interested as well as areas that they deem important yet are not naturally drawn toward. Other lifelong learners are not so curious and need to kick themselves in the seat of the pants to get moving. Some lifelong learners prefer a more structured and traditional approach, attending community colleges or community lectures. Others prefer a less-structured approach and learn as they experience life by talking to others who have mastered areas of knowledge. They like to go and see someone who knows what they want to know, watch them apply the knowledge, and then ask questions and maybe try it themselves. Whatever your method of learning, keeping up with the flood of knowledge in our world is part of survival in a highly developed society. An individual with a BS degree is obsolete within 5 years if he/she does not continue to stay current with the day-to-day developments in his/her field.

It should be obvious, then, that companies—or for that matter, an officer, manager, or employee of a company—cannot remain relevant or useful unless they continually learn. To stay abreast of current advances in technology and best practices, a company must offer incentives to employees to continually learn and upgrade skills and knowledge. Companies must provide time for employees to do this learning. Companies cannot survive unless they are lifelong learners, and that means they must continually train the people who make up the corporate family.

Lifelong learning is necessary for growing relationships. We each have an area of expertise. The fact that we are in one area of knowledge can block us from meaningful relationships with those in other areas of knowledge. It can cause us to fail to understand—even to misunderstand—why one department or group responds to us the way it does. Increased knowledge of the other areas opens doors of communication and a more effective, efficient, and adaptable work environment. If an employee studies only within his or her respective field of knowledge, he or she becomes an expert in one area. However, if an employee also studies other fields of knowledge, he or she becomes a better communicator who happens to be an expert in a certain field. The same principal applies to companies.

This power of learning and knowledge to open relationships also extends to relationships with other companies. Learning and staying relevant can allow us to recognize when certain companies would make good partners for a strategic alliance. Not being a learning organization—learning from our own experience and exploration as well as studying others—leads to bureaucracy or extinction.

Is your company efficient, effective, and adaptable? If it is not involved in lifelong learning, then it is not. Lifelong learning is necessary to stay in business in a world that is learning as fast as ours is learning. This is true in regard to two aspects:

- Knowing what the new normal is in our field
- Developing the willingness and motivation to change as an organization

First, learning involves knowing the new normal. Department managers and C-level management must keep up with the world and what is happening. If a line manager is learning and keeping up and sees the changes that need to be made and his up-line support does not see it, his life is one of stress and despair. He cannot change anything. The up-line management must lead the charge in learning. When significant change takes place in the world of technology, politics, or public opinion, a company must be ahead of the curve to stay in business.

Second, learning is a factor in a company's ability to be nimble. Learning changes people and makes people desire change. It does the same for companies. When we understand something, it no longer threatens or scares us. We also become valuable to the company to help the company make the change. Also, as a company we become more valuable to the marketplace and continue making profits as well as become an example of how to make the change.

When a subgroup in a company is involved in lifelong learning and the balance of the company is not, it will cause conflict. Once we learn, we become discontent with not living at the level of our learning. Marriage counselors know this. If one mate gets more and more education and the other does not, it increases the chance of divorce.

Lifelong learning is not optional for the twenty-first century. The better we get at lifelong learning as employees, management, and a company, the better communicators we will become—and that means more *money*.

SUMMARY

The hidden factor in business success involves the improvement of communication in a company. Communication as a process is overlooked because it is so much a part of our everyday lives. We think it is easy even though it is difficult. Because of this thinking, we are plagued with poor-quality communication. Poor-quality communication costs businesses money. Therefore, if business communication is improved, it is like money in the bank.

The four types of poor-quality communication are (1) miscommunication; (2) noncommunication; (3) misunderstanding; and (4) withholding information. By identifying the processes of communication in a company and tracking them, they can be studied and improved. The instances of miscommunication, noncommunication, misunderstanding, and withholding information can be lowered significantly. The bottom line will increase.

Quality communication creates the possibility for high-performance teams as well. High-performance teams improve the bottom line. Teams are powerful when the members are in communion around a shared mission. An environment of quality communication is the seedbed of organizational life, and a healthy organization is the seedbed of high-quality teams. Leaders of organizational life serve their organization when they create a climate of communication. The endeavor to create a climate of communication will force the development of quality relationships, which will lead to the emphasis on virtue, integrity, and trust. To sustain and maintain this culture, leaders, managers, and employees must become lifelong learners.

Remember the quotation by Lee Iacocca that said, "The ability to communicate is everything." He was right. Let me make Iacocca's point a different way. What if you and your employees each spoke and read different languages. Would running your business be difficult? Yes, I know you would answer that it would be a business-killing situation if that were true. Yet, even in the same language, we struggle to communicate clearly and effectively half the time. Think what your business, your government, your not-for-profit organization, or your family would profit if you could move your communication effectiveness from 50% to 75%? And, what if you could move its effectiveness to 90%? What if you could move its effectiveness to 99%? What a difference you would be making in the world and in the life of your employees. And, you would be rich. You have a clear choice. That choice is to pick up the money you are leaving on the floor of your enterprise because of poor-quality communication.

The words *companionship* and *communication* are synonyms.

—**R. D. Lewis**

REFERENCES

1. Collins, Jim (2001). *Good to Great: Why Some Companies Make the Leap ... and Others Don't*, Harper Business, New York.
2. Maslow, Abraham (1987). *Motivation and Personality*, Addison-Wesley, New York.
3. Geddie, Tom (April 1994). Leap over the barriers of internal communication, *Communication World*, 11(4): 12.
4. Fisher, James R., Jr. (July/August 1999). How a culture of contribution gives your company a grow-up call, *The Journal for Quality and Participation*, 22(4): 10.
5. Frost, Peter, and Robinson, Sandra (July/August 1999). The toxic handler: Organizational hero—and casualty, *Harvard Business Review*, 97–106.

2

What Happens When Two People Talk—At Work?

Eighty percent of the people who fail at work do so for one reason: they do not relate well to other people.

—Robert Bolton, *People Skills*

The term *close relationship* means two people have entered the zone of quality communication.

—R. D. Lewis

People skills determine a person's success in the workplace. It has been said that success in management is 15% technical skill and 85% people skills. These numbers ring true to those who are veterans in the workplace. People skills are communication skills. On a purely academic level, communication skills can be divided into two large categories: micro and macro.

Microcommunication refers to interpersonal communication theory and skills.

Macrocommunication refers to the system and processes in which microcommunication is nested.

Microcommunication is characterized by two-way communication between individuals or teams. Macrocommunication is characterized by two-way communication from an impersonal system, culture, or environment with large groups of people. Even though by definition macrocommunication is two-way communication, practically speaking, it seems like one-way communication to an individual or a small group on the microlevel.

In this chapter, we concentrate only on the microcommunication level. Specifically, we focus on the two basic microcommunication processes faced by businesspeople: the communication loop and the interorganizational communication systems and processes. What happens when two people talk—and we mean really communicate—at work? The company makes more money, of course. So, let us talk *talk*.

THE BASIC SCOOP ON THE COMMUNICATION LOOP

If you have not met, let us introduce you to the communication loop. The communication loop is a lot like an electrical circuit. If the circuit is broken, electricity does not flow. The circuit has to be complete for the lights and computer to function. Electrical circuitry illustrates the concept of communication between persons. It is not communication unless it takes place within an intact loop.

Another example would be the dependence of human and animal life on plant life and vice versa. One aspect of this dependence would relate to humans breathing the by-product of the plant world, oxygen, and the plant world breathing the by-product of the human and animal world, carbon dioxide.

A similar relationship is necessary between two communicators. When two communicators interact with the give-and-take of ideas, it makes the two communicators become one regarding the understanding of ideas. Language and the skill in using it make communication possible.

This section of the chapter introduces the details about the communication loop between two persons. It breaks down its parts and discusses factors that influence its functioning. We use the term *loop* for the idea of a completed circuit of communication. It takes a completed circuit to experience good communication.

Meet the Loop

A minimum of two people are required for communication. These two people must be motivated to share. Then, you can have some give and take. To share productively requires an environment of integrity and trust. The first person must send a message. That message must be heard and understood by a second person. Then, the second person must respond. We say that the original message must loop back to the person who initiated the message. Let us learn more about this communication loop.

Communication is the process of exchanging ideas and feelings between persons. The word *communication* comes from the root word *commune*, which means to hold in common. Synonyms of the verb *to communicate* are the verbs *to convey, to impart,* and *to reveal.* Antonyms are *to conceal, to suppress,* and *to keep back.* Communication deals both with the positive and with the negative. The positive refers to the abilities of understanding and executing efficient and effective communication. The negative refers to the need to remove barriers and blocks to positive communication.

Communication theory is relatively new. The bulk of studies and scholarly works on communication were done in the twentieth century. It was not brought together into a unified theory that was widely accepted until the end of the twentieth century. An article, "Communication Theory as a Field," by Robert T. Craig, a professor at the University of Colorado, Boulder, has been credited as the catalyst for recognizing communication theory as a field of study, that is, a branch of knowledge.

Now, certain basic truths in this field of study have been identified and widely accepted. The process of interpersonal communication involves formulating a message, encoding the message, sending the message, receiving the message, decoding the message, and giving feedback. This happens so naturally and often people believe communication is simple and easy. Of course, this is not the case. Miscommunication and misunderstanding take place more often than good communication. People experience on a daily basis the hurt emotions, time loss, and financial cost of being misunderstood. It happens at home as well as on the job. The following is an example.

> Dave walked into the office, his head down and his eyes staring at the floor. He made his way to his desk. He wasn't his usual self this morning. He usually whistled happily as he walked in the door, but not today. He usually said "Hello" to others in the office, but today he didn't make eye contact or say "Hello." Dave looked troubled.
>
> As Dave came in the room, a colleague named Gene looked up from his desk and smiled. "Good morning, Dave. Did you see our team win the championship last night?"
>
> "Nope," Dave said in a clipped, emotionless response and kept walking.
>
> "That's too bad. They were awesome," Gene said with feeling and went back to work.

A miscommunication took place in this illustration. By *miscommunication,* we mean that the message one party sent was not received or else was improperly decoded by the second party. Did you catch it? Admittedly, the miscommunication was somewhat indirect. That is because it was committed predominantly on the nonverbal level. Dave communicated non-verbally with his body language, tone of voice, change in normal behavior, and facial expressions. Gene did not notice that Dave was in emotional distress and needed a friend to notice his pain. Dave would have worked better and produced more with just 10 minutes of someone hearing him share on a personal level. Of course, this is not usually permitted, much less encouraged, in traditional business settings for the mistaken notion that it costs the company by condoning nonproductive activity. Nothing could be further from the truth regarding the example given.

An Autopsy of the Loop

Understanding and improving the microcommunication process will help in the transformation of any organization into a world-class operation. The microcommunication process can be broken down into eight broad steps:

1. **Sender:** The originator who thinks something.
2. **Encoding the message:** The sender has to translate the thought into the spoken word.
3. **Medium:** The vibrations of the spoken word are sent through the airwaves.
4. **Receiver or audience:** The listener receives the vibrations.
5. **Decoding:** The listener then has to interpret the vibrations into words that the listener interprets into meaning and stores them in his brain.
6. **Feedback:** At some point in time, the listener needs to recall these stored thoughts, to translate them into spoken words, and to provide feedback to the communicator. Feedback means sharing with the sender in the receiver's own words what he or she heard the sender say.
7. **Analysis:** The communicator compares his or her interpretation of the listener's feedback to the original thoughts to determine if it was correctly understood by the listener.
8. **Either begin a new loop or end the loop when understanding is achieved:** If it was not correctly understood by the receiver (listener),

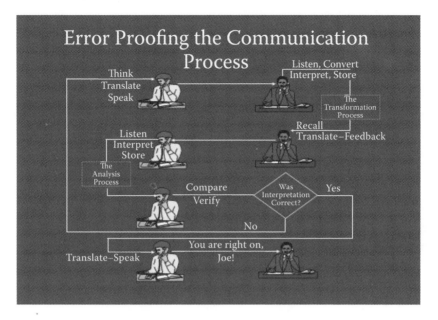

FIGURE 2.1
Error proofing the communication process.

then the cycle has to start again. If it was in agreement with the original thought, the communicator then translates this analysis into words that are sent back to the listener indicating that there is agreement.

Figure 2.1 illustrates this process. We call it error proofing the communication process.

The Loop Has Soul

Several things influence messages. The credibility of the sender is a factor. The degree of believability, trustworthiness, and authoritativeness determines the degree to which the receiver or audience listens. The mastery of material by the sender is a factor in how believable he or she is perceived to be by the receiver. Connecting with the receiver by understanding his or her concerns and by being on the communication "wavelength" is also a factor of influence determining how the message is sent and received. Even the personal style of communication can help or hinder the message. An abrasive style generally obstructs communication.

The message is always on two levels: the factual content and the emotional content. The *factual content*, what we refer to as *content*, comes in the medium of words and corresponds to the left brain's purported preference for facts and data. The *emotional content*, sometimes referred to as the *affective* content and in the vernacular referred to as *soul*, is the way the sender feels about the factual content. The soul of the message comes in the medium of nonverbal communication and corresponds to the right brain's purported preference for intuitive issues, which some now attribute to the so-called first-brain or brain stem.

Encoding the message means to put the information, ideas, and feelings into language, whether verbal, nonverbal, written, or hand signed. The medium refers to the channel through which the message is sent. Verbal communication channels include face-to-face, telephone, or video conferencing means. Written communication channels include letters, memos, reports, manuals, and technical means (facsimiles, electronic mail, the Internet).

The receiver or audience receives the message from the sender and seeks to understand it. Decoding is the process of understanding the information, ideas, and feelings of the message. Because all persons have different life experiences and different filters, perfect communication is a practical impossibility. Hence, the need arises for feedback to check for accuracy in communication and to error-proof communication. In feedback, the receiver reencodes the message in his or her own words and sends it back to the sender. The feedback loop is very important. Unfortunately, many people do not understand it. Sometimes, managers unconsciously discourage discussion and punish workers who give feedback, ask questions, and in other ways seek to gain better understanding. Managers who mistake honest questions for resistance make a big mistake and create a barrier to communication.

The Loop Has Issues

Two elements that influence messages are noise and context. Noise is a barrier to communication. It can be external noise or internal "noise" (blurred or smudged type, worried mind, or technical difficulties). One engineer at a large defense contractor told of being in a cubicle next to a group of six engineers who regularly met for telephone conference calls to other groups of engineers around the country. "They naturally would talk more loudly into the speakerphone. I finally had to ask my boss to move me so I could do my work," he told us. He was dealing with external noise.

External noise is a factor in the workplace and in communicating. Loud noises taking place in a communication zone are a barrier to communication.

Internal noise refers to a person's emotions and personal distractions that are so intense or "loud" that that the person cannot hear what he or she needs to hear in the workplace. For example, I have read research that shows that a person who goes through a divorce is of diminished value to a company for 3 years after the divorce. Does that not seem incredible? Yet, it illustrates how internal noise can hurt the bottom line of a company.

The Loop Has Culture

Context refers to the situation in which the communication takes place as well as the factors involved in the transmission of the message. The context may include the corporate environment or the broader culture of community, nation, or world. Some examples include the following:

- Being called to meet with the vice president during a merger as opposed to normal times.
- The context of a message, such as a camera crew and reporter from an investigative television news program asking you to report on how you feel about your boss versus the same question coming from your coworker in the break room.
- Giving directives to employees in a politically charged atmosphere versus doing the same in a trusting, highly motivational climate.
- One colleague telling you that you are incompetent versus the whole department of 19 coworkers telling you that you are incompetent.

Barriers to communication also exist because of the state of mind of the communicators. One that comes to mind is when a communicator experiences information overload. Cultural differences in communication styles also become barriers. Both of these barriers are increasing in frequency. Other contextual barriers are less obvious, such as the décor of a room, the style of architecture, the arrangement of the furniture, the color of the walls, and the smells in the air. These things are part of the context of communication, and they greatly influence the attitudes of people, either negatively or positively. Organizations that are aware of these things do a better job of creating a climate and environment for good communication.

THE FORMAL LOOP AND ITS SHADOW

Organizations have networks of communication much like the human body has a network of nerves that move impulses from the brain to the various body parts and back to the brain again. Because of the way the organization is designed, certain people and groups of people communicate with one another regularly and leave a record of this communication. This is called the *formal communication network* because it comes from the *form* or the *structure* of the organization. The organizational chart primarily draws a picture and a crude flowchart of this communication system.

Alongside the formal communication network is an informal communication network. This network arises because the formal network is either blocked or ineffective in providing adequate information. Informal networks move along the lines of human relationships rather than along the lines of organizational function or position.

Organizations are just collections of people and the materials with which they work. These organizations take on personality and soul. The communication systems define an organization's soul. Your company has soul. The formal structure lays the defining building blocks of a company's personality and soul. Let us take a moment to discuss the formal communication network of an organization.

Get Loopy with a Network of Communication Loops

If traditional organizational communication channels could touch all pertinent persons in the traditional organizational structure and be effective and efficient, then the communication of an organization would not need to be discussed in a book such as this one. However, the traditional communication channels are not effective or efficient, and sometimes they are redundant in some areas and missing in others. Besides these issues, there are those other informal channels of communication in an organization that are not mentioned on the organization chart or the policy manual.

As mentioned, the best picture of the formal network is the company's organizational chart (Figure 2.2). This chart draws the lines of communication. Notice how many positions have no lines of communication with other groups or positions. An organization of "functional silos" that have vertical communication within each divisional silo but no horizontal communication between divisional silos was once thought to be a workable and

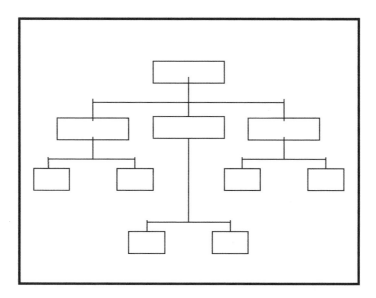

FIGURE 2.2
Organization chart.

superior organization. Now, this type of organization cannot thrive. The postmodern world changed dramatically the way that the organization operated. Technology increased the availability of information. People who once did not receive information now receive it before management. These changes are what pressures organizations to change, yet the older structures bend only so much. Corporate culture has formed around the old structure, and this strong corporate culture makes the structure even more inflexible. Even though the number of networks may be many, if they are not of adequate design for the needs of the organization in this age of such major advances in communication technology, they can make a company sick. The result is much like hardening of the arteries in the human body. And, the employees may get "loopy," that is, inexplicable, nonsensical, and zealously counterproductive. Another phrase to define *loopy* would be "unwitting agents of suboptimization."

Networks of Loops Loop in Different Directions

We need organizations. They will always be with us. In some fashion, organizational leadership must communicate with the managers and workers and vice versa. Perhaps at some future time these separate functions will be integrated. Until we reach that point, the organizational charts will continue to grow "flatter," and the three directions of internal communication will continue to be important: downward, upward, and lateral. Technology may have given us a fourth internal direction or non-direction: random.

Random Communication

A good illustration of random communication took place in the summer of 1998. A Carnival Cruise Lines ship caught fire off the coast of Florida. Several people were injured, and the ship had to be towed back to port. As passengers were disembarking the media interviewed a couple. They said they were in their cabin and heard about the fire when they saw a live picture of a burning cruise ship on CNN. It took them a few seconds to realize it was their ship. Perhaps you have a personal illustration of random communication events happening in your own family or circle of friends. For our purposes, we discuss the more common organizational directions: downward, upward, and lateral.

Downward Communication

Downward communication refers to the need for upper management to communicate clearly to lower management. Upper management has not always been good at doing this. In fact, upper management has often been horrible at communicating effectively to their management down line, relying on memos and reports. In the past, leaders have been able to rely on their high position to shield them from scrutiny. After time, a person in a high position usually becomes insulated from reality and begins to make poor decisions. Things used to move so slowly that these "fossilized leaders" would retire or die before totally ruining the company. Then a new, more "in touch" leader would come along, and the cycle would repeat itself.

That style of leadership no longer survives. Like many animals, it has become extinct because the environments will no longer support it. What is needed today is leadership that walks and talks to people throughout the organization. Today's leader must know more, be more emotionally balanced, be humble enough to be a learner, and be a model of what he or she wants the company to be. In other words, the leader must be a knowledgeable communicator because communication requires more than good grammar and a fast wit. Communication is, first of all, who a person is within his or her character. Communication is having a clear understanding of core values and ethical values. Finally, communication is emotional health resulting in transparency before the group.

As mentioned previously, things change rapidly, and the rate of change continues to increase. Excellent communication processes, as well as excellent communicators, are an important and essential skill in this environment. Because top management controls the degree of excellence in the communication of an organization, they need to understand these things. Communication will not improve beyond that which the leader allows. The first step in closing in on good communication, which brings higher profits, is for the leader to publicly model and declare the importance and priority of excellent communication.

Upward Communication

Upward communication means information flowing from lower management and workers to the people above them on the organizational chart. Upper management absolutely depends on information from below. Formal reports and statistics are mandated. Yet, if this is the only information that upper management receives, it will not be enough to let upper management make excellent decisions.

What valuable information escapes the formal reports? Information about employee morale cannot be counted or measured easily yet is valuable and needed information. Employee or managerial incompetence seldom is measured or reported. However, a company that wants to improve would definitely need this information. If a manager or employee notices a problem in the system itself, and no mechanism exists for this manager or employee to report what he or she has noticed, the system has a fatal flaw. These kinds of information need to flow upward, and a system change needs to be made that allows system issues to be reported.

Lateral Communication

Lateral communication refers to departments and managers on the same organizational level communicating with one another across organizational silos. One functional silo may be engineering; another might be sales and marketing. These two divisional silos might not have a formal avenue for meeting or communicating. Nevertheless, what one does definitely affects the other. Some departments are dependent on one another for pertinent information in doing their work. Formal networks for communication become critical at various times in a company's life. When managers on one level are competing for a promotion to the same position, withholding information to hurt the other manager's chances becomes the thing to do in American business. Yet, the other manager is not the only one hurt in such a situation. The whole company is hurt. Lateral communication needs to be made important and part of the criteria for giving promotions and awards.

The Complexity of Formal Networks of Communication Loops

The two charts presented in Figures 2.3 and 2.4 are actual drawings from a company with which Dr. H. J. Harrington worked to improve its operational efficiency and communication systems. It had 39 major departments that were working together, and the original chart shows the departments. Each department once spent 10% or more of its time coordinating with the other departments (Figure 2.3). After a redesign, the organization cut out two levels of managers and reduced the number of managers from 582 to about 420. The second diagram (Figure 2.4) shows the coordination required in the new organization. The object was to spend less time coordinating and more time communicating within the individual groups.

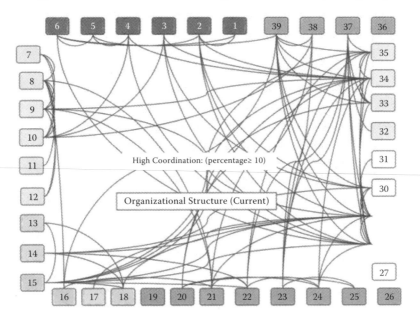

FIGURE 2.3
Original organization requiring high coordination.

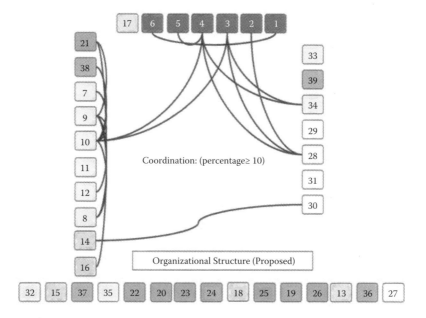

FIGURE 2.4
Redesigned organization requiring less time for coordinating.

Figure 2.5 is a typical knowledge map that shows how knowledge is communicated through the organization. After redesigning the organization just mentioned, Dr. Harrington defined two types of knowledge: tacit and explicit. Tacit knowledge is sometimes called *soft knowledge*. It is knowledge that is formed around intangible factors embedded in an individual's experience. It often takes the form of beliefs, values, principles, and morals. It guides the individual's action. Explicit knowledge, sometimes called

Create the knowledge map

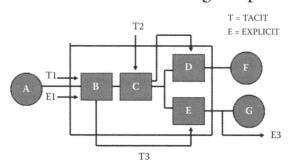

FIGURE 2.5
Typical knowledge map.

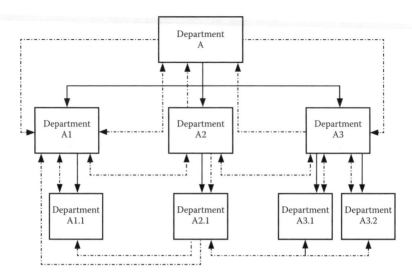

FIGURE 2.6

Typical information/communication flowchart.

hard knowledge, is stored in a semistructured content such as documents, e-mail, voice mail, or video media. It can be articulated in formal language and readily transmitted to other people. Knowledge management is now an accepted practice in many companies. It is an important part of the communication system. The payload of a communication system is knowledge.

The next diagram (Figure 2.6) is a graphic of how we have pictorially shown the changes in typical information/communications flow with the broken lines with dots and dashes. Typically, you would have the original information/communication flowchart along with the new one that would show the changes in information flow based on changes in operating procedures and culture. Often, when doing planning, this is shown as a desired future state around which the system is designed.

Shadow Loops

Alongside the formal communication networks are the informal networks. These communication loops operate in the shadow of the formal communication loops, so let us call them *shadow communication loops* or *shadow loops* for short. These can be more important in a business than the formal ones. The shadow loops are made up of friends and close colleagues within and across the formal lines who talk to each other about the company. These people know much about the personal and private lives of people at work, including their bosses. Through secretaries or maintenance personnel, they know about changes before the changes happen. The rumor mills are kept going in the informal networks called the shadow loops.

Shadow loops function to confirm formal communication. Suppose someone missed the day that an announcement was made in a group meeting. The next day, the person might talk to someone he or she knows and trusts about the formal communication. Perhaps the formal memo was ambiguous or unusual. The informal network is used to check it out.

Shadow loops also function to elaborate on formal communication. Often, key questions go unanswered in the official version. The "grapevine" or shadow loop goes to work and gets an answer—or makes up its own answer. When information is omitted, the minds of the people fill in the vacuum. That is a problem.

Shadow loops function to expedite formal communication. Formal communication does not reach everyone involved in the organization. The informal channels spread the word to those who did not hear.

Shadow loops function at times to contradict formal communication. When the formal "party line" must say one thing for political or other reasons, the informal network sets the record straight.

Shadow loops function to circumvent formal communication. This function of shadow loops is used often. It is used more in a bureaucracy. Often, the formal rules prevent workers from accomplishing the assignment. So, they circumvent formal channels and talk on the side or under the table. Everyone knows, yet no one knows, that this activity takes place. Sayings like, "It's easier to get forgiven than permission," or "If anyone asks, I didn't know about it," are common in such situations.

Finally, shadow loops function to supplement the formal communication. A formal system can never cover the bases. Therefore, an informal system buttresses the formal system. For this reason, people within an organization should be aware of both systems and learn to use them skillfully.

Intentional use of the informal network is actually recommended by some business writers as the way to promote oneself in a career. These writers use the phrase *office politics.* They include the use of the informal network to supplement the corresponding use of the formal network for personal gain. Of course, it is true that effectiveness in an organization requires skillful use of the informal as well as the formal communication network. For this to work, it must be done honestly and ethically, not in some Machiavellian fashion. In fact, the old industrial organization makes the use of politics to promote oneself an inevitable thing. As we changed to the new systems of the information age, office politics of a different genre have come to exist. Things posted on Facebook® or YouTube® have affected careers in many different ways.

How to Use the Informal Communication Network, Also Known as the Shadow Loop

How can a person in an organization make use of the informal network of shadow loops? As with most things in life, it starts with knowing oneself. What kind of personality do you have, and how do others perceive you? Without an objective view of oneself, good communication is difficult or impossible. An objective view of oneself would be like a man floating in the corner of the ceiling, looking down on himself and his office situation, seeing himself dispassionately as he interacts with others in the office. This ability to be reasonable and fair, to disassociate from oneself and to see oneself as others see, is the beginning of good communication. Another ability that follows this is the ability to empathize with others. This means putting oneself in the place of another and seeing and feeling from inside his or her life situation.

Next, using the informal communication network of shadow loops entails cultivating relationships at all levels. Some corporate cultures do not allow this. Some national cultures do not allow this. Yet, in today's organization, managing and leading from the middle is not optional but a requirement. Treat all persons with dignity and respect. Everyone in the organization has a unique and important view of the business. They each have information. It benefits the organization to open channels of communication with as many of these people as possible. Be a friend to secretaries, custodians, line workers, shipping clerks, and vice presidents. Everyone enjoys a friendly greeting and an easygoing conversation. That is how relationships start. The relationship must be in place before the information can flow. Do not wait until you need information to try to cultivate friends. And, the motives to cultivate friends must be for more sincere reasons than just to have them as a source of information. This is where virtue in a person intersects with communication and profits in a company.

Number one in IBM's seven IBM principles on which Thomas Watson Senior built IBM is "respect for the individual." IBM's basic belief is respect for the individual, for each person's rights and dignity. It follows from this principle that IBM should

- Help employees develop their potential and make the best use of their abilities;
- Pay and promote on merit; and
- Maintain two-way communications between manager and employee, with opportunity for a fair hearing and equitable settlement of disagreements.

Once you have a network of relationships that go beyond the usual, then cultivate the art of asking questions. Questions are like magic. Think about it for a moment. Questions elicit information. They are the buttons that activate a person's information dispenser. Resisting a question is practically impossible. Not answering a direct question requires a conscious effort. Asking good questions is a skill well worth developing, especially for leaders and managers. Help yourself excel in the workplace by learning to ask questions that give the information needed in a way that is comfortable to the one to whom the question is directed. Not only do questions cause a person to give information, but also they trigger the brain in both parties to search for an answer. Questions are even more powerful to the one who asks them. That is why it is so important to ask good questions. Asking bad questions can throw a person off course.

Using the shadow loop network also calls for being discreet. Do not embarrass another person by quoting this person to the wrong people or by being seen talking to the person at a time that might send the wrong signal to the person's department colleagues. Learn to politely *not* give certain information that may unnecessarily hurt or alarm. Always walk among your network of relationships with integrity. None of these ideas are mutually exclusive, but they do call for wisdom.

SUMMARY

An individual's success at work is dependent on people skills. The heart of people skills involves communication. Two spheres of communication exist: macrocommunication and microcommunication. Macrocommunication deals with impersonal communication from a government, corporation, or institution to a person or group. It is capable of two-way communication only on a high political plane or on the level of a social movement, yet for the individual, it seems like one-way communication. Microcommunication deals with individuals and small groups communicating using the communication loop. This chapter focuses on microcommunication.

Communication theory postulates that when two human beings talk, they complete a sequence that has give and take. The communication process is like an electrical circuit that must be completed for electricity to flow. The elements of this communication process are the following:

1. **Sender:** The originator who thinks something.
2. **Encoding the message:** The sender has to translate the thought into the spoken word.
3. **Medium:** The vibrations of the spoken word are sent through the airwaves.
4. **Receiver or audience:** The listener receives the vibrations.
5. **Decoding:** The listener then has to interpret the vibrations into words that the listener interprets into meaning and stores them in his or her brain.
6. **Feedback:** At some point in time, the listener needs to recall these stored thoughts, translate them into spoken words, and provide feedback to the communicator.
7. **Analysis:** The communicator compares his or her interpretation of the listener's feedback to his or her original thoughts to determine if the message was correctly understood by the listener.
8. **Either begin a new loop or end the loop when understanding is achieved:** If the message was not correctly understood by the receiver (listener), then the cycle has to start again. If it was in agreement with the original thought, the communicator then translates this analysis into words that he or she sends back to the listener indicating that there is agreement.

A large company has many of these overlapping communication networks or loops. The many communication loops in a company give it personality and soul. These networks come in two large categories: the formal networks defined by organization charts and the informal networks in the break room and water cooler that are like shadows of the formal networks. This informal shadow communication can be useful in an organization. It takes the development of people skills and networking skills to use successfully.

Improving the communication between departments, teams, coworkers, and the company and customers will increase the profits. Excelling in communication is no longer optional for companies and individuals.

An attitude of gratitude, a track record of integrity, and a high level of skill and diligence are understood in any language.

—**R. D. Lewis**

REFERENCE

1. Craig, Robert T. (1999). Communication theory as a field, *Communication Theory*, 9(2): 119–161.

3

How Do You Talk to Your Boss?

Life is 10 percent what you make it, and 90 percent how you take it.

—Irving Berlin

Learn to think like a boss and tell him what he needs to know to do his job: the "bottom line" of the issue with a couple of possible solutions.

—R. D. Lewis

INTRODUCTION

Talking to your boss can be scary. Speaking to a person who has supervisory responsibility over you and the power to help or hurt your career often strikes fear into the heart. How does one go about giving an oral report to the boss? How does one take the initiative to go to the supervisor with a problem, solution, or request? How does one dress, behave, and speak? What actions and behaviors contribute to successful encounters with the boss?

> Reverend Dr. Glen Paden, a member of the clergy and a church denominational executive in California, was visiting Wayne Reynolds, who had served previously under him in Sacramento. Wayne was currently a staff member at a church in the San Bernardino, California, area and was showing Dr. Paden the large facility when he came on a group of people in one of the buildings. He introduced Dr. Paden this way: "Dr. Paden used to be my boss, but he always treated me as a friend. In fact, he once told me, 'Don't think of me as your boss. Think of me as a friend who is always right.'"

That is funny, but it is not bad advice either. If you can think of your boss as a friend, you will have less anxiety in approaching him or her, and that is good whenever you talk to a supervisor or boss. On the other hand, even though a boss is not right all the time, we serve ourselves and the situation best when we understand his or her position of responsibility and treat him or her with the respect that is due. Someone must be in a position of ultimate responsibility, and the person in that position will be a flawed human being. If you, as an employee, can keep this in mind, then communication with the boss will sit on a realistic base. Not being nervous around the boss actually puts the boss at ease and makes him or her want to listen. Having an honest respect for the authority of the boss will also come through in your facial expressions and tone of voice. Having a disdain for your boss also comes through. Since you want to be taken seriously, work on showing respect for the person in the position of boss. That leads us to a discussion on overcoming fear of our boss.

Fear is not a sign of respect for the boss but rather of a lack of confidence in oneself. If one has a legitimate reason for fearing the boss, then it takes a highly developed character of virtue and self-actualization to respect the position of boss if not the person holding that position. Assuming a normal situation, our boss is worthy of respect both as a person and as the position he or she holds in the organization of which we are a part. Our boss also needs information about the area in which we work to do his or her job. A boss and the employees are not entities that can exist apart. Each is really part of the other. Therefore, let us work on eliminating our unfounded fear of talking to him or her.

NOTHING TO FEAR BUT FEAR

Franklin Delano Roosevelt, former president of the United States of America, in a radio speech in 1933 said, "It's my firm belief that the only thing we have to fear is fear itself." That belief holds true in so many areas of our life. Our emotional state of mind affects us. When we experience fear, it impairs our ability to make good decisions and perform with effectiveness. A positive state of mind enhances decision making and performance. Therefore, it follows that a positive, optimistic frame of mind is an asset to any employee when talking to his or her boss. The need to overcome fear related to approaching our boss has to be the first step in talking to the boss. How do we prepare to talk to our boss? Is there anything we can do to overcome our fear of talking to the man or woman in charge of our work? The good news is that there are steps each person can take to overcome fear and prepare to talk to the boss.

The Downside of Fear

Fear that is inappropriate can destroy opportunity and stifle improvement opportunities. Normally, fear is an emotion that warns us of danger and prepares us for fight or flight. Danger causes us to withdraw. It is a defense mechanism. Yet, psychologists have shown that a human being can be conditioned to fear things that are not a threat or danger. Often, we fear things irrationally that are not a threat. Many times, one bad experience with "the boss from hell," or even stories about bad experiences with bosses, can prejudice us and make us fear all bosses. These preconceived ideas about bosses subconsciously block us from building healthy relationships with the people in these positions of responsibility with a company, government, or school. For example, you could have been treated badly by a truly abusive boss. Some bosses are simply in over their heads, no doubt. Labor unions have strikes against management that cause residual feelings of anger and mistrust between these parties. This fear or antagonism against a boss could come from a bad family situation. A bad, abusive father can cause a child to grow up to have problems dealing with authority figures. The point is that fear can be associated with things we must face for our own good. Talking to our boss is actually a good and essential thing to do if we need our boss in order to do a job and have an income.

When we fear our boss, we filter out anything good and positive about our boss. We see only the negative. We find ourselves irrationally thinking that the boss is against us when he or she actually is not against us. This causes us to make career-limiting decisions.

Here is the inescapable fact. Bosses are here to stay. Bosses and leaders are needed when more than two people are on a common enterprise. Think about it. Surely, you have been in a situation in which no one took leadership of a group. It could have been your neighborhood baseball team, a combat situation, a family reunion, or a wedding rehearsal. Whatever the situation, bosses serve a purpose. Fear of bosses, then, is an abnormal and negative attitude and should be overcome for our own good and the good of society.

The Good Side of Fear

Fear—and nervousness—can be harnessed to motivate us into positive action. The fear of talking to one's boss can motivate a person to create a climate favorable to talking to the boss. That way, fear can serve a good purpose. Take the fear of the boss and rechannel that energy into an effort to counteract the danger that fear has created. Harness fear for a positive purpose. As a thoughtful, educated human being, you can take the negatives that life throws at you and think of ways to redirect the energy into positive and constructive uses. That is exactly what we can do with our unfounded fears about talking to our boss or supervisor.

Once the day comes in your relationship when your boss knows your name and you know better how to communicate with him or her, your fear will either be gone or so much diminished that it is not a stumbling block. And, you will remember that you got to this place because you harnessed your fear and used its energy to motivate and energize you to make a plan to create a climate conducive to building a relationship with your boss. That is the good side of fear. Because it is unpleasant, it forces us to do something with that negative energy or continue in our pain. It also causes us to think about the big picture of life.

Most of the things we dream about are not things we want. Dreams are often expressions of responsibilities we want to escape. We would probably panic if suddenly our daydreams came true. So, the main questions any human being must ask himself or herself are, "What do I really want? What do I fear? How well do I know my family and myself? How well do I understand my company and the business environment in which it operates? How well do I understand the government agency I serve and what we were created to accomplish? Where is my company going, and how realistic is my company in heading where it wants to go? What should my school, synagogue, civic club, mosque, church, and so on really be doing?"

By now, you have realized that one sometimes fails to get what one wants in life. However, working toward what one wants over time makes life challenging and gives a sense of value to what we achieve. A good exercise might be to analyze the elements involved in getting what we want. The good side of fear forces reasonable individuals to think about these things.

What would determine that a person would get what he or she wanted? Here are some factors:

- Personal expectation/desire (life mission)

- Personal skill and knowledge needed to realize the expectation/desire (expertise)
- External environment needed to support the realized expectation/desire (favorable economic/political conditions)
- The people and institutions needed to help an individual realize expectation/desire (interdependence and synergy)
- The wisdom and understanding to make the right decisions at the right time (experience, education, meditation, mentoring, consultation)
- A minimum of reversals and bad fortune (good luck or blessings)

In a book like this one, you may be asking, "Why are we discussing this topic?" It goes to the discussion of profits from good communication. Optimum communication between people comes when they know themselves, where they are going in life, and the effect that things external to themselves have on their lives. Communication is about people working in groups or on teams. Virtue and wisdom are not exclusively for discussions by philosophers and theologians. These are practical, fundamental matters that determine quality communication and thus personal, organizational, and business success. High-performance individuals and teams are dependent on these factors. Good government exists where these factors are realities in the lives of those who govern. Excellent business exists where these factors exist. Good-communication profits happen in such environments.

By applying these factors to the situation of talking to our boss, one can more accurately predict to what degree his or her talk has a basis for succeeding. If a person knows the long-term and short-term direction of his or her company or government agency, if a person understands the constraints of the business and political environment on his or her company or government agency, and if a person knows what he or she *really* wants, then that person can decide whether the meeting with the boss is worth the time and effort. The meeting could backfire and brand one as a nuisance or an incompetent. Only a person who has the larger picture and the depth of knowledge and character can read situations wisely.

Communication at its core is about developing the character and knowledge of people. It is about lifelong learning. And, it is more about knowing what you want than it is about getting what you want. The good side of fear is that it causes thoughtful people to think about the big picture of our lives and work.

Facing Fear

Creating a climate of communication requires initiative and simple social skills. Therefore, since the time to start talking to your boss is before you need to talk to your boss, face your fears and do it. In a large corporate setting, you will need a strategy. Take the initiative to say "Hello" to the boss, to attend meetings where your boss will be present, to ask thoughtful questions, and to make appropriate comments. That way, when you find yourself in a position where you must talk to him or her about business issues that are important, you will at least be recognized. Even if he or she is preoccupied, subconsciously his or her mind never forgets anything, and being where he or she happens to be will have a cumulative effect. If you are in a large organization, the more times he or she sees you with that pleasant smile and greeting, the sooner he or she will begin to recognize you as an employee who is a positive and pleasant person. Even bosses have fears and need encouragement, but never forget that he or she *is* the boss.

In most large corporate settings, a climate that leaves the door open to talk with one's boss must be developed over a period of time. If you talk to your boss regularly about good things and routine things, then talking to your boss about bad things becomes a less-traumatic and fearful event. You begin to think how to get into safe conversations with your boss that gradually lead to a solid relationship. Any relationship at all with your boss will aid you in a good way when a situation arises that demands the attention of your boss. At the very least, you want to arrive at a stage in your relationship with your boss so he or she recognizes you as belonging to his or her department, division, or company. The next stage would be when the boss remembers your name and the position you hold.

Do not panic or try to do something quickly. You need an approach to a one-on-one encounter with the boss that can move you deliberately and surely to your goal of a positive climate for communication with your boss. The word *approach* is just another word for a plan. We use the word *approach* because it is less intimidating than the word *plan*. A plan sometimes is perceived as an ingenious, detailed, complicated, sophisticated, and difficult-to-put-together piece of high-powered brain work. No, we are not talking about something that would be too difficult for a person to do. We are talking about taking time to think it through, maybe discuss with a friend or colleague, and in your normal routines check out the routines of the boss. Then, find a way to be around where the boss will be so that you are in the same room or hallway. You will gain some more information to decide on an approach of finding a time and place to say hello to the boss and introduce yourself. After this, you plan ways to "bump into" your boss at least four more times and introduce yourself. Then, you are on your way.

If you are in a small company, this scenario is not necessary, is it? In that situation, one looks for a chance *not* to be around the boss. Nevertheless, a person in a small business where the boss is always near also needs to overcome the fears of the boss. Such a person needs to do reading about personality types and about communication styles, to peg his or her boss's type of personality and style of communication, and then practice communicating to that style and type.

In a small business, where the problem usually is overexposure, it is more important to present yourself as a trustworthy and pleasant person. Use body language to say that you are a supportive, competent employee. Here are some basics that are appropriate in most normal situations in the United States:

- Maintain eye contact for the length of time that indicates acknowledgment of another person's presence and friendliness.
- Have a smiling and positive face.
- Have relaxed, open hands at the side during the greeting or else an open palm waving hello.
- Speak the word *hello* or the equivalent, if possible, and use the boss's name, showing the proper respect (*Mister, Ms.,* or other title unless he or she has let the employees know to use the first name).
- Stand straight and lean a little toward the boss rather than shrinking back.
- Demonstrate this respect of your boss when you are alone with the other employees because consistency is a virtue.

Study your boss whenever you get the chance. Ask the boss's long-time employees and friends questions about his or her personality, likes, and dislikes. Does the boss have a hobby? Does he or she like a certain sport or team? Is his or her personality basically one of an introvert or extrovert? Is the boss more task focused than person focused? Does he or she have any insecurity? All this information will help you determine how to approach the boss and what you will say to him or her should that need arise.

Finally, develop your skills in communication. Read about communication. Take advantage of the seminars offered by your company. Pay for a course in communication at a local community college or attend a 1-day seminar in the area. Join a club that teaches you to speak in public or take advantage of opportunities at your synagogue or fraternal organization. Improvement requires lifelong commitment and learning.

PLAN THE WHOLE PROCESS

When the time comes to see the boss about business-related matters and concerns, think through the process. Why do you need to see the boss? What is the nature of the need to see the boss? Is it a personal need driving the visit? Is it a need driven by your department and the normal course of work and business? Is it as a representative of your team or of the employees? Will your boss feel it is relevant to the company and worth his or her time? Write down the reason and nature of your visit. Then, imagine the desired outcome of your meeting. Be ready to tell the boss's secretary the nature of your request for a meeting in one phrase that will grab the boss's attention while remaining true to the nature of the meeting.

Next, think of the process you will go through to visit the boss. Figure 3.1 is a flowchart of a preplanning process for the meeting with the boss.

Mission

The activity of thinking through what you want to accomplish and the steps to take to reach your goal are invaluable preparation. This removes much of the tentativeness and discomfort. First, write out the reason or purpose for the meeting and what result you want to come from your meeting with the boss. Even if the result is an intangible, write it down. In other words, what is your mission for this one particular meeting with your boss?

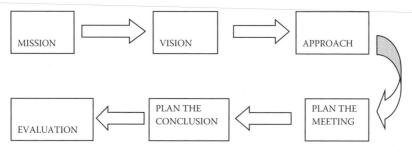

FIGURE 3.1
Meeting with the boss flowchart.

One of us heard a story that illustrates talking to one's boss. We will use this story to talk more about writing a mission statement for talking with the boss. The story is from a person who at the time served as the head of payroll for a school district in California.

This boss worked at the time with an associate who was classified by the government as a member of a minority race. This fact is pertinent to the story. According to the head of payroll, the employee was unreliable (did not complete assignments); as a result, this associate stopped getting any assignments classified as critical. As the story went, the associate openly used work time to fill out and file the complicated racial discrimination complaint with the labor relations board, citing, among other things, that the district only gave menial assignments to the associate. The school district decided not to look into the merits of the accusation but to take the very cheap way out. They settled with the plaintiff for a sum probably less than it cost to maintain the position for a month.

Well, the head of payroll was distressed at the implications of not answering the charges of racial discrimination. It made it seem that she was discriminating on the basis of race. She was not sleeping at night, and it was hard to focus on work. As a result, she decided the only way she could put aside some of her strong emotions over the action of the district and get back to business, side by side with the complaining associate, was to talk to the boss. She decided to tell the superintendent of her great disappointment in the action of the school district. The head of payroll said something like the following about her experience:

> I made an appointment. When I went to his office, I was very nervous, but I knew I had to do it. I didn't expect anything to change. I just needed to tell the district what I felt. He told me to take a seat and asked me what was on my mind. I told him I disagreed with the decision of the school district not to fight the charge of racial discrimination since it was without basis. He explained to me that the school board decided that the expense in lawyers, time, and stress on the district was too big a price to pay when the plaintiff would settle for such a small amount. I told him that I understood that, but that if every business decided to pay off people who lied, it would only teach more employees that they could get away with it. Well, nothing changed, but at least I was able to go back to work and begin to focus.

If you had to write a result that the head of payroll wanted to accomplish by her visit to the superintendent, what would it be? She stated that she knew nothing would change, so she did not expect to reverse the school district decision. Neither did she want to change district policy for future employee lawsuits. What she wanted was emotional relief so she could cope with the emotional stress and the slap in the face she felt her employer gave to her. We could state her mission this way: "I want to express my feelings of anger at not being backed by upper management to reduce my emotional distress so I can redirect my energy to doing my job."

Vision

Once you have written down the mission of your meeting, visualize how you will look and sound at the meeting with your boss and how he or she will look, sound, and feel. Hear what you will say and how you will say it. Hear your boss talk and hear how the boss will sound. Imagine the result of your talk as though it had happened, that is, as if the result were already accomplished at some time in the future. How will this result change your workplace or resolve the issue? How will it change your status with the company? How will attitudes and the work environment change? Write down your vision of your meeting with the boss as though it were already true, that is, use present tense verbs to describe what you see, hear, and feel in the future.

Writing it as though you were in the future will seem strange at first. Pretend you have a time machine and have used it to travel to your meeting a few days in the future. You are looking at you and your boss talking in the future. Imagine a best-case scenario for positive results from your meeting with the boss that are realistic and attainable. Then, write what you see from the future in the present tense.

If the mission statement speaks to purpose, then the vision description speaks ultimately to the track or direction a plan is taking. Both of these steps in planning are foundational in importance. Do not think of them as busywork with no practical value.

Approach

Next, plan how to approach your boss. Will you stop the boss in the hallway? Will you e-mail? Will you call the boss and talk to his or her secretary to arrange an appointment? What time of the month, the week, and the day will catch your boss in the best frame of mind to give you positive attention? This is an area where knowledge you have gathered about your boss's personality type and communication style will help.

Some people have a reluctance to contact the boss for an appointment. They cannot pull the trigger. You probably have experienced this feeling about other matters. If so, you also know that when you do execute and do it, one generally has a good experience. Afterward, one wonders why the fear. This is a common experience when a person faces personal fear. So, just do it.

The Meeting

When you meet with your boss, what will you do to gain his or her trust and goodwill in the first 5 seconds? How will you dress? What kind of look will be on your face? What will your posture be saying? What tone of voice will you use? What will be the first words?

What will you use to segue from the mutualities to the meat of the meeting? How will you clearly and convincingly make your issue known? Will you bring papers and data to leave with the boss or in anticipation of questions and objections that the boss will have? What can you do or say to show your boss how helping you will help with his or her front-burner issues? Remember, a boss has a different agenda than a lower-level manager. The boss is concerned with strategic issues and the bottom line. The boss must please a board and the stockholders. How can you help the boss while helping your department or team?

Concluding the Meeting

Now, you need a good and satisfying conclusion to your meeting. How will you wrap it up? Will you ask for a decision then and there, or will you ask for another meeting? How will you summarize what you and the boss have said and decided at this meeting? How will you say goodbye and exit?

We have learned that just before leaving a conversation or presentation, if one changes the subject to something of mutual interest that is unrelated to the topic that has been discussed, it causes the parties to lock the important information into the brain and acts as a seal. So, the discussion might be of a football game, a favorite television show, or any subject that is being talked about in the popular media. If your boss is too busy for small talk, then you cannot change that fact. Nevertheless, keep this tactic in mind and use it if you can.

Execute the Plan

Until now, nothing has actually happened. You have been planning and thinking. Now, you must carry out your plan. As you move into action, you will receive information that may lead you to modify your plan. Do not be afraid to change your plan to adapt to new information that you did not have when you first started planning. Be sure to communicate any changes in writing with your team and those who need to know. Use this as a learning experience. Keep notes about what you are learning and how you are improving your skills.

- Make the appointment with your boss's secretary or catch the boss in the hallway.
- Dress for success if you have made a formal appointment.
- Once in the meeting, do not focus on the written plan; focus on the meeting.
- Keep your body language nonthreatening and relaxed, yet professional.
- Evaluate your meeting.

When it comes to evaluating your meeting, write an account of what happened at the meeting as soon afterward as possible. Have your method of recording these notes ready ahead of time and your filing method in place. Try to write out who said what as well as you can remember. Write down things you noticed in the body language and facial expressions and tone of voice of both yourself and your boss. Write down what was decided and what you think will eventually come from the meeting. This document will serve as a learning tool as well as a tool to help plan your next meeting with the boss. When you put this document in the folder with your mission statement (purpose), your vision (direction), your planning steps, and the notes of how you changed and adjusted your plan as you began to implement it, you will have a valuable collection of materials.

Now, write one more paper. After reviewing the materials mentioned, write out how you would improve your process or actions if you could go back and do it again. This exercise will focus your mind on your next meeting with the view of improvement and excellence.

Follow-up to the Meeting with Your Boss

Write a card or thank you note to your boss and other people who helped you with the meeting and mail it the following day. Do not wait too long to mail it, or it will ruin the effect. Thank them for giving their valuable time and express your appreciation for them as people and for the job they do. As you gain experience in talking to people above you in the organization, you will notice that you will write your notes even before the meeting takes place and have them ready to go. Just make sure notes are not mailed before the meeting in case something goes wrong.

Should you use e-mail communication instead of the postal service to send your thank you notes? More and more people are doing this. Know your company and situation well enough to know if this is appropriate. However, nothing says, "You are special enough for me to go to all this trouble for you," like a mailed, handwritten letter.

Next, take steps to carry out the tasks that fell to you as a result of the meeting. Keep a positive attitude no matter what your boss decides. You are in this for the long haul. You can afford to lose a few skirmishes and battles as long as you win the war.

SUMMARY

From time to time, an employee may need to talk to his or her boss. This usually strikes fear into the hearts of employees. This is normal. Do not let fear be a negative force that holds you back in your company. Channel your fear into energy to create a climate for communication with your boss.

The main component of creating a climate is to plan the whole process of talking to your boss. The process steps are these:

1. Mission: Write a statement giving the purpose for talking to your boss.
2. Vision: Write a statement describing the event in a positive way as though it had already happened successfully.

3. Approach: Write a description of the way you will make your appointment with the boss.

4. Meeting: Write a detailed plan for each segment of the meeting from how to dress, to the first greeting, to where to sit, and to the agreement to be made.

5. Concluding the meeting: Write a summary of what was agreed on, what action assignments to make, and how the meeting will be followed up.

Now that you have planned what to do, execute the plan. Make the appointment. Dress appropriately to match the type of appointment you have made—informally dressed or formally dressed. In the actual meeting, do not be distracted by your plan by focusing on it. Rather, focus on the boss and the meeting. Be conscious of your body language and send a message that is one of a relaxed professional. Finally, write a thorough account of what happened in the meeting as soon as you can and file it. Use these notes to improve and to plan for the next meeting with the boss.

Send thank you notes the next day to your boss and the others who helped you with the meeting, especially the boss's secretary if the secretary was involved. This is important.

Finally, be sure to carry out any action items you were assigned. Remember: You are in this for the long haul. Do not worry if the meeting did not come out exactly the way you wanted. Keep a positive and pleasant attitude.

> When you talk to your boss, make eye contact, don't be over familiar, don't be afraid, and give the boss the short version of the facts. Bosses are busy, and so are you.
>
> —R. D. Lewis

4

How Do You Talk to Your Employees?

A manager might not want to be "buddies" with an employee, but a manager certainly needs to be friendly with his employees. Being friendly includes conversation.

—**R. D. Lewis**

Always leave your employees feeling you had time to listen to what they had to say and thought it was important.

—**H. J. Harrington**

INTRODUCTION

IC can stand for intensive care. But wait—it also stands for internal communications. When communications happen within an organization, they are called *internal communications*. And, by the way, effective internal communications might be just the kind of intensive care many organizations need. Since management historically talked to employees and employees were not expected to talk back, a synonym for IC (as used in this chapter) is *employee communication*. Therefore, this chapter discusses how managers and other leadership talk to employees.

IC has arrived as a department in corporations. IC departments began breaking away from the human resources department and reporting directly to senior management in the last third of the twentieth century. Although less expensive to a business than external communications, IC produces as large a profit as external communications, if not more. Think of the profits made from the money spent on marketing, advertising, and communications with suppliers, distributers, retailers, resellers, and, customers. IC can at least duplicate this profit.

The notion that company information did not concern employees has been debunked. The leaders in the field of business communication and total improvement management believe that today's employees need access to company information to do their jobs. In the beginning of the Industrial Revolution, perhaps sharing information with employees was not mission critical. The employees were not educated. They did mindless work. Today, it is different. We have an educated workforce. Add to that fast communication, and providing information to employees becomes a necessity. If nothing else, it is a defense against rumors and against angry employees who learn of company activity from their next-door neighbor who read it on Facebook.

Rapid change and the convergence of these changes across most areas of human existence caused a work shift. A disconnection between top managers and the workers has been one of the results of these cultural forces, and this disconnection in the corporate hierarchy and structure kills communication in the workplace. This rapidly changing social environment has caused an effect on people akin to moving to a new country and living in a foreign culture, which causes a psychological effect called *culture shock*. Alvin Toffler's book *Future Shock*[1] combines these two cultural phenomena into a single phrase. Here are some of Toffler's observations about the 1960s changes in Western society:

- The shift from mechanical labor to knowledge work
- The shift from unskilled to highly educated employees
- The shift from decision making only at the top level to decision making at the point of implementation

These changes caused the firing of one class due to the elimination of what they did and the hiring of more highly educated employees. Of course, these new employees cost more and sometimes knew more than the manager about the job they were doing.

Since then, the world has shrunk and flattened. The terms *globalization* and *global village* surfaced. Large companies began to downsize, to outsource, to move certain operations offshore, and to use part-time and contract workers from the cheapest labor markets anywhere on the globe. Job security was gone with the wind. Companies in the United States like IBM had built a loyal, trusting, highly motivated workforce assured of lifetime employment if they performed well. This cultural shift eliminated that practice. Japanese industry gained dominance in many industries using a trusting, loyal workforce based on lifetime employment, yet even in Japan that practice is now practically nonexistent. The result of this has not only affected the ability to communicate between top management and the workers but also generated an inability for employees to talk to one another. In addition, middle management became disconnected from both the workers and top management. What a mess.

So, exactly how would managers go about talking to their employees? It is back to basics for the solution: Create an environment of openness and trust in your organization. And how, pray tell, is that done? The first step is this: The organization relearns to listen. The second step is this: The organization relearns to communicate effectively.

CREATE AN ENVIRONMENT OF OPENNESS AND TRUST BY FIRST BEING A LISTENER

Good communication in an organization starts on the personal level. Personal trust must be built between employees and the manager. Without an environment of trust, communication cannot happen. The dream of good, complete communication requires an open, honest, and virtuous environment in government and in the corporate workplace. So, how does an organization go about creating a new environment of openness and trust that will reconnect management and employees? To create an environment of trust, management and workers must learn and practice good listening.

A manager is a good listener when he or she concentrates on listening, but this in itself is not enough. Managers need to be trained to listen. To produce managers, leaders, and bosses who are good listeners takes effort and a firm commitment on the part of a board of directors and the corporate leadership. In government, the support has to go all the way to the legislature and the unions. The virtues, about which the ancients wrote, are indeed pillars on which civilizations stand. This quality listening thing is a big deal. This should start from the top.

As managers, we need to be good listeners. An old adage that many have heard goes like this: God gave us two ears and only one mouth. The point being made was that people should learn to listen twice as much as they talk. Our employees cannot tell us their problems or their observations when we are talking. As managers, we need to make effective use of silence and active listening to encourage employees to talk. Take the time to develop good listening habits. Some useful guidelines are as follows:

- Gather as many ideas as possible before making a decision.
- Look directly at the person who is talking to you.
- Use words of encouragement like, "Yes, I understand; tell me more."
- Put your telephone on hold when someone comes in to talk to you.
- Ask probing questions and do not jump to conclusions.
- Take time to chat with coworkers.
- Understand what is behind their words.
- Listen with your eyes and ears.

A simple illustration of this would be an educational classroom. A certain kind of environment must exist for learning to take place. Here are three of the key ingredients:

- A classroom must have an environment of respect.
- A classroom must have an environment of rapport.
- A classroom must have an environment of safety.

Let me ask, how does the environment of a classroom differ from a workplace? The modern organization has been called a *learning organization*. New hires need to learn, and with change constantly facing us and our corporation, we have to learn as we go. How can we learn in an environment in which we are not trusted? How can trust exist in a situation in which management does not respect the employees or vice versa? How can we ask the hard questions in an environment in which we think we will be fired for asking them? Remember, the essence of communication is rapport.

By listening, management can understand the employees. By understanding the employees, empathy and reasonableness develop. When empathy and reasonableness exist, an environment of openness and trust develops. Within an environment of openness and trust, even more efficient and effective listening takes place. When high-quality communication happens, profits go up.

To train managers to listen and then help them improve in this area, a measurement tool is needed. The Harrington Institute and other organizations have assessment tools that measure listening effectiveness in a company. Using this tool would create benchmarks. Continual improvement in listening has four phases.

Phase 1: Assess listening effectiveness using an assessment tool. Add a new question to the Employee Opinion Survey asking the employees of their impression of how well managers listen to them.

Phase 2: Train managers and employees in listening skills immediately after conducting the company-wide assessment.

Phase 3: Eight months after the assessment, conduct interviews with managers about their progress and conduct interviews with employees concerning the listening effectiveness and efficiency of managers. Share the results in group settings and use the results to start discussions and to learn.

Phase 4: Continual improvement: Begin again with phase 1 after 12 to 18 months.

Besides training and a benchmark to measure progress in management improvement efforts, other key areas have to be addressed for management to be able to communicate effectively with employees. Let us talk about these.

One of management's top priorities in the process improvement area is to build a competent, close working team that performs both efficiently and effectively without stifling the creativity of the individual. This requires that every member on the team trusts and understands each other. Management needs to trust their employees and share the power that information about the organization provides to everyone. In the past, when management spoon-fed employees with only enough data to do their job, holding back most of the key operational information was standard operating procedure. Whenever this happens, it builds a false sense of power for management and fosters a feeling of distrust in the employees. Providing everyone with as much data as possible is always best because it short-circuits the rumor mill. A rumor gains the status of a fact in a process something like this one:

- Unknown (first person): "I don't know if there will be a layoff or not."
- Rumor (second person): "We could have as many as 1,000 employees laid off."
- Fact (third person): "There will be 1,000 employees laid off next month."

As an ancient prophet said, "People perish from the lack of knowledge." To earn trust and understanding from employees, management must provide them with a secure environment. Management must realize that any improvement process will cause the employees to ask themselves the following questions:

- What is in it for me if I make the organization more productive?
- Will productivity improvements cost me my job or reduce my standard of living?
- Am I willing to change jobs or relocate to stay with the organization?
- What will my future be with the organization?

These are known as "silent questions" that management must help the employee to answer to provide a secure environment. This can best be accomplished by management's positive, proactive action.

Tell Them Why

Everyone wants to have self-respect and be respected by others. This is a universal need that we all have, and it is a need management needs to fulfill more today than ever before. Without self-respect, it is impossible to build trust and loyalty. Showing that you respect a person is a sincere form of flattery. Think of how you handle people. The higher level a person is, the more you respect him or her, the more time you take to explain why you are doing something. When you do not feel a person is important or that the person is not intelligent, you have a tendency to tell the person what to do. You tell your children to take out the garbage or to do the dishes. The more you respect an individual, the more time you take to explain why he or she should do something. Management often falls into this trap of telling employees what to do without explaining why it is worth their time and effort to do it. It is always better to tell employees why they need to do something in preference to how to do it.

A boss tells an employee how to do something. The modern manager tells the employee why it needs to be done, taking the manager out of the role of boss and putting him or her in the role of a modern leader and associate. As the manager, no longer are you ordering employees to do something. You are providing them with an understanding of the results that need to be accomplished, the impact that the activity has on the organization, and a sense of urgency. Telling an employee how to do a job may get it done but explaining why the job needs to be done will get it done with enthusiasm. People who understand why develop their own approach for accomplishing the task, make fewer errors, and complete the assignment faster because they have a sense of ownership. They will also feel free to change their approach as the situation changes. If employees do not understand why they are doing a task, they charge ahead, implementing management's direction until they are stopped even though a critical factor in the equation may have changed.

Do It with a Smile

A smile goes a mile, while a frown drives you down.

—H. J. Harrington

A smile unlocks the door of acceptance. It denotes friendship, caring, and a willingness to listen to both sides of the story. Managers who have a smile on their face, a twinkle in their eyes, and sincerity in their voice project an environment of friendship and cooperation into the entire workplace. The energy level of the total department surges. People like to work for managers who are friendly and likable and have a positive attitude. Too often under the pressure of the job, managers forget that everyone looks to them to set the attitude of the organization. Other managers think that they will not be taken seriously if they do not appear to be a little aloof, firm, and stern. They rely on this harsh personality to give them stature and respect, but that is not true. A manager can get short-term results by threatening people yet can build long-term team relationships and a higher level of performance by creating an enjoyable work environment. People just perform better when they are happy and satisfied with their job—when they are not threatened by their job and their manager. What are the key management characteristics that make a work environment enjoyable? Managers should be

- Sincere and interested in the employee;
- Approachable, communicative, and easy to talk with;
- Kind, showing respect to everyone and treating everyone equally;
- Comfortable to be around, with a presence that conveys warmth;
- Friendly. with a pleasant personality;
- Helpful and a role model, not above doing any job;

- Aware and taking into account that other people are also busy too;
- Emotionally healthy, not bringing personal problems to work;
- Dependable and of steady composure;
- Organized, remembering commitments; and
- Sharing and accepting both success and blame—"the buck stops here."

President Dwight D. Eisenhower typified this style of person. There was never any doubt that he was in command and meant what he said. But, he always had a smile for everyone. Although a smile or a frown can make management convincing, they still need to follow through to show that they mean what they say and to make sure the desired result is accomplished.

Adopt a New Philosophy about Organizations and Employees

Boards, legislatures, and managers are encouraged to change their philosophies and beliefs about employees. They must understand that employees are trustworthy, and that they are smart. If your employees are not trustworthy and smart, we believe they will become trustworthy and smart when they know that they are trusted by their bosses. Yes, exceptions will exist, but doesn't that just prove the rule?

The top leadership and policy-making groups should initiate a culture of trust because they set the standard for the rest of the organization. They may need to change the mission statement and the policy manual to reflect the commitment to good communication. By doing this, these leaders would speak the first word in the conversation, breaking the ice. Managers could follow by initiating discussions with employees. The act of modeling the type of sincere communication that management desires to see in the organization says to employees, "We are sincere and serious about quality communication in the workplace. We trust you and value you, and we want to hear what you have to say." This is where creating an environment of openness and trust ideally should start.

Why would this be so difficult? The reason is that we become vulnerable as persons when we demonstrate that we trust others. Others can see who we really are when we communicate openly and honestly. That is why virtue is a necessary part of communication. No one respects a manager or a legislature or a union that cannot be admired, emulated, and trusted. And, if a legislator honestly communicates yet is not an honest person, well, constituents discover that the legislator is not honest. Why do you think used car salespeople are the brunt of so many jokes? If you are in the used car business, you have such a big opportunity before you if you can add virtue to the mix.

When employees are treated with respect, they live up to that level of trust. It changes them. That in turn changes the organization. This kind of environment allows high-performance individuals and teams to exist. It also allows good communication to exist.

Adopt a New Philosophy about Management

Adopting a new philosophy about employees must be accompanied by a new philosophy about management. Management will become a position of support and coordination, not a position of privilege and control. The manager moves the organization toward fulfillment of the vision through enabling and supporting the teams in reaching their objectives and goals. When teams take ownership and devise a way of reaching the objective, the team members work harder.

Management gives the teams what they need to do their work. Dr. Kenneth C. Lomax, founder of Business Improvement Associates, Roseville, California, teaches his clients the 4 Ts that every employee needs:

- **Time** to do the work
- **Tools** to do the work
- **Training** to do the work
- **Team** environment in which to work.

Macrocommunication is communication structured into society and its organizations. Microcommunication is on a more personal level between individuals and groups. A manager straddles both of these worlds. Here are some of the ways a manager communicates with his or her employees on the macrolevel:

- Providing performance goals
- Producing performance plans
- Sharing and taking feedback
- Evaluating performance
- Rewarding performance
- Handling performance problems
- Performance improvement activities

Listen with Your Eyes as Well as Your Ears

> In emphatic listening, you listen with your eyes and with your heart. You listen for feeling, for meaning. You listen for behavior. Emphatic listening is powerful because it gives you accurate data to work with.
>
> —**Stephen R. Covey,** *Daily Reflections for Highly Effective People*

The facts about how people communicate reveal amazing things. The first amazing fact is that 93% of face-to-face communication is nonverbal. It includes the way a person stands or sits. It involves the expression on a person's face or the tone in a person's voice. Even the position of a person's eyes and what they do with their hands and arms are in synchronization with the message being sent. Only 7% of communication consists in the actual meaning of the words used. That is why written communication and verbal communication are entirely two different types of communication. Each must be learned and practiced to be clear and effective.

You already understand many facial expressions. Most women are naturally gifted in this area. They teach each other and study it informally. "Did you see that look on his face?" they will ask each other. And, of course, what mom has not said to her child: "Wipe that look off your face!" Men also learn to do this if they are poker players or communication researchers in a scientific setting. Women clearly have the reputation for doing it better. We call it "woman's intuition."

In the last section of this chapter, you can read more about body language, a form of nonverbal communication. We hope it inspires you to do independent study and attend classes in the subject. Good communication must include reading nonverbal clues and skillfully asking what the person is really saying. These tools are absolutely essential for managers who communicate with employees.

Listen to the Person and Not Just the Employee

> If I were to summarize in one sentence the single most important principle I have learned in the field of interpersonal relations, it would be this: Seek first to understand, then to be understood. This principle is the key to effective interpersonal communications.
>
> —**Stephen R. Covey,** *Daily Reflections for Highly Effective People*

An employee has a larger life than what happens at work. An employee is also a father or mother, a religious person, a sports person, a sick person, an abused person, a political person, and so on. When an employee is acting out of character, the time for a face-to-face talk has come. The stimulus for uncharacteristic behavior often lies outside the workplace.

An appropriate question, followed by focused listening, can help the manager or team leader understand the situation. This act more often than not also relieves the pressure the employee is feeling. The act of talking releases emotional pressure. Asking clarifying questions that dig deeper can help a person to share the real burden. A question like, "What happened?" or "What's bothering you?" may be all that is needed to get a person to begin to open up. You do not need to make it too difficult. A question like, "Why did you say that?" can lead to the real issue causing the abnormal behavior.

The person you are helping generally does not know why he or she is acting out of character. Of course, some personalities "act-in," known as "stuffing it." This can lead to diseases and illnesses. A quiet, introverted personality type usually acts-in. So, when you ask questions and listen, you are helping to bring the issue that the employees are dealing with to their conscious mind. This act alone brings relief, which helps a team member return to top efficiency and effectiveness.

Listen to the Behavior over a Period of Time

People are consistent in behavior in their personal life. Families develop a culture. Individuals develop a personality and a set of habits. After knowing and being with a person, you learn how the person does and says things. Individuals have a rhythm and pace all their own. When the behavior changes, you notice, right? Do not ignore it.

Deborah Lewis, wife of one us (Robert Lewis), talked about her 23 years as office administrator for a K–8 public school. She could definitely read her colleagues. When something was not right at home, one of her principals during her career would get moody and overwhelmed and would resort to outbursts in the office setting. If the job were stressful, another, different principal's thinning hair would stand up like he had static electricity. Yet another principal would paint rooms in the office over the weekend during periods of anxiety or stress. Another would always take vacation days and go fishing. One employee at the school would become quiet, and she would need her extra space during periods of stress. Another would consistently become ill when things were not right. These were all indicators of stress at work, a difficult home situation, or bad news about health.

What can a team leader or manager do in such a situation? A team leader would need to exercise patience and thoughtfulness in this situation. By knowing why the behavior change is taking place, a team leader would not read into the behavior the wrong message. The wrong message would be to take the behavior personally or to think these team members were just being jerks who needed to be disciplined or denied a promotion or raise.

Listen to Themes, to Metaphors, and to What Is Conspicuously Not Discussed

Did you know that we communicate through storytelling, metaphors, and deletions in our communications? Our minds are marvelous and complex and do give us hints regarding what is happening in our unconscious minds. For example, when children are traumatized, they often cannot or will not talk about it. Psychologists began to notice, though, that children would draw pictures that held the themes of what had happened to them. Dr. John Savage, founder of L.E.A.D. Consultants, now called *Lead Plus,* located in Atlanta, Georgia, told me that he asked himself why adults did not do the same thing. He eventually realized that they did the same thing except they drew word pictures. These word pictures are metaphors, themes in a story, or sometimes a deletion of information from a story.

Listen for metaphors. A metaphor is a figure of speech in which one thing is compared to another, suggesting a resemblance of some kind. For example, "Let's go the whole nine yards," is a metaphor. We use metaphors all the time, but learn to listen for them.

Also, pay attention when something that should be said is not mentioned. For example, a colleague has both a living mother and father, and he constantly tells stories about his mother, yet he never talks about his father. What causes deletions from our conversations? Do you have a guess? Obviously, it is something we are avoiding.

How could we know what another person's metaphor or deletion means? We cannot. We must ask because everything else is a guess. Do not ask unless you have a solid relationship with the person. Ask in a private setting shortly after the person uses the metaphor. But, do not ask if you cannot deal with the emotion and see the discussion through to the end. You should talk to your company's counselor or mental health professional if you feel that you are dealing with a deeper, mental health issue in an employee with whom a mere friendly conversation cannot bring closure.

With stories, listen for themes. For example, a woman tells you about a recurring dream in which she is at the edge of a high cliff looking down, and she freezes. Dr. John Savage would ask, "What's going on in your life right now that's like standing on the edge of a high cliff looking down and you freeze?" He uses the exact words. If some kind of physical reaction occurs—a startled expression, tearing of the eyes, a flushed face—then you know that the conscious mind very likely realized the answer to your question for the first time. This realization brings emotional relief, making your workplace more efficient and effective.

Listen to Learn

The old saying that even a stopped clock is right twice a day makes a sage observation about other people. We can learn from anybody if we will overcome our prejudices and preconceived ideas about them. A leader must be a learner. This takes humility, something in short supply among so many managers and leaders—but not great leaders, as the book *Good to Great*[2] revealed.

Some of the smartest people in the world work beside us and right under our noses. They are the employees who actually make it happen; that is, they produce the output that their internal or external customer needs. They have learned from years of doing, watching, thinking, and learning. Think about it: They carry the history of the company and their department. Why not talk to them and listen to their knowledge and wisdom. Why not consult them about issues and obtain their unique perspective? Truth is, that is a leader's job.

We recently heard a story that applies here. We do not remember all the details, but here is the gist. You will recognize this story from your own experience because it is common.

> A small manufacturer had a contract for 250 units of a product. The manufacturer was running at full capacity. When asked by the contract holder to increase production to 325 units, the company vice president (VP) did not think it was possible. He pinpointed where the bottleneck was in the production. He knew the company did not have the money to enlarge the capacity for that area—besides it would take too long. He decided to do a study. He put together a task force of three engineers from his company and

an outside consultant. They spent a day studying and reported that production could not be increased without increasing the size of the production facility and adding employees.

The next morning the VP was stopped by the lead operator in the sector where the bottleneck was located and was asked what was going on with the consultant. The VP told him that the customer wanted another 75 units or more, but that his department did not have the capacity to do more than currently.

The lead operator said to him, "We could probably do that many more units. By the way, the break room needs a new microwave and coffee machine. If we can reach that number of units, do you think you could replace the microwave and coffee machine?" The VP agreed, and the operators spent the day reconfiguring the computers and machines. They were able to produce 350 units a month, 25 more than the minimum requested.

As we said, that story has been duplicated repeatedly in workplaces over the world. The sad truth is this: The people who get the work done are overlooked by the leaders. What we are saying is that these people ought to be the first consulted, and smart management will consult and learn from them.

CREATE AN ENVIRONMENT OF OPENNESS AND TRUST BY BECOMING AN EFFECTIVE COMMUNICATOR

Peter Senge wrote, "The traditional model of change—change that is led from the top—has a less-than-impressive track record."[3] Wherever change starts, you know it has been accepted when the board of directors officially adopts a policy underwriting the change. That would be a goal of the change agents seeking to bring a climate of openness and trust to the workplace and boardroom. Making this new policy part of the policy manual and mission statement would send a powerful signal of commitment and would give managers a leg to stand on.

Meanwhile, as a middle manager or team leader, do not lose heart. Change can start with you. In fact, it must start with you if you see the need to change your work environment to one of openness and trust. That means you need to develop good communication in your department or group by learning to be a great communicator. Start the ball rolling by becoming a warm, approachable manager who is not threatened by employee comments, complaints, or frustration. This means that you must begin to grow as a person yourself. You cannot bring improvement to your department unless you first improve yourself and commit yourself to lifelong learning.

As you build an environment of openness and trust by becoming an effective communicator, use several methods of communication with your people. Develop these into highly reliable and respected tools. Enlist talented people to help. Openly sharing mission critical information and making an effort to discuss strategic plans with the various employee groupings would emphasize the commitment of management to the success of their employees. Let us share a little more about some of these methods of communication.

Talk to Your Employees

Face-to-face communications are the bedrock of microcommunication. Research shows that employees would rather hear news directly from their supervisor than from any other source. Unfortunately, supervisors often shy away from face-to-face conversations with those they supervise. Others put off scheduling group meetings. One reason for this stems from time and pressure issues. Also, supervisors sometimes have personal doubts about their abilities to handle face-to-face communications, whether one on one or in a group.

Companies have a huge stake in hiring and training skilled supervisors. As important as communication is to the bottom line, management and line supervisors need to be trained in the basics. They also need support from the top to do all that they need to do to develop good communication and create an environment of openness and trust.

One on One

It actually takes quite a set of interpersonal communication skills to be effective in a one-on-one situation. If an employee makes a comment that can be taken as critical of the supervisor or company, it may put the supervisor on the defensive. If a supervisor is somewhat insecure, he or she might respond in a way that escalates the emotion or creates an issue that was not an issue.

A secure and skilled personal communicator will listen and ask questions. Usually, that is all that is required. Listening and asking good questions seems lame to those who do not understand the power of skilled listening and the skill of asking the right questions. Questions are powerful. Think about it. *Not* answering a question is difficult. Ask a person a question, and it takes a deliberate effort not to answer. Questions focus the brain and pull all the thoughts to the subject triggered by the question. Even after the discussion, the employee's brain will work on the answer to the question. That is why asking the right questions is so important.

Training is needed for management in what to do and how to do it when talking to an employee in a one-on-one situation. Great training is available in these areas that absolutely changes the way a person understands listening and eliciting information using a question aimed at the right subject matter. Good communication is a skill, like piano playing, that can be improved through training and practice.

Although face-to-face talks can be difficult for managers and supervisors, sometimes nothing else but a face-to-face talk will do. When a personal matter would embarrass an employee in a group setting, or when it is of no concern to anyone else, face-to-face communication is the only good communication. If an employee has been accused of some impropriety or some illegal act, face-to-face communication, again, is good communication, and public communication is bad. If a supervisor has developed a routine of regularly talking to employees one on one, less stress is generated when the supervisor must call an employee into his or her office for a talk.

Face-to-face talks can also be used to build a climate of openness and authentic communication throughout the department. The consistent *act* of talking one on one with employees becomes like another reinforcing voice speaking to everyone in the department. It says, "Management supports and appreciates you." This activity is important to do to create more trust and mutuality between the supervisor and the employee.

In a Group

Managers need to talk to the employees as a group from time to time. We are not talking about messages you would say over a public address system. We are talking about 20- to 30-minute meetings that have been well planned. Managers need to regularly communicate the heart and mission of the organization and department. Group meetings are also a time of building group identity, company pride, and strong relationships. If employees could meet each month for the manager to address them, it would go a long way to creating camaraderie and team spirit. Recognitions could be made and value-added information shared. A regular meeting also gives a natural forum for sensitive and important issues that arise. It gives a place to invite top management to come and be exposed to a large number of their employees for question-and-answer sessions. And, after it has become an accepted practice in the department, it can give a manager skilled in public speaking a bully pulpit.

As you learn about public speaking, you will learn the importance of the place you are speaking and the arrangements:

- The apportionment of the room—the shape of the room, the height of the ceiling, the arrangement of the chairs and the kind of chairs, the color of the walls, the focal point for the speaker, the decorations, and the cleanliness
- The temperature of the room
- The acoustics of the room
- The lighting of the room
- The quality of the sound equipment, if needed
- The size and quality of the screen used for audiovisual materials
- The availability of flip charts or whiteboards
- The availability and professional quality of printed materials handed out to employees
- The skillful use of other people to convene, focus attention, and introduce you
- Prepared material—well-organized, relevant, skillful use of illustrations and humor
- Audience participation
- A good delivery—eye contact, enunciation, volume, proper dress, confident bearing, opening, body, and a closing that flows

Even if you are not trained and skilled at public speaking, having the setting well apportioned and organized, having an agenda and sticking to it, involving other people, and writing out what you want to say will make it a successful event. You will find that the event itself is bigger than any one person's speech or part on the program.

Write to Your Employees

Management and leaders need to use writing as a communication avenue if they plan to create a climate of openness and trust. Written instruments are a powerful tool for so many reasons. Here are some reasons:

- Written instruments like newsletters, blogs, and e-mails can be used to inspire and build team spirit.
- Written instruments can be used to reinforce decisions or directives.
- Written instruments give the recipient an opportunity to study the communication for greater clarity.
- Written instruments like memos or newsletters can be attached to a bulletin board or computer screen and act as a reminder for recipients.
- Written instruments serve as a record of what was communicated as checks and balances for the communicators.
- Written instruments can be used to give a permanent record for historical, legal, and planning purposes.

A manager who can use written instruments effectively can triple his or her effectiveness and increase efficiency at the same time.

Newsletters

A newsletter is a printed letter or pamphlet that is delivered through the postal system or sent over the Internet. It is written and published at set intervals during the month or year. It contains articles, announcements, advertisements, and pictures. It is used to communicate with a group and to promote events and ideas. An indirect result is the building of group identity.

An organization could use a newsletter to increase the effectiveness of ongoing communication with its people. The newsletter would include a regular article or opinion piece by the manager. This would allow the manager another venue in which to talk to his or her employees at their place of residence through the postal service. A manager could promote, recognize, problem solve, and teach with the written word. Some personality types respond to this kind of communication better than the spoken conversation.

Each issue could highlight a different employee. The newsletter could print the pictures of employees with brief background minibiographies and what they do at the organization. Included also could be information they have chosen to share about their life away from work and then some interesting story about them that happened at work. The newsletter could also reinforce the organization's mission and its news in the business world. Newsletters can be great tools for building community.

As you will see in Chapter 11, newsletters sent via the Internet are fast putting traditional printed newsletters out of vogue. Managers now are moving to the practice of blogging and using social media. We discuss electronic newsletters (e-newsletters) later in this chapter, too.

Town Meetings

The days of the pilgrims and wild west are on the way back to American business. Henry Ross Perot, an American businessman best known for running for president of the United States in 1992 and 1996, embraced town meetings as a way to develop open communications between all levels of management and employees. The new town meetings are used to manage the organization. They are used to provide upper management and the employees a way of exchanging ideas and obtaining a better understanding of each other. Some organizations schedule town meetings that are open for anyone to attend, while other organizations invite specific individuals to attend. Typically, the agenda for these town meetings is a short presentation by upper management followed by an open question-and-answer session on any subject. Someone should be assigned to take notes at all of these meetings so that upper management can follow through on any problems that are defined by the audience and on any commitments that were made. After the minutes from these meetings are prepared, they should be posted on a bulletin board without the names of the people in the audience who ask the questions. This allows everyone to share the outcome from these meetings. Posting the minutes from the town meeting on the bulletin board has proven to be good practice because the questions asked are frequently questions that are on many people's minds, but they have not had the opportunity to ask them or they are too shy to ask them. Again, Chapter 11 shares about social media and its use in a corporate environment. Online bulletin boards, calendars, and reminders sent to a smart telephone are now available and used widely. Nevertheless, sometimes when standing near a water cooler or in a break room, a person looks for something to "kill time." A bulletin board with material to read does the trick.

Memos

Memo writing is used for an organization's IC. A memo is used to direct, persuade, or share information. With a memo, less is more. People are busy and hate to be interrupted. Also, shorter is more powerful. A memo leaves a paper trail and can be referred to later to clarify instructions or appointment times. The memo is divided into these parts:

- Heading
    From:
    To:
    Re: (subject or topic)
    Date:
- Body
    State the purpose of the memo clearly. Give all the important information that the receiving party will need to take action or comply with any requirements. The body should have an introduction that states the subject. The body gives a brief reason why. A conclusion or summary ties it up with a couple of sentences. It is good to end with a call of action of some kind.

A memo does not need to be signed. You do not need to type the sender's name at the bottom because the originator's name is included in the heading. Memos of a social nature, like announcing a birthday celebration in the break room, might add the name as a friendly gesture and could be on colored paper. Check to see if your organization has a standardized memo form (see Figure 4.1).

E-mails, Blogs, and a Tip of the Hat to Texting

Electronic communication tools for managers start with e-mail (electronic mail) and blogs (weblogs). They take place because of the Internet. A blog can be what you want it to be. It is a place people can go to read about you or to read about an organization. It can be like a newsletter in its content and purpose, or it can be like an online journal or diary. Blogs occur on a web page. Managers can use these tools with their employees to communicate and build team spirit.

An e-mail is different from a blog in that it is sent to people at specific computer terminals over the Internet. An e-mail is not on a web page. However, an e-mail can be written and sent with a newsletter or other documents attached to it. Or, an e-mail can be the formal letter. E-mails can be used by managers to communicate with a specific employee or with a group of employees. Your e-mail software will allow you to put employee

---

Harrington & Lewis Manufacturing Co.

5300 San Marcus Street, Somewhere, CA USA

MEMO

FROM: Jim Harrington & Bob Lewis

TO: All Employees

RE: Bonuses Issued —please read carefully!

DATE: July 1, 2012

MESSAGE: We reached our company's five year improvement goals 3.5 years early. To show our thanks for your work and commitment, we have issued an employee $10,000 mid-year bonus that you will receive with your next paycheck. Also, each employee will receive at least that size bonus at the end of December.

At the end of the year, you can receive your entire bonus in cash, or you can choose a special gift for both you and your wife or for you and a friend or family member. The special gift, in lieu of cash, is an all-expense paid Mediterranean Cruise, including airfare and spending money. The cruise will take place during the factory's shutdown for refitting from Dec. 26 thru Jan. 3. We will fly from San Francisco to Barcelona and board the cruise ship.

Please contact HR for more details and with your decision to join us for the cruise. Cruise sign-up deadline is December 1.

FIGURE 4.1
Sample memo.

e-mails into groups that you can label. That way, you can send any team an e-mail, and it will go to every team member.

Emails and blogs never disappear and should be treated as permanent records. Be wise what you say electronically. Even when an e-mail is deleted, it is not deleted. A technical person can find your e-mail's ghost on your hard drive, on the recipient's hard drive, or on a server (a computer) located in some computing cloud (also known as a data center). Also, your e-mail to one person could be read by another accidentally, or a person could hack into your e-mail.

As an employee of a company or as a professional, always use proper form and grammar. If you are writing to a friend or close team member, you can afford a few typos and some slang, but not to customers (internal or external), clients, or management.

Write important e-mails and wait a day before sending them. Let a trusted associate read them for errors, content, and clarity. Good writing takes time and effort, which includes letting it sit a day or two if you can. If not, heed the previous advice and let another person read it and give feedback.

The only electronic communication for which the writing is a world unto itself is text messaging, which takes place on your cellular telephone. However, if you are texting a boss, at least use complete sentences and spell correctly. Do not use acronyms and initials, like this one: ADBB (all done bye-bye).

Understand Your Employees

To be a good communicator, a manager needs to understand the employees as persons. Of course, that means to understand something of their families and interests. That knowledge comes naturally with relationship building. What we want to focus on now are three categories that do not necessarily come naturally. These are important for a manager, leader, or boss to understand to communicate effectively and efficiently:

- Employee personality types
- Employee communication channels
- Employee nonverbal communication usage

A person tends to react in similar ways in varied situations. When a person's behavior or personality changes suddenly, it is a sign that some event exerting influence on the person caused it. Once we know a person and that person's personality, the assumption that the person will react in a predictable way in the workplace is a good bet. Following this line of thought further, managers who know and understand the major types of personality can better understand employees and put them in situations where they will succeed and flourish. The act of doing this is an act of communication on the metacommunication level. It is indirect, yet it sets the stage for a happier employee, which sets the stage for positive and more effective communication.

Different persons also have different communication channels. Remember the famous phrase, "Breaker, breaker: one, nine"? That is a way of talking used by CB (citizen's band) radio people. Saying "breaker" on your CB radio means you want to talk, and "one, nine" means you are using channel 19. We really need to be that specific when we talk to each other if we want effective communication. A manager needs to be speaking in the same channel as the employee.

Nonverbal communication is a large category that includes body language. People instinctively pick up on some body language, like certain stances mean friend or foe. However, most people miss the more everyday, subtle body language. When the words and body language do not match, the truth always lies in the body language.

Let us explore just a little more about these topics. To fully understand and have proficiency at using each of these communication and team dynamic components, a manager needs extensive training and practice.

Personality Type of Each Employee

Don Stediman drove up to the Waltz's house to pick up Jamie, his toddler. Mrs. Waltz had watched Jamie at her day care center for 6 months. She was wonderful with the kids, but like many day care providers, she was weak in business skills. As Don greeted his child, he looked up at Mrs. Waltz. She had a tentative look on her face. Then, he remembered it was the day he was to pay her. He stood and took out his wallet. The check was written, and he handed it to her. She took it and looked at the total.

"Mr. Stediman, I have a new policy. If you are late, there's a $5.00 fee."

"Late?" Don was bewildered. "I thought it was due today like always," Don said.

"Today at 3 p.m.," said Mrs. Waltz, trying to be business-like. "We've been having some problems with people being on time, so I've had to make a policy."

"I don't mind your policy, but shouldn't you give notice. I could have paid last night."

"Oh, didn't you see the note on the front door this morning?"

Don hadn't. He paid the extra $5.00 and left, thinking that the one thing he did not need to do was let aggravation at Mrs. Waltz lose her as his day care provider.

The next Monday, Mrs. Waltz was her cheerful self and acted as if nothing unusual had happened. When Don asked to have a copy of her new policy, she actually responded with a blank look as though she never had heard the word *policy* before.

"Don't you remember that just last Friday evening you charged me a $5.00 late fee because of some new policy you talked about? I assume you have it written down somewhere," Don said.

"Oh, the late fee," Mrs. Waltz responded. "Of course, I remember. But I haven't had time to write a policy yet. Couldn't you just remember it?"

The next week, Don talked to Mrs. Waltz on Thursday evening. He told her that he had forgotten to write the check and asked if she would take it Friday evening and waive the late fee. That would save him from having to go home, fire up the computer, write the check, and drive the 6 miles back to give it to her. She smiled at Don and cheerfully said she understood that the late fee was a hassle. She put the coat on Jamie while waving to another parent who was leaving. Don thought that she had agreed to his proposal and left.

The next day, when Don paid her the usual fee, Mrs. Waltz asked for the late fee.

"But we had an agreement. You said you would waive the late fee," Don quietly protested.

"Oh, I was hoping you would understand about the late fee," Mrs. Waltz said. "I just had to make the policy. I really can't stay in business if everyone doesn't pay on time."

The miscommunication between Don and Mrs. Waltz led Don to spitefully pay the late fee in unwrapped pennies and to the "firing" of Jamie by Mrs. Waltz. Someone skilled in personality type would have realized that the interchange between Mrs. Waltz (an ESTP personality type in the Myers-Briggs Type Indicator) and Don Stediman (an ISTJ personality type in the Myers-Briggs Type Indicator), especially in the context presented, would usually have ended the way it did. The reason is that these personalities grate against one another. The ESTP personality type is described as spontaneous and challenging to be around. They like risk. They are competitive. The ISTJ, on the other hand, is characterized by the words tradition, predictability, and duty. In fact, they have an unshakable sense of duty.

Most people assume that everyone else communicates on the same basis as they do. This is the assumption that personality type theory helps to correct. People have different reasons for communicating and different criteria for gathering information. Understanding this and observing it in everyday interactions is the beginning of improved communication on the microlevel.

A famous modern personality inventory is called the *Myers-Briggs Type Indicator*. We can pair Myers's four groups with Plato's:

- The Sensing /Perceiving Type (SP) = Artisan
- The Sensing/Judging Type (SJ) = Guardian
- The Intuition/Feeling Type (NF) = Idealist
- The Intuition/Thinking Type (NT) = Rational

Whichever modern theory of personality your organization decides to use, it will be helpful in improving communication.

Variables Style Management

In Dr. Harrington's book, *Total Improvement Management*, he introduced the methodology of variables style management.[4] He points out that in this environment, management styles must have many facets. Yesterday, we expected managers to adjust their management style to meet the personality traits of the individual employee. Today, we need to adjust our management style to meet the individual's personality and to his or her job assignment. Employees' working personalities can be divided into four categories.

1. Planners: People who excel in taking an idea and laying out a systematic approach to its implementation. Planners tend to be introverts.
2. Networkers: People who establish excellent communication systems between groups. They are excellent negotiators and politicians. Networkers tend to be extroverts.
3. Doers: People who like to take a plan and implement it. They like to be assigned to a problem that needs to be corrected. They make things happen.
4. Leaders: People who, through their charisma, appearance, technical knowledge, or example, attract others to them. People follow them because it is unpopular to do otherwise.

Each of these personality traits imposes very different needs on management. Their general needs can be classified into two types:

- Social needs: These needs are satisfied by management contact, public recognition, and a demonstrated interest in the individual's career, personal interests, and personal life.
- Technical needs: The skills required to perform a given task.

Two factors drive the degree and frequency to which both needs have to be fulfilled:

1. How well the individual can perform the assigned task.
2. The type of personality that composes the individual's makeup.

Figure 4.2 shows why management style needs to change versus the employees' performance level. It is easy to see that, based on how the

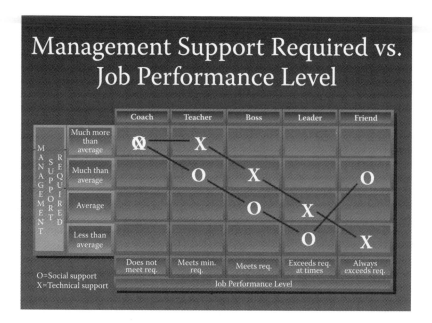

FIGURE 4.2
Management support required versus job performance level.

individual is performing, the management style may need to be changed to meet the employees' needs.

- Employees who do not meet requirements need a "coach." That is, they need someone who will tell them what to do and show them the correct way when they cannot accomplish a task. They need someone who will help them feel good about themselves, even when they are not doing well, and minimize their chances of making an error.
- Employees who meet minimum requirements need a "teacher." That is, they need someone who can help them understand the concepts, someone who will measure their performance and show them when they make an error. They need someone who recognizes their success and helps them to succeed.
- Employees who meet requirements need a "boss." That is, they need someone who gives them assignments and follows through to be sure that they are accomplished and who helps them develop and improve the quality of their output and their productivity. They still need more-than-average social support. They need someone who tells them that they can do better and takes time to discuss social issues with them.

- Employees who exceed requirements at times need a "leader." They need someone who knows what needs to be done and has empowered the employee to take on responsibilities and accountabilities for his or her job. The leader works with the employee to ensure that barriers to completing the job are limited. The leader focuses his or her effort on coordinating the employee's interface and provides feedback. The leader sets the example for the employee with his or her technical and personal style while at work.
- Employees who always exceed requirements need a "friend." At this level of performance, management can delegate responsibilities for the assignment to the employee and hold the employee accountable for its outcome. Management should develop an open, two-way personal relationship with the employee, sharing experiences and family concerns. Technical interests and understanding are developed by providing a ready ear to discuss project operations and exchange ideas, but the technical decisions are made by the employee. The employee is empowered to make decisions and take control of all tests assigned to him or her, without management direction. Much more effort is put into satisfying this individual's social needs while minimum effort is required in providing technical support.

It is easy to see that a management style must change from coaching (the most dictatorial management style) all the way to friendship (the most dissipative, that is to say, laissez-faire, management style) based on the varying degrees of performance. The performance is as much the responsibility of the manager as it is the employees (see Figure 4.3).

If a person has a networking personality and is assigned to do networking (coordinating between areas), his or her chances of meeting requirements are extremely high with little effort on the employee's part. But, if a networker is assigned to do a planning activity, it will be hard for him or her to meet requirements even though he or she extends significant effort in trying to accomplish the task. Unfortunately, in today's and tomorrow's complex environment, most job assignments require the employee to be moved back and forth through many types of assignments often during a single day. As a result, management style for an individual employee will have to vary based on the tasks that the individual is performing. Management cannot hold an employee responsible for poor performance if management misassigns the individual and does not give the individual the required level of technical and social support.

Expected Performance Based Upon Personality Traits and Types of Assignments				
		Type of assignment		
PERSONALITY TRAITS		Planner	Networker	Doer	Leader
	Planner	Outstanding	Very poor	Good	Poor
	Networker	Very poor	Outstanding	Poor	Good
	Doer	Good	Poor	Outstanding	Very poor
	Lender	Very poor	Good	Poor	Outstanding

FIGURE 4.3

Expected performance based on personality traits and type of assignment.

Five-Way Communication

For a long time, organizations have been trying desperately to establish effective two-way communications (up and down), and just as we have started to make real progress, now we find that this is not adequate. Many organizations are now trying to establish five-way communications (up, down, horizontal, customer, and supplier). This five-way or star communication process is a key part of a participative team environment that is based on a strong supplier-customer relationship (see Figure 4.4). Today, the complex organizational environment makes this five-way communications system an essential part of an effective operation. In our information-rich society, management can no longer ration the information they believe that the employee needs to know. Likewise, every employee has an obligation to maintain active communication with all those he or she interfaces. The day of management being responsible for keeping the employee informed disappeared when we began to empower the employees. Management's responsibility is to provide the communication process and the media. It is everyone's responsibility to use it. Everyone has a personal responsibility to manage a personal communication network within his or her own star. At a minimum, every employee is involved in four of the five points of the star.

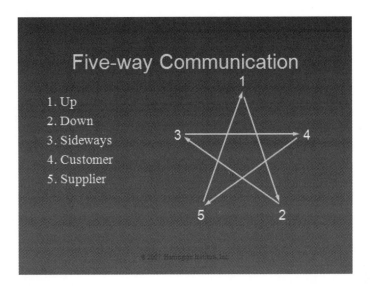

FIGURE 4.4
Five-way communication process.

The actions that need to be taken to effectively make the five-way communication process work are the following:

- Management needs to trust the employee with information previously restricted to management.
- Management must establish the process.
- Everyone needs to be trained in how to use it.
- A reward system needs to be put in place to encourage the use of the process.

Today, technology and personal initiative can easily take care of the communications problem if both are used correctly. Computer networks, voice mail, centralized databases, telecommunications, video conferencing, town hall meetings, and bowling leagues are just some of the means of communicating; the list goes on and on. The five-way communication process in today's environment is not only desirable but also mandatory.

One of the weaknesses in most communication systems is the inability or reluctance of the employee to use them. In most organizations, communication training has been limited to management. This was a realistic approach in a one-way, downward communication process. Why would you want to train employees in communication skills? If they knew how to communicate, they would want to be listened to, and who had time to do that? But today, with everyone having shared responsibilities in making the communication process work, everyone needs to be trained in how to use it and have access to the required media. The biggest problem we face in establishing a five-way communication process is getting the data into the process. A well-designed data system that is user friendly will group information into relative packages that minimize the time and effort required to obtain the needed information. The biggest roadblock to making this happen is upper management, who for years believed that information was power and therefore were unwilling to share this power with employees. Add to this the feeling that most employees could not be trusted or were not intelligent enough to understand the business, and it was easy for management to justify not putting most of the information they controlled into the communication process. The fact of the matter is that most employees can be trusted, and the ones who cannot be trusted have already found ways to get the information they want. When managers start to share their information openly, the communication process is legitimized and becomes effective.

Communication Channels

Increasingly, consultants to business are adapting the findings in various fields of science to the business arena. One of these fields is neurolinguistic programming (NLP). NLP is becoming a foundational field in communication. In the 1970s, a totally new understanding of how humans make sense of their world was shared with a select group of practitioners, researchers, and teachers. Slowly, it became more widely known. It was developed by a linguist and a man who was both a programmer and a mathematician. The linguist was John Grinder, and the programmer and mathematician was Richard Bandler. Drawing from many discoveries from the earlier part of the twentieth century as well as their new findings, they came up with the theory they called NLP.

Neuro refers to the brain and the nervous system. This word indicates that Grinder and Bandler were proposing a theory for how the brain uses the five senses to understand and explain the world in which people live.

Linguistic refers to language. The brain and nervous system convert the feelings, smells, sights, sounds, and tastes into language. Specific words are stored in the brain to correspond and *represent* the real world. People use this language to represent the world to both themselves and others. Language patterns are expressions of who people are and how they think.

Programming refers to the coding of experience. A program is a series of steps in a process designed to produce a certain result. NLP states that the results a person achieves and the effects created by a person's actions are a result of these personal programs. Once recognized and understood, these programs can be changed. NLP explains how a person changes through drawing new maps of the territory we call the world.

NLP believes that although people live in the world and the world is real, they do not operate directly on the world. Instead, people use maps of the world. These maps are *representations* of the world residing in the brain. Think for a moment of an actual map of a territory. It is a representation of that territory produced on a piece of paper or computer screen by GPS. We carry the same kind of map in our brains of our experiences in the world.

A person has a maximum of five representational systems to guide behavior in the world. These correspond to the five senses. Because smell and taste are used so little in representing the world, they are usually combined into the feeling system. A representational system called *nonspecific* has also been created for people who seldom use language of the sensory channels. However, some have recognized the nonspecific system as a heightened auditory system.

Therefore, the different ways people think are

Visual	A person thinks in pictures or mental images.
Auditory	A person thinks in sounds.
Feelings (kinesthetic)	A person thinks in feelings, either outward feelings of touch or inner feelings of emotions.

People generally have a preference for one of these systems over the others. They develop this one system while exercising the others minimally.

How can a person discover which representational system (visual, auditory, kinesthetic) another person prefers? A number of ways exist, but the easiest ways for nonlinguists are to notice predicates (verbs, adjectives, and adverbs in a sentence) and to notice eye movements (where they are positioned when a person speaks).

To become proficient at knowing a person's preferred channel and speaking to them in their preferred channel takes many hours of training. This training would be worth a company's time and money.

Body Language

The chief executive officer (CEO) of Allied Copper & Nickel made a sweep with his right hand as he described the large division of the company that would be included in the reorganization.

"We can save a lot of employee burden and several middle-management salaries. Then, with the rightsizing efforts and the new restructuring, we will actually increase productivity. What do you think, Herb?" the CEO, Roger Baines, asked.

Herb, the VP of operations, put his right hand to his mouth, rubbed his nose with the index finger, looked at the floor, and said, "Sounds like a great idea." Then, he folded his arms.

CEO Baines smiled and said, "I'm glad you're open to this, Herb. Of course, we have a lot of planning to do to implement the idea. I'll be depending on you. Do you think we need a consulting firm?"

Herb shifted positions and rubbed his neck. "Sure. We're going to need all the help we can get."

After the meeting with CEO Baines, Herb was distressed. Of course, he would never let anyone else know how he felt. But, restructuring was a difficult thing. He had friends he would have to lay off. And, he was not sure about all this high-performance team business. He believed in running a tight ship, not letting the crew do whatever they wanted to do. Herb found himself standing in front of Ed Johnson's office, the VP of the research and development division.

"Ed, do you have a minute?" Herb asked.

Ed had just hung up the phone. "Sure, come in, Herb. You look worried. What's going on?"

"Has Roger talked to you about his plans?"

"No, but what's new?" Ed said with a weak smile as he looked at the desktop and put down his pen. He nonchalantly scratched below his earlobe five times. Then, he picked at what appeared to be some lint on his left sleeve.

"He wants to restructure the whole company from bottom to top—except for us, of course. He's in a downsizing mode. I think it's a big mistake."

Ed brushed the rest of the lint off his sleeve. "Well, you may be right, Herb. He's been under pressure lately from the board to increase profitability. All our competitors have already restructured. Have you read anything about what Baines wants to do?"

"You know I don't read anything, Ed," Herb intoned, then sighed. "So, are you with me on this? Can we do something to stop it?"

Ed looked at the floor. "Sure, Ed. I'll help you."

"Great. I knew I could count on you, Ed," Herb said as he left.

This conversation is representative of business communication. The CEO wanted to restructure, but not the two VPs. However, the CEO believed they were in agreement with him. Is that what you understood from the conversation? A person trained in gestures and nonverbal communication would have understood something different. Had CEO Baines been trained to watch nonverbal clues, he would have understood that Herb, the VP of operations, really did not agree with him and said as much—nonverbally. And, the person versed in gestures would have known that Ed, the VP of research and development, had also lied to Herb. CEO Baines had talked to Ed, contrary to what Ed had told Herb; furthermore, Ed had agreed with the CEO. What are the gestures that told us these things?

- Putting right hand to mouth (deceit)
- Touching nose (lying)
- Putting hand to back of neck (gesture indicating "you're a pain in the neck")
- Looking at the floor (lying)
- Folding arms (defensive)
- Giving a weak smile (insincerity, remorse)
- Putting down the pen (a sophisticated looking down gesture—lying)
- Scratching below earlobe five times (lying)
- Picking imaginary lint off sleeve (withheld disapproving opinion)
- Sighing (heaviness of spirit)

Can you see how speaking or "reading" body language and other nonverbal cues can reveal the real message? This skill will serve to open communication and bring health into an organization if all people trust and value one another and know how to call someone when they are saying something but not meaning it. A huge gap was evident in the communication of the three executives in the example. To close the communication gap, nonverbal communication must be one of the skills of every person in a company, beginning with top-level executives.

SUMMARY

To talk to employees, an environment of openness and trust must be created. Fortunately, this environment is created when a manager and his or her organization begin listening to employees and communicating with employees. When a manager listens to employees, it signifies a change in attitude in an organization. It signals a shift from distrust to trust. It signals a shift from thinking employees are not part of the team to thinking and recognizing they are part of the team. The employees have information the manager needs. The manager has information the employees need.

To talk to employees also means that the manager must become a communicator. A manager must talk to employees one on one as well as in groups. Doing this routinely builds rapport and understanding.

A manager communicates by writing to employees as well. The manager must use each avenue well and effectively: newsletters, memos, e-mails, blogs, and texts.

To talk to the employees means a manager must understand them. A manager needs to understand personality types, communication channels, and body language.

> The knowledge worker needs knowledge about the organization or they're just workers.

—H. J. Harrington

> Unambiguousness in our relationships leads to quality in our communication.

—R. D. Lewis

REFERENCES

1. Toffler, Alvin (1970). *Future Shock*, Random House, New York.
2. Collins, Jim (2001). *Good to Great: Why Some Companies Make the Leap … and Others Don't*, HarperCollins, New York.
3. Senge, Peter et al. (1999). *The Dance of Change: The Challenges to Sustaining Momentum in Learning Organizations*, Doubleday, New York.
4. Harrington, H. James (1995). *Total Improvement Management,* McGraw-Hill, New York, pp. 207–208.

5

How Do I Hear What My Teammates Are Really Saying?

I have been listened to therefore I am.

—**Anonymous**

Forming, storming, norming, and performing are phases that a group of people follow when becoming a team. The more stormy the storming phase in the team development, the less the quality of the communication that has been taking place. The degree that the team learns to change this reality and to commune with one another will determine the quality of the communication in the norming phase.

—**R. D. Lewis**

INTRODUCTION

Lindsay was telling her boss about a time-saving change for the production line that she had been considering, but she felt her boss was not interested. He was not making eye contact with her; in fact, he was looking over her shoulder, watching the work group in the area of the receiving bay. She finally trailed off what she was saying, a little embarrassed for him, but he did not seem to notice. When she stopped talking, he gave her a glance, a pat on the shoulder, and a quick smile. "Keep up the good work, Lindsay," he said and walked over to the receiving bay.

Six months later, the competition made the exact same changes in its production line that Lindsay had suggested to her boss that day. One year later, Lindsay and her boss were victims of layoffs, but they both got jobs with the competition.

Lindsay's boss may seem like a terrible person, but he was not worse than Lindsay herself. Truth be known, they both had the same problem, and neither knew. Do you know what it was? Both could hear yet neither could listen. Both, however, were highly skilled at telling. Why do teammates lack the learned skill of listening?

Listening is like a door to the world. How we choose to listen structures our perception of reality. How do you listen to the world? What preconceived ideas do you bring to the listening experience? These preconceived ideas and key life experiences change the way a person hears other people and determines that person's reality. A listener must be open to personal improvement to become a high-quality listener. Quality listening requires thoughtful, informed, and skilled listeners. This takes commitment, training, and objectivity. It also takes unselfishness, humility, and valuing the group over the individual. Remember the message of that book we have mentioned several times, *Good to Great*?[1] The standout leader can be good, but not great. In today's business environment, teams take precedence over the individuals. This requires many changes in the individual, with high-quality listening as the starting point.

The most powerful listening is done in dialogue, which takes place in a team environment. When individuals change into a group, thinking and acting as a single person, bound into one entity by trust, respect, and a common mission, then the power of listening multiplies exponentially. High-performance teams are like that. So, I ask again, "Why do teammates lack the learned skill of listening?"

RUGGED INDIVIDUALISM DIES WITH THE TEAM

When a person works alone, that person can do as he or she pleases regarding how the work is done. Add one more person and doing as he or she pleases is not going to get any work done. More than one person working on a common endeavor requires high-quality and professional-level communication. A team environment requires more than two-way communication; it is multidirectional. Yet, talking as a group requires each person in the group to purposefully choose to give up monologues in favor of dialogues. No more shut up and listen kinds of top-down, rugged-individualism, one-way communication. Community and mutuality are the key descriptive words for high-level communication used by high-performance teams. The team becomes one and then joins the larger community of teams.

On a team, each member adopts the attitude of first listening with understanding, then talking about his or her own ideas. Dialogue with no egos attached brings a team into accord. When accord happens, everyone on the team embraces this new idea, and it is no longer the team's idea alone; it has also become each team member's own idea. That is the ideal. In reality, accord cannot be reached in most situations, but compromise can be attained. Either way, the team takes priority over rugged individualism.

Generally, people know how to talk about interests and ideas. Listening to others talk about their interests and ideas, however, takes a concentration that must be learned. Generally, teammates do not have this learned skill of listening because listening is not commonly taught. A child or student is punished, though, for not listening, so the parents and the teachers know the importance of listening.

Schools emphasize writing and public speaking but not listening. Part of the issue is that listening is considered by many to be the same as hearing. That idea could not be more wrong. Hearing is what an organ of the body performs, but listening is an intellectual activity and a skill that must be developed like any other skill. If a person listens, then that person has almost certainly learned how to do it. Few teammates are "natural" listeners. They need to learn to do it just as they learned to read and write. Those who learn this skill are the highest-regarded and highest-compensated people in our society. Yet, their colleagues think their success is related to some other factor. Teams need teammates who have learned to listen to become high-performance teams. And, as an aside, that also applies to the team of husband and wife—no charge for that bit of marriage counseling.

Listening, according to Larry Baker, author of *Listening Behavior*,[2] is a "selective process of attending to, hearing, understanding and remembering aural (and at times visual) symbols" (p. 17). Most studies indicate this listening process is poorly done. According to research, a person spends 70% of his or her day in communication. If communication can be broken down into writing, reading, speaking, and listening, most of this time is spent in listening. Around 40% to 45% of a manager's time goes to listening, and at least 25% of that listening time is thrown away. If a company has a manager who earns $100,000 per year, then the manager is paid $10,000 for wasted listening time. And we know what that is called: an improvement opportunity.

A physiological reason exists for giving teammates the opportunity to be effective and efficient listeners. This physiological reason is the rate at which we hear versus the rate at which we talk. We listen at the rate of 400 to 800 words per minute. We talk at the rate of 120 to 180 words per minute. We generally use this lag time to think of other things while a person is talking. We can clutter our mind with static, or we can use this listening gap to focus all our listening capacity on listening. When we concentrate totally on listening, we call this *deep listening*.

What Makes a Standout Leader?

A standout leader can be good but not great; this is the message of the book *Good to Great*.[1] Do not be discouraged if you are the team leader who wants to make your mark in your chosen life's work like many of the great men and women of history. Leading a team, a church, a company, or an army division is not about a John Wayne kind of leader. According to the author of the book *Good to Great*, it is about being a level 5 leader, a leader who has a unique blend of personal humility and professional will. John Wayne was good, but the characters he played in the movies had only professional will and little-to-no personal humility. On the other hand, a leader with the blend of professional will and personal humility has the potential to be great, and listening does take a large dose of personal humility.

Of course, the team leader has a responsibility of getting the right people on the team doing the right thing. The leader and team need to have listened and watched one another long enough to know one another's strengths and comfort zones. Collins uses the metaphor of a bus. He says you have to have the right people on the bus. Do not make the "what" decisions until you do this. Also, he extends this metaphor by saying you also need the right people sitting in the right seats. Listening to what your teammates are saying is necessary to accomplish these things.

The Team Takes Precedence over the Individual

High-performance teams have members who understand that the team takes precedence over the individual. It is not about any one person on the team. It is about the team. Everyone contributes. Everyone shapes the end result, including the ones who put forth ideas that are discarded. Everyone shares the credit and the glory. Everyone has humility.

Psychology has studied and continues to study whether groups make better decisions than individuals. As you might guess, it all depends. Generally, some research shows that individuals make better low-risk decisions, and groups make better high-risk decisions. Sometimes, groups fall into a way of thinking called *groupthink* when people simply agree to keep the status quo. When groups excel in making decisions, the people in the group feel safe to share, which means the teams have high trust and the right people, and they love and respect one another. These conditions come when team leaders and team members put the team first. You know that the team has precedence over the individual when each teammate is hearing what each of the other teammates says, and each teammate has the humility to choose the best solution, even if the suggestion made by that teammate is discarded. Only then can teammates truly know one another and hear what contributions are being made. On a higher level, each team member knows that the wrong suggestions need to be voiced to help select the right suggestions. Therefore, nothing that is said in a sincere attempt to reach the goal is wasted.

Maturity Is Imperative for Good Teamwork

In a person, maturity has an age component and a character component. We say that someone is mature of age when he or she has reached full physical, emotional, and mental development and when he or she is able not only to take care of himself or herself but also to take responsibility for the care of others, like children, a household, or a business. A person is of mature character when he or she treats others with respect, integrity, and love in the "platonic sense."

The very nature of teamwork would require the people making up the group to be mature of character. A mature person understands that the individual is of intrinsic worth and therefore worthy of respect. Also, each individual has a point of view different from others and can give a unique perspective on the subject under discussion.

In describing the basic idea behind quality circle (QC) circle activities, Kaoru Ishikawa listed these three points on the "basic idea behind QC Circle Activities":[3]

- Contribute to the improvement and development of the enterprise.
- Respect humanity and build a happy, bright workshop where working in it is meaningful.
- Display human capabilities fully and eventually draw out infinite possibilities.

This is the Japanese way of saying "team maturity."

The Ancients Were Right

Each generation in the United States tends to think it is smarter and wiser than previous generations. Of course, that belief is not true. They have certainly been richer over the last 250 years. The endless scientific and financial progress in the United States for the last two and a half centuries has led each succeeding generation to believe that they are also getting wiser than the older generations when it comes to the basics of human society and interaction. To illustrate this, a few years ago, my then-35-year-old son saw that I had a copy of an old, 1930s vintage, Humphrey Bogart movie. He said he wanted to take it and watch it. When he brought it back to me, he said, "I really enjoyed watching that old movie. I couldn't believe the way the women flirted with Bogart—like that lady cab driver. I didn't know women talked that way in those days." I got a laugh and some insight from his comments. Men and women today are little different from the way they have been throughout history. Wise men have lived in other times and learned the same lessons about life and human nature that all wise and discerning people learn through the decades. Here are two ancient principles that are relearned every few generations: Know thyself and do unto others as you would have them do unto you.

Know Thyself

To be wise and successful in the ultimate sense, a person must learn to understand self, whether himself or herself. Our greatest obstacle to happiness and success is our self. If we cannot differentiate between others and our self, then we cannot have relationships. When we see other people as not having thoughts, opinions, or aspirations of their own but see them as an extension of ourselves, we are said in psychological terms to be subjective. When we are able to differentiate between others and our own self, we are said to be objective. An objective person has the ability to see another person's point of view. This is one aspect of knowing thyself, understanding that self is unique and different from other selves.

Another aspect of knowing thyself is to be able to see self the way that others see self. Some are said to be blind to how they affect other people. When we say a person has no *couth*, although discussing a lack of cultural polish, we might be talking about an accompanying blindness this person possesses related to how he or she is affecting others in an offensive or disturbing way. One component of being uncouth is being too subjective.

To "know thyself" has another dimension, one that is not only outwardly focused but also inwardly focused. A team member must understand his or her own motives, desires, strengths, weaknesses, and limits. The team member must love his or her own self and respect the self as well as other selves.

How can one judge whether a person has enough balance in the area of objectivity and subjectivity to be a good teammate? There are psychological profiles and analysis tools that can be used to measure these attributes. Your human resources department and some business consultants are certified to administer and interpret these psychological and personality profiles.

A team made up of members that know self is destined to become a high-performance team. Only when we know and respect self are we able to join with other selves in a common endeavor and as a team work with one mind.

Do Unto Others as You Would Have Them Do Unto You

This saying, "Do unto others as you would have them do unto you," appears in different forms from ancient times. It was stated as a positive in the Bible; Confucius stated it as a negative. The idea of reciprocity appears in many ancient writings and laws.

I have heard some humorous rephrasing of the Golden Rule, as it has been called. One such is this: "Do unto others before they do unto you." This sounds more like the natural bent of human nature. Yet, the longing of humankind for a higher moral level would point to the classic statement. If all people practiced the higher road of treating others the way we would want to be treated, the results would be a happy, prosperous society for all. The same is true in a working environment. Encouraging and helping one another, rather than desiring that the other workers fail in order to make oneself look better, actually brings greater prosperity for everyone over the long term. Greed ultimately destroys a person and the things that person loves, including businesses.

USE THE FEEDBACK LOOP

Remember the feedback loop introduced in Chapter 2? Begin using it as you communicate with your teammates. The concept is basic and simple enough for teenagers to learn. By consistently using it, you will lower listening errors and increase the quality of your team's listening. Here is the shortened version of using the feedback loop. It is called *a loop* because a message is sent from a sender (the person talking) to a receiver (the person listening). When the receiver receives the message and it is heard and understood, it is then sent back to the original sender in the receiver's own words. The resending of the message is to check the accuracy of the understanding by the receiver.

This is simple, right? In concept, yes, it is simple. In practice, it takes concentration, skill in listening, and patience. That is because we have deadlines, and the process seems as though it is such a waste of time. Besides that, our egos get in the way. It takes a lot of humility and unselfishness to have what you said critiqued. It takes a different view of life than the one portrayed by the actor Michael Douglas in the 1987 motion picture *Wall Street*, in which greed was the motivation.

In high-performance teams, the good of both the group and the company has to take precedence over the good of the individual while respecting and valuing each individual. The balance has to be such that by putting the group first, all the individuals also better themselves, which is exactly what happens. It seems a contradicting phenomenon. When an individual does what seems to him or her the quickest and sometimes the only way to get ahead, it limits or destroys the individual, like in the movie *Wall Street*; yet, when an individual does what seems will limit or destroy him or her—helping others also get ahead—it ends up putting the individual further into the realm of success than would have happened otherwise. So, it is a matter of balancing personal wisdom and drive with love and good will toward men. That is why the virtues taught by the ancients are relevant today. They lead to the well-being of those who practice them, including teams and businesses.

Listen to Your Teammate

When you really, deeply understand each other, you open the door to creative solutions and third alternatives. Our differences are no longer stumbling blocks to communications and progress. Instead, they become the stepping stones to synergy.

—**Stephen R. Covey**

How do we listen to a teammate? We do it with the feedback loop and our total attention. We have gone over that part. But, what would one do differently at a more formal meeting? You do it like a professional goes about doing his chosen field of work. When an appointment is made to discuss your work project, here are some reminders and suggestions:

1. **Come to the listening table with the right tools.** Tools used to help one listen with comprehension would include a writing tablet (whether electronic or paper and pen), in some instances a recording device or a digital camera, a copy of any documents that will be part of the discussion, and your mind. Yes, your mind needs to be present and prepared. Give your mind ample time to think about the topic under discussion and the person with whom you will be having a dialogue.

2. **Take a few moments to establish mutuality.** *Mutuality* is the formal acknowledgment of one another's presence and engaging in a moment of "small talk" unrelated to the topic to be discussed. This creates an affinity and support for one another and rids the mind of what has been its focus, allowing the mind to refocus on the new discussion to follow.

3. **Dialogue with the person, following each "whisper of a thought" that surfaces to your mind.** A dialogue is give and take, like the feedback loop. You listen, establish understanding, and then probe the subject using questions. Take notes, take pictures of items or things pertinent to the dialogue, and refer to documentation as needed to establish mutual understanding.

   What is meant by a "whisper of a thought"? Can you remember ever having a vague thought when talking to a person and never getting back to query the person related to the subject of the thought? Later, it became apparent that your thought was right on target and could have been of positive benefit to the person or yourself. That is what I meant about a whisper of a thought. Make a note to remind yourself to ask the whisper question later in the conversation.

4. **Write or state a summary of the discussion, including the action items of each member of the discussion.** This is just like the feedback loop, is it not? The distinctive characteristic of this restatement of what has been communicated is that it is a summary of the results of the entire meeting itself rather than simply the summary of a statement of one of the participants during the dialogue.

5. **File a report of the meeting in your storage file and send copies to the team and other pertinent parties.** According to a Chinese proverb: "The palest ink is better than the sharpest memory."

Repeat Back

Repeating to your teammate in your own words what you understood him or her to say is a critical success factor in listening. We call this a *perception check,* and we talk about this practice as error-proofing communication. Your teammate is not a mind reader, and neither are you. Even after years of working together and knowing one another's body language, this practice continues to be necessary to avoid career-limiting mistakes. Ask for any clarifying information. If body language is incongruent with the words coming out of the teammate's mouth, describe the body language you observed and ask if the teammate is comfortable with what he or she is proposing. Go around the loop—"get loopy"—as many times as needed to establish understanding.

When we get loopy and repeat to a person what we have heard them say, we paraphrase that person's statement. In paraphrasing, a helpful tool to use is a standard phrase to start our paraphrase. The paraphrase can be in question form or in a statement form. Most of us have several of these standard phrases that we use repeatedly as starter phrases. They are called *stems.* Here are some examples of stems to use when paraphrasing as offered by Dr. John Savage:[3]

- "You are saying that …"
- "What I hear you saying is that …"
- "You are telling me that …"
- "If I am hearing you right, you are …"
- "Let me say what I am hearing …" (p. 24)

A paraphrase might go like this: "You are saying that you didn't attend the meeting because your mother had a stroke, and you had to call the paramedics and follow them to the hospital to admit her."

Listen to the Feedback

Now, if miscommunication has happened, the first speaker will tell you that he or she has been misunderstood. Listen to the feedback concerning your feedback coming from the teammate. Listen with the same intensity that you listened to your teammate when the message was first sent. Each person in the communication loop needs to practice deep listening throughout the total conversation until clear understanding is achieved.

One more thing needs to be said about being on the receiving end of a perception check. If you are sensitive about not being completely understood, you might become defensive. Ask yourself, "What is there about my personality or my conditioning that causes me to be defensive about being questioned or about being fully understood?" This is a personal growth opportunity. Learning and growth in excellence are lifelong endeavors. Maybe you are being checked for understanding by a much younger new hire. As long as the person means no disrespect, he or she should be commended for the effort to communicate clearly and not resented or rebuked for being insubordinate. Remember, unless you are in a military or paramilitary organization, the day of business using the command-and-obey structure is over.

Repeat the Feedback Loop for a Second Time

Usually, two times around the loop bring clarity of understanding. If not, do not let go of the conversation until total clarity is achieved. In a team environment, understanding must be crystal clear. Each person must grasp the content of shared information and communications taking place. Every point of view should be in focus. If not, then the team needs to be made aware of the information that one of the team members does not fully understand.

I know—asking for clarification on meaning of a communication for the fourth time is embarrassing and potentially insulting. So, then, say as much after the third time. Acknowledge the unspoken thought that each party is thinking. "I'm so sorry to ask again. I know this seems insulting to you, but it is not meant to be. It is so important for me to understand this. What am I missing?" Frank and open talk like this will ease the emotion of the situation and help each party think about the missing piece of information that will get you and the sender of the information back on track.

Use the Feedback Loop with Verbal and Written Team Communication

The same process can be used with written communication as with verbal communication. Written communication also uses themes and metaphors that can be helpful in building good communication. Continue using the communication loop with written communication until understanding is achieved. With e-mails or letters, you can copy all teammates who can follow your conversations.

DISCUSS FEELINGS AND BODY LANGUAGE

A listener needs to know four things about the message sent by a sender:

1. The content of the message
2. The sender's unspoken and hidden content attached to this message
3. The order of importance of the first two items to the sender
4. The degree of objectivity of the listener toward the conversation

Miscommunication generally takes place when the listener fails to correctly analyze these four aspects of a message.

Messages have two components. The first component is the literal *content* or the subject matter of the message. The second component is the *affect* or the emotion conveyed by the sender concerning the content. That is, how does the sender feel about the message? Which component is most important to the sender, the content or the feeling he or she has about that content? The sender determines which component has priority. It can be either one. The listener, in the decoding process, must determine which component carries the most value to the sender. Also, often part of a message could be "deleted" or omitted, usually unconsciously.

Listeners often choose to focus on the content of a message rather than the emotional content that is communicated. At one time, business schools concentrated only on the content. Most businesspersons are highly trained and skilled at understanding data and content. Yet, embedded in the content, the listener will find an emotional response to it on the part of the sender or speaker. The listener has little chance of understanding the meaning of a communication unless he or she identifies the emotion connected with it. Those highly analytical minds may have difficulty with this. Nevertheless, facts are facts wherever we find them.

Although we ultimately make decisions based on facts, the effectiveness of the execution of our decisions can also be greatly influenced by teammates' feelings about the decisions. Execution of a decision might or might not take place based on a person's motivation and belief about the decision.

The trust level in a team must be high to allow total openness and safety in discussing the feelings and emotions of teammates related to the content of the communications.

How do we know other teammates' feelings? We know through body language and nonverbal communication. At least, we get a clue regarding what the feelings and motivations are through these means. We must do perception checks, however, with our teammates to verify our guesses based on body language and nonverbal clues. Also, always be aware of the environment in which the message is being sent because that environment also has an effect on the sender and the message being sent. If I said, "Give me another round," it would mean one thing at a bar in a club and entirely another thing in a combat situation. The miracle is that we understand each other as well as we do. The reason for our having a functional understanding of each other is that our understanding is framed by a common context. The more a listener understands about the self and his or her teammates, the more precisely the listener understands the message.

What causes feelings? While many things evoke feelings, one word explains why many people react to certain things with emotion. The word is *filter*. We have filters in our mind that stop us from hearing or understanding certain things. We become emotional when these filters are threatened or challenged.

Listening Filters

The saying that a person hears what he or she wants to hear has truth to it. The reason teammates become emotional about certain subjects or even hear something different from what was said is because they have the equivalent of mental filters that block certain stimuli and messages from being heard. Filters have been installed in all of us through the socialization process—that is, through our growing-up years. Few are aware of this, of course. It is all on an unconscious level. Listeners really need to overcome the blindness, or "deafness," to the fact that these filters exist. These filters change the messages being sent to us or else filter many messages that do not fit existing paradigms or set opinions. These filters are created by the experiences of our life and the beliefs that have come from these experiences. Teammates are blind to these beliefs and how they influence what they value about work and the attitudes they have toward the actions of fellow workers. Microcommunication is hindered in the workplace because of the filters that every person has. Challenge a person's paradigm that functions as that person's communication filter and feelings and emotions surface.

A simple example of how unexamined beliefs lead to miscommunication and conflict would be a belief about silence versus noise at work. Say that a supervisor believes that when teammates enjoy their work or talk at work they are not getting their jobs done. The supervisor values silence and seriousness on the job. He was socialized by his family and his school to believe this, and it became a filter. But, let us say his best producer does not hold that belief. Let us say the best producer believes talking to coworkers and enjoying work causes everyone to produce more. How likely will these two get along and be able to communicate? What is the chance that emotion will be generated between the two? This blockage to their communicating, no fault of either of them, has become a filter that does not allow them to truly hear, see, or feel what the other is saying.

The Johari Window

A tool that dovetails with our discussion of filters that hinder listening and illustrates the idea of filters is the Johari window (see Figure 5.1). The Johari window aids teammates in understanding and identifying our listening filters, which hinder communication and are the triggers of our emotions in the communication process. This is a conceptual model for describing, evaluating, and predicting aspects of interpersonal communication. The Johari window has been around for several decades as a training tool for interpersonal communication. It is an old tool of cognitive psychology and was developed by Joseph Luft and Harry Ingham in 1955. The window has a two-way pane through which information moves to and from sender to receiver. The window is dynamic. That is, the size of

	Known by Self	Unknown by Self
Known by Others	1. Free activity area or open/public self	3. Blind area or blind self
Unknown by Others	2. Hidden/avoided or private self	4. Unknown area or unknown self

FIGURE 5.1

The Johari window.

the panes in the window are designed to grow or shrink relative to the other panes to illustrate the levels of trust, vulnerability, denial, control, and other states of mind on the part of the sender or receiver of messages. The window is a grid that points out the blind spots in teammates' lives or, for our discussion, "dead spots" in people's hearing. Pane 1 represents the area of our lives visible to us and others. This is the public self. This represents the free and open sharing of information. It is healthy communication. Healthy communication, to which we have alluded, is direct and open. This pane increases in size, to push the metaphor, as trust increases between a manager and an employee. The element of trust and healthy, good communication go hand in hand. As both parties are able to share more and more personally relevant information, the pane becomes larger. This describes teammates with capacities for open relationships and for vulnerability. If the employee is unable to be as open as the manager, this will shut down the relationship. The windowpane needs to be two way, not one way.

Pane 2 represents the private self. This area is known by the self but unknown by others. For one reason or another, our private self hides some information from others. It could be the need for protection of the self from criticism. It could be for the purpose of manipulation of others. Or, perhaps the "self" withholds information in the belief that it is tactful to withhold certain thoughts from others.

Pane 3 represents the blind self. In this area, a person does not see his or her attitudes, behaviors, or motives, but everyone else does. These are behaviors and attitudes that a person chooses not to see. When this pane grows larger than the other three panes, a difficult situation arises. A person who does not have an objective view of self cannot communicate. Communication requires that we be able to see the other person's point of view.

Pane 4 is the area of the unknown. Although it is a reality, neither the self nor others have knowledge of it. Life commandments learned in the first year of life may lie hidden here, holding back the person from complete communication with another person. Psychotherapists, psychologists, and other counselors work to help many teammates whose fourth pane in the Johari window model has become disproportionately large. How do they help them? They help them by practicing deep listening of the highest order. What are the life commandments? What are the deep *pains* that enlarge pane 4? One of the listening tools that certain therapists use is called *story listening*.

Story listening is used as a technical term by therapists and people trained as skilled listeners. Story listening describes the skilled listening (deep listening) done when listening to a person who is telling a story or who is repeating key words and phrases. *Storytelling* is the term used regarding the activity of a person to whom the skilled listener is listening. We also use these deep listening skills in a team setting when general conversation is happening. The team could be discussing a solution to a delay in the delivery system of the company when someone in the team makes a comment that fires off a memory in another teammate. That other teammate might say, "That reminds me of something that happened to me when I was at my former company," and then tells a story. Teammates would listen for metaphors and key words used that give clues to deeper issues that are unspoken and that could help reveal hidden filters in that person's mind that block communication.

Story listening aids teammates in hearing important data in teammates' past that need closure and emotional healing to facilitate quality communication in the present. Remember, emotional issues in our past act as filters to what we are hearing in the present and distort communication.

Story listening as a discipline has been used throughout the twentieth century. It has been used with children who were victims of trauma and abuse. Through their drawing, role-playing, or storytelling, the children revealed the deep pain they were burying within. Usually, a common theme or a common metaphor would be noticed in the stories and drawings of the children. Talking to them about the theme or metaphor would help therapists understand what the children had experienced. Finally, the connection was made between the pictures and stories of children and the verbal speech and stories of adults.

In our example, the teammate will tell the story, and all the team members will listen carefully for any metaphors, key words, or obvious omissions of things that should have been mentioned but were not. When high levels of trust exist, teammates can probe for deeper messages within these metaphors, key words, and omissions by asking the storyteller questions that contain a reference to the identified metaphors. These skills would need to be taught to team members by experts in these fields. Hours of training are needed for most and are helpful for all, but once learned, these can become basic communication tools.

"Storytelling is a form of self-disclosure," said Dr. John Savage,[3] "You cannot avoid telling your story. You can only try to make it abstract, in an attempt to hide the deeper struggles you are experiencing" (p. 77). The mind protects a person from the pain of emotion or from the judgments of others. Some teammates who have witnessed an atrocity or have been in a horrible accident may have no memory of the event. At the same time that the mind hides these feelings and fears from our self and others, it also sends veiled messages about these still-living and open-ended events through our stories, words, body language, and tone of voice. When something taps into this emotional pain, the unconscious mind seeks to protect the conscious mind from the emotional pain by keeping the memories stuffed in a secure vault in our unconscious mind. Just as persons who have been in combat have flashbacks, all persons experiencing emotional stress need to be debriefed immediately or suffer the emotional scars.

Four levels of storytelling have been identified:[3]

- Data back then
- Feelings back then
- Feelings now
- Self-disclosure, sometimes called the moment of "Aha!" (p. 79)

Data back then stories are in the past and contain data but no feelings. The further back in time they go, the deeper the emotional pain of the person telling the story. This first level also indicates a lower level of trust between the teller and the listener. As the teller gains more trust and feelings of safety with the listener, he or she moves to level 2, or *feelings back then*.

Feelings back then, as the name implies, adds the new element of feelings to the level of data back then. The storyteller may not name feelings, but the emotion can be detected in the body language and voice. This shows that the storyteller feels safe with the listener and is gaining trust in the listener.

The third level is called *feelings now*. Notice that the title of this level indicates a moving of the story and feelings closer to the present. At this level, the nonverbal language is more dramatic. The face especially reveals emotion through all the normal physiological indicators: flushing or color change in the cheeks, nose, ears, and neck. The tone of voice shifts. The eyes may be moist. The verbal language is more direct and less abstract.

The fourth level is called *self-disclosure*. At this moment, the storyteller becomes conscious of that which was once hidden to the self and unknown to others. The person, at this moment, may cry or laugh, depending on the type of story. When a listener helps a storyteller come to the "aha" moment, it enhances the relationship. It also gives both parties a different perspective on life and emotional relief and life-changing insight to the storyteller.

Three Rules in Dealing with Emotions in a Team Setting

- Pick up on emotions that teammates display or state; describe to the teammate the emotion or state of mind you detect and ask for corroboration or attempt to alert the teammate to what might be a subconscious or denied state of mind
- Be caring and nonjudgmental.
- Do not become sidetracked from the mission of the team by letting feelings dominate the discussion and activity of the team, but realize the overarching purpose of discussing the feelings is to accomplish the team's mission and goals by improving team cohesiveness and quality communication.

USE THE SHADOW COMMUNICATION LOOP TO FURTHER THE TEAM MISSION

Remember the discussion of the shadow loop in Chapter 2? We use the term *shadow* as a nickname for the informal communication system in a corporation or organization. When people take a break from work or go to lunch and talk about work, information is exchanged. Often, the true feelings of people are shared at these times. Why do women talk at the beauty salon? Why do men take each other golfing and talk? It is because in a more relaxed setting, people are more relaxed and able to have a lengthy conversation. Lots of decisions, sales, and commitments are made in these informal settings. Your team should be aware of this powerful communication tool.

Talking at the Water Cooler

Talking at the water cooler with team members can indirectly help or hurt the team process. The term *water cooler* in the United States is the place where breaks from work take place. It may be a room with tables, chairs, vending machines, and a coffee pot. It is casual, and people are not working, but they are in the work environment. Other places where informal communication could take place would be in the company gym or at the after-hours watering hole. It could be at the children's school event, Little League baseball game, or soccer game. Fellow workers are not working, they are together, and they talk to each other.

They might be talking about their families or ailments. However, they also talk about their work. What are they saying? Who do they know in the organization that matters to your team? What free information can one overhear at this time of casual talk that can be helpful information for your team? What kind of information can you purposefully and casually insert into the conversations at the water cooler that you would like other teams and departments to hear? What kind of information would kill your team's progress and reputation? Remember the following saying in American defense industries and in the American military in World War II: "Loose lips sink ships." The same idea applies to the wrong kind of casual talk at the water cooler.

Use the Shadow Loop to Further the Team's Progress

Mature team members will use the shadow loop to further the progress of the team. If an organization has a particularly robust shadow communication loop, teams might want to strategize on how to use it to further their objectives. Here is a list of questions that might stimulate your team's imagination in how to formulate a *verbal packet* that could circulate in the shadow communication loop and ultimately get to the right ears. A *verbal packet* is a formal, team-approved topic with an outline, commonly referred to in the media as "talking points," to be casually inserted into conversations taking place in the shadow loop.

- What information does your team need to complete its assignment?

- What equipment does your company need to invest in for your team's objective to be realized?
- What key person in your organization needs to become aware of the important project of your team and how it would be a solution, catalyst, or ally for his or her assignment?
- What training does your team or even other divisions of your corporation need to create the skills and environment necessary to make your team's solution feasible?
- What adjustments in management and personnel need to take place to make your team successful?
- What other teams are a bottleneck to your team's efforts and the efforts of your whole department?

These questions should stimulate your thinking and imagination. Drop your team's verbal packets skillfully and strategically at the water cooler. And, stay away from casual conversations that would damage your team's success.

HEARING IS NESTED IN A RELATIONSHIP WITH FOUR STAGES

Dr. John Sherwood developed a model to explain how long-term, productive relationships are maintained. Although it is called a *role renegotiation model*, it could be called an *interpersonal communications model*. Every employee and every team member benefit from understanding and reviewing this archetype of a relationship. It is a different style of flowchart for the process called *relationship*. We are indebted to Dr. Savage in our understanding of this model. Dr. Savage has done a lot of work with the model on relationships initially developed by Dr. Sherwood. In the intimacy of a team relationship, understanding how relationships are developed and maintained becomes essential to the functioning of the team. Relationships are central to communication in a team or anywhere else people associate. Companies are a system of relationships. Thus, communication must affect the bottom line. Figure 5.2 contains a diagram of the role renegotiation model of relationship contracts. Begin reading it at the top center column and read downward. It has four stages:

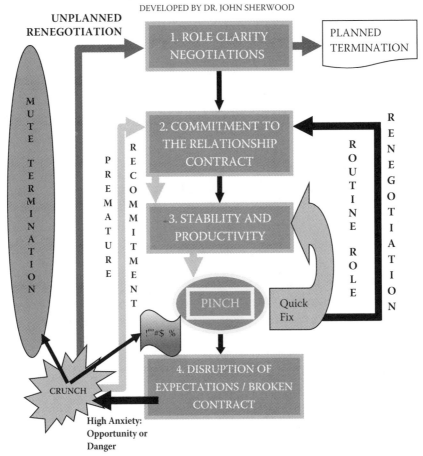

FIGURE 5.2
Four stages of a relationship with renegotiation and termination loops.

1. Role clarity negotiations
2. Commitment to the relationship contract
3. Stability and productivity
4. Disruption of expectations/broken contract

Developing Role Clarity: Developing Expectations and Gathering Information

The life of a relationship can be understood as a process with a loop. A long-term relationship must build into the process a planned and routine renegotiation loop. In other words, every few months sit down together and ask, "How are we doing?" If this loop is not set up and used, the maintenance of a relationship becomes difficult and cumbersome, and it soaks up more and more of the energy that should be used on the mission. Absence of this loop or ineffective use of the renegotiation loop results in the unpleasant loops shown on the left side of the diagram.

All relationships begin with activity 1, role clarity negotiations: Who are you? Who am I? And, do we want this relationship? High-performance teams must be successful in performing this activity. Role clarity, development of expectations, and data gathering occur in this stage and set the stage for all that is to follow.

Go into a restaurant and notice the couples. The body language shows who is in a mature relationship and who is in stage 1. A couple building a new relationship and enjoying it are leaning toward each other and engaging in lots of eye contact. They are speaking with animation and telling stories about themselves and what interests they have. They are unmindful of the people around them. The couple married 20 years talks occasionally, but generally without as much energy or eye contact. They sit reading the paper or rummaging through a purse. They enjoy watching the others around them and saying hello. After all, they already know everything about one another and are in a committed relationship; all they have to do is keep up with the day-to-day events and keep the relationship intact by regularly fixing the "pinches" in the relationship.

Stage 1 is so important that if the work is not done properly, the relationship will categorically fail. This activity of role clarification can be done informally, like the dating couple mentioned. Or, it can be done formally, like scheduled meetings with lawyers to discuss the possibility of entering into a joint venture or negotiating a prenuptial agreement. One of the most important aspects of stage 1 is developing expectations and clarifying them. Too often, employees, teams, and corporations assume agreement on the relationship contract and are burned. Whether or not persons or entities enter into relationships with mutually clear expectations, the fact remains that both entities and persons do indeed have private expectations. This makes microcommunication skills important to the entities that enter into activity 1. Without crystal clear communication at this level, the entities enter into the relationship with built-in conflicts waiting to reach fruition.

Commitment to the Relationship of Boss/Member of Staff

Once the two entities are satisfied with the work done in activity 1, they move to activity 2. Activity 2 is the commitment to the relationship. At this point, the boss says, "You're hired," and the staff member says, "I accept the job." In a relationship between a man and a woman, this would be the marriage vow. In a business partnership, this might be signing a legal agreement. Commitment, however, is much deeper than a ceremony or a signing. Commitment is a decision of both the heart and the intellect.

What is a decision? A decision entails inclusion and exclusion. It involves a separation. One thing is chosen. Everything else is eliminated. A decision is as much about what the team does not want as it is about what the team wants. Commitment to a decision is an act of the will and the heart. The English language has an expression: "He doesn't have the heart for it." It means that a person may see the opportunity in doing something on an intellectual basis, but emotionally and spiritually the person has reservations, and perhaps the person has other important interests that he would have to give up to commit. A real commitment and a clean decision have no reservations.

A business decision generally involves others, so it falls into the purview of communication. Great microcommunication involves the need for people to make decisions and then make commitments to those decisions. If not, clarity in communication is impossible. In other words, do what was mutually agreed on or else come to me and renegotiate. Otherwise, we have problems in our relationship. High-performance teams understand this.

Have you been part of a company that states one thing and then does something else? On the inside, the leadership fully intended to do what was stated publicly. Then, unforeseen or overlooked information came to light. Under time constraints or under the false belief that making a public statement of a change would make them look weak, leadership changed decisions and implemented them without "planned renegotiation." Instead of looking weak, now they look like liars and dishonest businesspersons. Humility is still one of the seven virtues, and virtue is appropriate in all situations. Virtue has a place in microcommunication. And, because we live in a world of change, new information affects decisions previously made. This is one of the reasons for renegotiation in relationships. Sticking to what we agreed, unless first renegotiated, is universally understood and expected by all humankind.

Stability and Productivity for a Period of Time

Now, the relationship enters into a period of stability and productivity. The mission and vision are clear. Goals and activity planning are commenced and productivity started. During activity period 3, a company produces its products or services. During this time, improvement in the business processes takes place. Profits are made in this period. Yet, the health of an organization, the length of its life cycle, and the ability to stay flexible and responsive to the market changes are determined by the use of the planned, routine renegotiation loop. The loop helps to prevent organizations from becoming dysfunctional and conflicted. The planned renegotiation loop is a part of the initial contract of the relationship. It is a built-in time of evaluation and adjustment in the relationship. It is a formal time of sharing positive and negative information about the relationship and leaving with a renewed contract. This activity keeps the relationship functional and healthy.

Experiencing a Pinch in the Relationship

Pinches in a relationship will happen. We do not live in Utopia. It is called a *pinch* because it usually is painful enough to evoke a scream, but not fatal or life threatening. A pinch is a breach of expectations in a relationship. If you call a team meeting for 3 p.m. and do not show up, you have disappointed the team and robbed them of their time. If you never mention it or apologize, you may think you have gotten away with it because the team did not confront you. However, teams never forget.

Another example of such a pinch would be like a husband calling his wife and asking her to meet him for lunch at noon at a certain restaurant. She arrived on time, but he did not. After 20 minutes of waiting, she called him at the office. He had forgotten and was dictating a letter. This is a pinch. A breach of contract like this can be fixed immediately and quickly by the husband: "I'm so sorry, honey. I got caught up in work and completely forgot. If you can wait another 10 minutes, I'll be right down." The apology is accepted, the incident is forgotten, and life goes on. However, if the husband had not "fixed" the pinch, what would have happened? For example, let us say he lied and said that they had agreed to meet at 12:30 p.m. instead of noon. Or, perhaps he said he was so busy he would have to cancel and then did not apologize. Or, let us say for a period of 1 year he called his wife to meet him for lunch once a week and forgot her every single time. Now, substitute "team leader" and "teammate" instead of "husband" and "wife," respectively, in the scenario.

When a pinch is not fixed, it does not go away with time. It is not forgotten. It does not carry an expiration date. Pinches pile up. Someday, in the distant future, when one too many pinches is added to the pile, an explosion erupts in the relationship. To prevent this, pinches should be fixed immediately.

Dealing with the Pinches in the Relationship Is Crucial

It goes without saying, then, that for profitability, a company, or a family for that matter, should maintain as high a degree of health as possible. That means taking care of the pinches when they happen rather than avoiding them. This includes the pinches you might not be aware that happened. Teams need regular times to sit together and say, "How are we doing? Is anything on your minds? Have any of us left anything undone?" An atmosphere of trust and mutual respect allows these meetings to be successful.

Let us look at what happens in organizations that fail to deal with pinches? The first premise is that an entity, including a team, has a limited amount of energy to expend. Would you agree? When pinches add up, it sucks the energy out of a team. This is true for a corporation, government, school, family, or house of worship. The whole company becomes less effective, efficient, or adaptable when pinches pile up. The environment of an unhealthy team or company makes the people within it physically sick and mentally unhealthy.

Dr. Savage has noticed four broad stages in the degeneration of group health. The first stage is optimum performance. Of the energy of a group, 80% is used on accomplishing its mission, and 20% is reserved for maintaining the relationships. The second stage in the degeneration of group health is called the *neurotic stage*. At this stage, a group uses 60% of its energy on mission and 40% on maintaining the relationships of the organization. Dr. Savage defines *neurotic* as the refusal to face painful reality. Triangulation begins in this stage (Figure 5.3), with people in the group or organization refusing to talk directly to the people with whom they have a problem or a pinch. Instead, they talk indirectly, through a third party, forming a triangle of communication. This situation is the equivalent of a human body getting a virus. The whole organism slows and may be in bed for many days with a virus. An organization also can become sick.

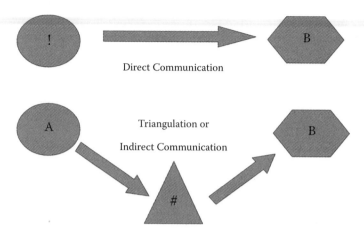

FIGURE 5.3
Triangulation in human communication.

Stage 3 in the aging of a group or company is called *exodus* or *decline*. At this stage, the relationships are so strained that 40% of the energy is expended on mission, and 60% is expended on group politics, group conflict, and holding the corporate pain in check. At this stage, the healthy people leave the group or company. The healthy people—those who are not totally neurotic—have tried to point out corporate dysfunction. For the rest of the group to listen to the healthy people would be to face painful reality, something it cannot do. So, the healthy people are perceived as negative and troublemakers. The healthy people leave. Only the unhealthy people stay because they cannot leave. They are stuck. They are unable to face reality and the pain of maintaining healthy relationships. After a while, only unhealthy people are attracted to the unhealthy group or company. So, the situation worsens. Then, the group or company finds itself in stage 4 of the aging and death of an organization or team, which is called *death*. Death of a company may take many years, or it may take a few weeks. Yet, in this stage it is not much more than a paper organization that uses 80% of its energy to deal with corporate pain and only 20% on mission.

Dealing with Them Immediately and Effectively Maintains Healthy Relationships

Avoiding sweeping relationship contract pinches under the rug maintains healthy relationships. Good communication, by definition, is about good relationships. Yet, no one, no matter how skilled in communication, detects all the strains of a relationship—not even his or her own. That is why the planned renegotiation loop is built into the process. But, mature teams with high trust and mutual respect have a way of dealing with them before the planned, routine renegotiation meeting comes around. Good communicators read body language. Good communicators also learn to "hear" the cries of their own hearts. Sometimes, when we are hurt because of a broken agreement or unmet expectation, we bury these things in our soul. We stuff them and play the tough guy. This is not good for the individual or the team. When a team member becomes aware that the contract was broken, that team member must take the initiative to approach the offending team member and bring up the issue. By all team members being honest with their feelings and needs, less and less will be on the table for discussion at the planned, routine renegotiation meetings. This is the way to maintain healthy relationships and lay the fertile ground for a high-performance team.

Ignoring Pinches in Relationships Leads to Disruption and Conflict

Until this point in our examination of Dr. Sherwood's model of the process of human relationship, we have had happiness and constructive conflict. Constructive conflict means that, although the parties in the relationship find themselves at cross-purposes from time to time, they are using these times to improve the relationship and to learn. Unfortunately, not all conflict is constructive. Destructive conflict takes place when so many pinches in a relationship take place that are not fixed that the relationship moves into disruption and role confusion. In a functional relationship, the roles are clear, even when occasional violations of the expectations take place. Stage 4 in the flowchart of a relationship represents a broken relationship. The relationship contract has been broken. Usually, the parties in the relationship are hostile toward one another. Experts in conflict resolution talk about the different stages of conflict. These are discussed next.[*]

---

[*] This list is from Speed B. Leas, *Moving Your Church through Conflict*, Alban Institute, Herndon, VA; it is currently an out-of-print book available from the Alban Institute through digital download, http://www.alban.org.

Problems to Solve

The *problems-to-solve* stage is the first level. The objectives of the parties are to find solutions. The disputants exhibit a high level of trust at this level. They believe a solution is possible, and they want a win/win solution.

Disagreement and Efforts to Save Face

The *disagreement* stage is next. The objective is to save face. The language is more general. A shift in the subject from the issues to the people begins at this level. Hostile humor is used. The confidence in the ability to find a solution is diminished, and the parties are looking for something close to a win/win situation.

Contest Stage and Efforts to Win

The *contest* stage is third. The objective at this stage is to win. Factions are clearly formed, and communication is distorted by using generalizations. The rumor mill is in high gear. Bizarre stories start because no way exists to test reality since the walls are up. Parties are even less hopeful for a solution. The conflict itself is a lightning rod that brings people out of the woodwork with their complaints. If a consultant is called in, he or she receives a list of problems, most of which are smoke screens.

Fight/Flight Stage: Eliminate or Harm the Character of the Other Side

The *fight/flight* stage is fourth. The priority of the parties is to eliminate or harm the character of the other side. The situation for everyone involved moves from win/lose to lose/lose. The language becomes lofty and righteous. The factions now have identifiable leaders and hold regular meetings. Outside parties are drawn into the conflict. The people can justify all sorts of means because the ends have become defined.

Holy War: The Object Is to Destroy

The final stage is *holy war*. The objective is to destroy. The language is threat and violence. At this stage, opponents are pursued if they withdraw. Continuing the struggle takes precedence over all else. Communication in this setting emphasizes universal principles. It is time to call the police.

RESTORING A RELATIONSHIP

Restoring a relationship that has deteriorated is usually handled in unhealthy ways. Dr. Sherwood's model, which we are considering, does not have it in its purview to discuss the levels of conflict. Notwithstanding, it is helpful to note that some situations in the relationships of a company grow to a murderous point, as witnessed at the number of incidents in recent years of disgruntled employees who have returned to their offices with guns and have murdered their bosses or colleagues. The first step to this condition is called *role confusion*, when what was agreed has been ignored or changed without honest and mutual renegotiation.

When a relationship reaches the breaking point, the stress and tension have a positive side and a negative side. The positive side is that, in this condition, people are open to change. The negative side is that this condition brings instability and the likelihood of destructive conflict. In many companies, experts say that a condition of instability must be deliberately created to have any hope for change. The classic wisdom of change masters has three stages:

1. Unfreeze a situation,
2. Institute change, and
3. Refreeze the situation.

When the relationships in a company reach this stage, change may take place whether or not the leadership wants it. The leadership needs to be proactive and take advantage of the positive side of such a condition rather than let things happen by chance.

The next event is called the *crunch*. Sooner or later, the crunch will come. When it does, five different outcomes are possible:

- Ennui
- Mute termination
- Premature reconciliation (or recommitment to the relationship without discussing the issues)
- Unplanned renegotiation under extreme stress
- Learned termination (the healthy, mature way to leave a broken relationship)

Ennui: Settling for the Status Quo and Limbo

Ennui is a French word that means "boredom." The connotation in English for ennui expresses a state of existence that is unhappy, yet "settled for." It is a less-than-pleasant situation in which a person is stuck. Frank Sinatra sang, *I Get a Kick Out of You*, in which this word is used in the introduction to the song—the bored singer is "fighting vainly the old ennui." Some relationships have grown to be dysfunctional and harmful, yet the parties involved feel they have too much to lose by resolving the problems or leaving the relationship. Others simply do not have the knowledge of what to do to change their situation. Thousands of managers and employees are settling for a horrible situation because they fear change more than they dare to risk a better life. Is a reminder needed that this situation is the epitome of noncommunication and the opposite end of the spectrum from good communication? You will not find a high-performance team in ennui.

Mute Termination: Quit Job or Fire Employee or Staff Member

Mute termination means that one or both parties walk away from the relationship without talking. If this happens, neither party will know for sure what went wrong or how the other party feels. In marriage, it is like a person finding a note on the kitchen table announcing that the spouse has left. In business, it is like having the boss walk in with no warning and telling the employee to clear out his or her desk and pick up a final check at the personnel department. Or, it is the employee who walks into the boss's office, emotionally vomits all over the boss and his desk, and then screams, "You can't fire me 'cause I quit." The macho man thinks that "bucking up" and moving on is all that is needed in this situation. Years later, if he is maturing and learning to communicate, he discovers the meaning of "closure" because he realizes that he is still affected by the incident and needs to deal with it.

Pretending to Fix the Relationship: Premature Reconciliation

Premature reconciliation describes an effort in a relationship to go back to a level of trust and productivity that was known in the past. The idea is that both parties just cooperate and pretend like nothing ever happened. The flaw in this course of action is that the real problems are not addressed.

The real problems will continue to produce the same effects. If this course of action is used repeatedly, then you have a circle of controversy, one after the other.

Unplanned Renegotiation of a Relationship under Extreme Stress

The only healthy direction after entering the crunch in a relationship is renegotiation of the basic contract. Parties debrief one another on the old contract. They learn about where things went wrong. They develop a new set of expectations. When they reach a new agreement or an informed recommitment to the old agreement, they restart the relationship.

Ending the Relationship

If the parties are unable to agree, then they terminate the relationship. Because they have talked it out and learned from the mistakes, this is called a *learned termination*. Absolutely, when a relationship has gone bad, this is the best way to leave it cleanly. This takes maturity, and it may take a third-party consultant to aid in the process.

In high-performance teams, the members understand, usually on an intuitive level, these rules of healthy relationships. They follow them in some form and thus are able to produce more together than they could do alone. This basic process for relationships is universal and should be understood by every person in an organization.

SUMMARY

> Knowing I need to listen and knowing how to listen is not enough. Unless I want to listen, unless I have the desire, it won't be a habit in my life.
>
> **—Stephen R. Covey**

Rugged individualism dies with the team. The team has to think and act as one. Enter good communication skills. This chapter talks about the nature of a person who has the capacity for good communication. It also talks about the relationship contract and how to keep it healthy and intact.

High-performance teams are made of individuals with the capacity for good communication. Good communication takes mature people who are self-actualized individuals. They need to be people of virtue. This is because great communication is honest, responsible, accurate, and transparent. Only virtuous individuals and companies are capable of this kind of great communication. Great communicators understand and conform to what the ancients meant when they advised: Know thyself and do unto others as you would have them do unto you.

Teams are a group of people in a relationship who have a common mission. Therefore, they have a relationship contract with one another, most of it unwritten. The members need to keep the contract in force by abiding by the terms and confessing or confronting in love when the terms are breached. The role renegotiation model helps teams understand how to keep the team relationships healthy by dealing with the pinches in the relationships immediately and honestly.

Good communication requires informed and skilled individuals. They need to be able to listen with both the ears and the eyes. They need to understand the emotional component of listening and that a message always carries the factual details attached to a person's emotions. High-performance teams are experts not only in their areas of technical and business work, but also in communication.

An individual may not always tell the whole truth but their body communicates the real story.

—H. James Harrington

REFERENCES

1. Collins, Jim (2001). *Good to Great: Why Some Companies Make the Leap ... and Others Don't*, HarperCollins, New York.
2. Baker, Larry L. (1971). *Listening Behavior*, Englewood Cliffs, NJ.
3. Ishikawa, Kaoru (1980). QC Circle Koryo: General Principles of the QC Circle, Union of Japanese Scientists and Engineers, Tokyo, Japan.
4. Savage, John (1996). *Listening and Caring Skills in Ministry*, Abingdon Press, Nashville, TN.

6

How Do I Hear What My Boss Is Really Saying?

You've been playing the game of body language unconsciously all of your lifetime.

—Julius Fast

Before babies have words, they have communication. Adults don't lose this ability. It's instinctive, it's powerful, and it's where the real truth in communication lies with adults.

—R. D. Lewis

INTRODUCTION

Your boss may be intimidating, but she is a person. She has pressures and deadlines like everyone else. And she communicates like any other person, which means you can hear more of what she is really saying than just the words coming out of her mouth. You can read her body language like a book.

Your boss may seem like a regular guy and be unpretentious, but he is your boss. So, do not think he is not the boss just because he is one of the guys, and do not think that he is telling you everything he knows with the words coming out of his mouth at the water cooler. But, take heart. He is a person. You can read his nonverbal language and get a lot more information than he knows he is giving.

To start, though, use the basics with your boss like you do your fellow workers. Use the feedback loop. When he or she speaks to you, repeat back in your own words what you understood him or her to say. Let him or her verify whether you did indeed understand. Reverse the process when you communicate to the boss, if you can, by prompting the boss to repeat back what was heard, although I realize this is not always possible given the difference in some bosses' status consciousness.

Allow one point to be made before we go further. You will learn that you can often read a boss's real intentions through nonverbal communications. Your unconfirmed interpretation is always an educated guess. Never take an action based on the boss's nonverbal cues. How could you ever prove you guessed right about the nonverbal clues? Any review board or arbitrator would favor the exact words spoken. If the nonverbal messages contradict the verbal directives and concern you greatly, the following are suggestions:

1. Ask the boss to put his or her directive in writing; or, if that is not advisable,
2. Repeat back what you understood a second time and double confirm the directive;
3. Describe to the boss a verbal description of his or her body language, if you are really secure in your job; tell the boss what you are reading into it and verify that he or she indeed wants you to carry out his or her verbal instructions.

A good relationship with your boss helps when you question his or her directives. And, that is the point of this book. Good relationships with your bosses and fellow workers are the essence of good communication. The better you understand them—and yourself—the better the communication will be.

LEARN TO SEE THE NONVERBAL MESSAGE IF YOU WANT TO REALLY HEAR YOUR BOSS

Nonverbal communication is a language. Of course, it has no words as such. It communicates attitudes, emotions, and intentions through tone of voice, facial expressions, eye movement, posture, body movement, distance separating the communicators, touch, timing, and the dominant channel of communication used by the sender.

In human communication, each of the affective parts of the message is transmitted through voice quality and tone, while most of the content comes through the bare words. So, nonverbal communication can also convey content as well as emotion, making it the largest part of communication. The content portion of some nonverbal messages can be conveyed by pointing a finger—and be careful which finger you choose.

Albert Mehrabian, an author and professor who is known for his pioneering work in the field of nonverbal communication, has studied the impact of verbal, vocal, and nonverbal communication on a message. He discovered the now-famous, and surprising, relationship of 7% verbal (words only), 38% vocal (tone of voice, inflection, etc.), and 55% nonverbal (gestures, posture, and facial expressions). In this book, the term *nonverbal communication* refers to both the vocal and nonverbal categories as used by Mehrabian. The term *body language* is also used in this book to mean both vocal and nonverbal communication as used by Mehrabian. When all three factors studied by Mehrabian are sending the same message, a person's communication is said to be *congruent. Incongruent communication* is when one or all of these factors are sending different messages. *Sarcasm* is deliberately misaligning voice tone or body language with the verbal message to show a contrast, so it is a figure of speech and therefore congruent. A person of integrity is one who is congruent in his or her communication, and a person is lying or conflicted when the communication is incongruent.

Dr. Suzette Haden Elgin, author and founder of the Ozark Center for Language Studies, shared the following about body language:[1]

- For American English, at least 90% of all emotional information, and at least 65% of all information whatsoever, is carried not by your words but by the body language that goes with those words.
- The most powerful mechanism for body language is the voice: its quality, its tone, and the intonation it gives to words and parts of words.
- There is a grammar of body language, just as there is a grammar of words and sentences. You *know* that grammar, although you have probably never taken a course in it—but most of this knowledge is stored in your memory in a way that gives you no convenient or reliable access to it. (p. 45)

Nonverbal communication has been divided into at least seven parts:

- **Proxemics,** the use of space in communication
- **Chronemics**, the use of time in communication
- **Oculesics,** the use of eye contact in communication
- **Haptics**, the use of touch in communication
- **Kinesics**, the use of your body and body movements in communication
- **Objectics**, the use of objects in communication
- **Vocalics**, the use of the tone quality of your voice in communication.

What do these funny looking words have to do with hearing your boss? It would take you months of serious study to learn everything about these academic terms. Nevertheless, awareness that nonverbal communication uses the whole person helps you be aware that your boss's behavior is part of the message. You will instinctively pick up on more meaning by this awareness.

IF YOUR BOSS BELIEVES IN YOU, HE OR SHE WILL TRUST AND THEREFORE TELL YOU MORE

Bert Decker,[2] chairman of Decker Communications, Incorporated, said, "Communication is a contact sport" (p. 4). He went on to point out that he meant *emotional* contact. His whole theory on communication effectiveness can be summarized with this statement: Reach the brain stem with a message of believability. The brain stem is the "heart of the mind" according to Decker. This nonverbal communication happens in a split second and is primarily visual. The eye is the only organ of the body that actually contains brain cells. The nerve pathways from the eye to the brain are at least 25 times larger than those from the ear to the brain. In the first 2 seconds of seeing a person, our brain stem processes the verbal and auditory clues and makes a basic decision: I can trust this person, or I cannot trust this person. This first impression about a person is so strong that some research showed it took another 4 minutes to add 50% more impression. Make a good impression on your boss when you meet him or her. Then, whether you talk to the boss or the boss talks to you, you will get more from the interaction.

What the Boss Sees Determines What You Get

For people to listen to you, you must make a good first impression. This is the first rule of nonverbal business communication. Pay attention to dress and a friendly, confident air. If a boss trusts you enough to listen to you, that same trust will be present when the boss starts talking. Communication is a two-way street.

Eye Contact (Oculesics)

Oculesics is the study of eye movement, eye behavior, gaze, and eye-related nonverbal communication. Eye contact must be made to make contact with the brain stem of the other person and thus to establish a "meeting of the minds." The brain stem opens or closes the way to the conscious mind of the other person. Eye contact shows openness and nothing to hide. The brain stem likes this openness in another person. Some common problems with eye contact that you have no doubt observed in others are "eye flit," "eye evasion," and "eye flutter."

Eye Flit

Eye flit was a problem Fran experienced. Whenever she got in a conversation with upper management, her eyes would dart and flit like a high-strung thoroughbred. Her habit prevented her from making brain stem contact and caused her listeners to be annoyed to boot.

Eye Evasion

Eye evasion describes the condition of Pastor Jenkins, who always looked at the back wall of the church sanctuary as he delivered his sermon. His congregation felt he was not interested in them, and they even wished he were somewhere else.

Eye Flutter

Eye flutter describes the practice of keeping the eyes closed for 2 to 4 seconds between glances and, from time to time during this sequence, fluttering the eyelids as they are opening. These problems are treatable. The first step is self-awareness. Make no mistake, for good communication, these problems must be overcome. Otherwise, believability becomes difficult, if not impossible.

For effective eye communication, look at a person in the eye while talking for at least 5 seconds. Another rule of thumb is to look at a person's eyes as long as it takes to speak a sentence. If you are in a group, move your eye contact to another person for the same amount of time or a little bit longer. What you are after is involvement, not intimacy or intimidation. Intimacy or intimidation involves eye-to-eye contact for a longer period of time, sometimes up to a minute or more. Remember, we are talking about achieving believability and trust. This is the first step in interpersonal communication.

Posture and Movement (Kinesics)

Kinesics is the study of nonlinguistic bodily movements, such as gestures and facial expressions, as a systematic mode of communication. Posture and movement are the second most important part of the visual impact. Posture has a greater bearing on your believability than the clothes you wear, although your clothing is important. Straight, upright posture communicates confidence. Posture is so powerful that good posture overcomes other physical drawbacks to gaining trust and respect, such as shortness of stature, obesity, and unattractive looks.

First, *stand erect* and tall. A chiropractor told his patients to imagine that they had a string attached to the top of their heads with a large helium-filled balloon on the other end pulling them up. He said good posture took away back pain. It also exudes confidence that others see and use in making their first impressions. In addition, to increase the effect hold in the stomach if you are a person who needs to and is able to do this.

Lower Body Posture

Lower body posture also deserves mentioning. Do not stand back on one hip. This communicates that you do not want to be there. The only place this might work is for a door-to-door salesperson to initially allay fear in the person who opens the door by communicating that the salesperson does not want to enter the house. In other business settings, this is exactly the opposite of what you want to communicate. Also, rocking from side to side or forward and backward should be avoided.

Another piece of the posture cluster is the *ready position*. This means to lean slightly forward. When speaking to a group or standing in a meeting, this communicates energy and interest. When seated, the leaning forward can also convey interest unless you are sitting on the edge of your chair with your hands on your knees or on the arms of your chair ready to push you up. This would indicate the conversation was over.

Movement

Movement while speaking is necessary to make emotional contact. Standing behind a lectern or sitting behind a desk does not provide emotional contact. Movement conveys excitement and enthusiasm. At the 1996 Republican Convention, Elizabeth Dole made a great speech. It was better than any of the candidates, including her husband, Senator Bob Dole, who received that year's presidential nomination. She left the dais, walked down into the crowd, and spoke directly to them as she moved from place to place. The content was good, but it was the emotional contact that made it a great speech.

Dress and Appearance (Objectics)

Objectics, also called object language, is the study of the human use of clothing and other artifacts as nonverbal codes. Dress and appearance are the third elements in the visual impact. Dress and appearance are very visual, of course. The way we dress communicates who we are. It communicates our values, self-esteem, and self-image. To make an impression on the brain stem, our dress needs to be congruent with whom we are as people, and it needs to be appropriate to the values and culture of the listeners. Some of you remember the book *Dress for Success*.[3] It made many good points about how a person is treated in public based on his or her dress. A person in a well-fitting and coordinated suit or outfit receives more respect and premium service. Those who are slovenly dressed or casually dressed are often ignored. The way we dress affects our feelings about ourselves as well.

Studies have been done on the effect of how a man or woman dresses in his or her office setting. Everything from the kind of clothes, the color of clothes, and the fit of clothes affects the response a person gets from those around him or her. In business, conservative business suits and ties are best. A minimum of jewelry on a man or a woman is best, although women get to wear more jewelry than men. Even the thickness of a wristwatch and the type of band have an effect on the people around us. Thin, dark leather watchbands with a thin watch face are better than thick ones. For an executive, a thin briefcase communicates importance; a thick or bulky briefcase or two briefcases indicates more work and less seniority.

Gestures and Smile (Kinesics)

As we defined previously, kinesics is the study of body movements, gestures, facial expressions, and the like as a means of communication. Gestures and smiles are the final elements to watch in the visual impact. The brain stem of a person learned as an infant, and perhaps knows instinctively, that if we believe what we say, we will be animated while we say it. Words that communicate the ideas of openness and warmth are *enthusiastic, excited, conviction,* and *passion.* The brain stem wants to know what you *feel* about what you are saying, not just what you are saying. The basic ideas to remember are openness and warmth. Openness is shown by open, outstretched arms with open palms turned up and a neutral stance (legs apart at shoulder width and facing forward). An unbuttoned coat also is a part of the openness cluster.

A smile breaks through to the brain stem. It disarms in most situations. And, it is such a simple thing to do. The muscles of the face pull up the mouth and the corners of the eyes. A smile goes deeper than the corners of the eyes, though. A smile that comes from the "heart" also shows in the pupils of the eyes. Everyone knows when the smile is phony. Our brains catch all these data on an unconscious level. Smiling also changes a person's attitude. Try it now. What power it has over our disposition and that of other people.

Once a person understands the basic openness gestures, he or she only needs to become aware of and eliminate the negative gestures. When communicating, unless you deliberately want to communicate lack of confidence or suspicion, avoid any nervous or closed gesture. A nervous gesture would be jingling keys and coins in a pocket. Another would be to hold your clasped hands over the area of one's crotch or to fold the arms while speaking.

What the Boss Feels Determines What You Get

The following section deals with the fact that putting energy and enthusiasm into our communication makes one believable and, therefore, listened to. Again, if your boss feels good about listening to you, it will translate into feeling good about talking to you.

Voice and Vocal Variety (Vocalics)

Vocalics refers to anything that is spoken and heard except for words. Voice and vocal variety is an animation skill that has tremendous influence and power. Think of the voice as the vehicle of your message. Learn to drive it with skill. The voice is such an expressive instrument that deep listeners intuitively pick up the nuances of its signals and instantly know about the emotional state and sincerity of the person using the voice. In addition to the affective elements, different cultures and languages have preferences for certain vocal tones and qualities that express energy. Preferred voices in the culture of the United States can be characterized as low, resonant, and full. The contour of the preferred voice in the United States is a smooth curve rather than a sharp angle or flat line. The worst voice to use in America today would be characterized as high and nasal, like Fran Drescher, the American television actress. This type of voice is a definite handicap to success—unless you can use it as a comedic prop as Fran Drescher has done.

Voices can be trained. A good learning exercise is to listen to the radio announcers or television newscasters and mimic them. Work on your telephone voice. On the phone, a person has no nonverbal communication other than the vocalic. Over the phone, resonance and intonation count for 84% of the emotional impact and believability. Remember the basic components of the voice: relaxation, breathing, projection, and resonance. These elements can be strengthened and improved.

Words and Nonwords (Verbal Technique and Chronemics)

Chronemics is the study of the use of time in nonverbal communication. Words and nonwords also deal with animation impact. Our words become conduits of energy and vitality. First, develop vocabulary and the feel for the sound and power of words on an audience. Learn to draw pictures with your words like Martin Luther King, Jr. Second, take out the nonwords that drain the power of your speech. Nonwords include filler words like "ahh," "umm," "you know," "and," "like," "sort of," "whatever," or "okay." Finally, learn to use the power of the pause. A period of silence can be effective for driving home a point or emphasizing a concept.

Boss Involvement (Objectics)

Listener involvement, or boss involvement for our purposes, gives animation to a discussion, dialogue, or speech. It keeps interest, aids clarification, and stimulates new thought. Ways to involve the boss include eye contact, movement, visual aids, and asking questions. These days, you can use your smartphone to take a video of an issue and show it to the boss.

Humor (Verbal Technique Using Kinesics, Vocalics, Chronemics)

Humor used skillfully is magic. Ronald Reagan used humor to win an election and to communicate with the American people. Maybe you have seen the video of the quip made to Walter Mondale in a televised debate when the question of Reagan's old age came up: "I want you to know that also I will not make age an issue of this campaign," Reagan responded. "I am not going to exploit, for political purposes, my opponent's youth and inexperience." Reagan was a master at delivering the one-liner not because he was a "natural," but because he practiced for years.

Some guidelines to follow in using humor are the following:

1. Do not tell jokes unless you are good at it.
2. Create a fun and happy atmosphere.
3. Discover the kind of humor that works for you and improve it.
4. Keep a friendly disposition.

In summary, accessing the attention of a receiver is the first job of a sender. The sender must communicate a "premessage" of believability. This is done nonverbally in the "twinkling of an eye." It is like getting a dialing tone before being able to dial a telephone number. Everyone instinctively knows how to do this. Be friendly and disarming. Just do it, especially when talking to your boss.

WHAT IS NEUROLINGUISTIC PROGRAMMING?

In the 1970s, a deeper understanding of how humans make sense of their world was developed by a linguist named John Grinder and a programmer and mathematician named Richard Bandler. They developed a theory called *neurolinguistic programming* or *NLP*.

- *Neuro* refers to the brain and the nervous system. Grinder and Bandler were proposing a theory for how the brain uses the five senses to understand and explain the world.
- *Linguistic* refers to language. The brain and nervous system convert the feelings, smells, sights, sounds, and tastes into language. Specific words are stored in the brain that correspond to the real world and

represent it. People use this "brain language" to represent the world to both themselves and others. So, your boss's language patterns are expressions of who he or she is and how the boss thinks.

- *Programming* refers to the coding of experience. A program is a series of steps in a process designed to produce a certain result. NLP states that the results a person achieves and the effects created by a person's actions are a result of these personal programs.

NLP asserts that although people live in the world and the world is real, they do not operate directly on the world. Instead, people use maps of the world. These maps are *representations* of the world residing in the brain. Think for a moment of an actual map of a territory. It is a representation of that territory produced on a piece of paper (or computer screen) that we fold up and put in our pocket. We carry the same kind of map in our brains of our experiences in the world. A geographic map is never equal to the territory and can never exactly represent the territory. Neither can our mental models of experience truly equal reality. Your boss has a representative map of his or her world and your business in his or her brain. If you learn to read the map, you can know how to communicate with your boss on a deep level.

A person has a maximum of five representational systems to guide behavior in the world. These correspond to the five senses. Because smell and taste are used so little in representing the world, they are usually combined into the feeling system. A representational system called *nonspecific* has also been created for people who seldom use language of the sensory channels. However, some researchers and practitioners have recognized the nonspecific system as a heightened auditory system.

Therefore, the different ways people think are as follows:

Visual	A person thinks in pictures or mental images.
Auditory	A person thinks in sounds.
Feelings (kinesthetic)	A person thinks in feelings, either outward feelings of touch or inner feelings of emotions.

People generally have a preference for one of these systems over the others, and so does your boss. Your boss develops this one system while exercising the others in a diminished or support capacity.

These mental representations or maps differ from the territory they represent by three universal processes: generalization, deletion, and distortion.

- *Generalization* refers to the habit of people taking a specific experience and forcing its truth into different contexts. For example, the statement, "I always catch cold in winter," would be a generalization for most people.
- *Deletion* refers to the practice of omitting parts of the meaning in our language. For example, a person would say, "They don't tell us what's going on around here." The response would then be, "Who are they, and what don't they tell us?"
- *Distortion* occurs when a person twists an experience in his or her language to reach a conclusion that is incorrect. A common statement, like "You make me furious," is a distortion. The owner of these words has abdicated personal responsibility for his or her emotions and given control to someone else. No one can make another person "anything" when it comes to emotional state.

Technical practitioners of NLP use a complete model of language called *transformational grammar*. This model, in and of itself, is a representation of the structure of human language. Language is a model of human experience.

Transformational linguists (practitioners of the NLP theory) believe that human language systems are themselves, also, derived representations of yet a larger model: the entirety of an individual's life experience. This language system is unique for each individual. It influences how each person speaks. If we can analyze how a person speaks, we can better understand that person's experience. Thus, we can communicate. This being true, your boss is communicating his or her life to you every time you communicate.

One of the concepts transformational linguists have developed to describe human speech is surface structure versus deep structure. The surface structures of language are those that other people can hear (verbal communication and writing, mostly) and see (nonverbal communication). On this level, we can analyze the generalizations, distortions, deletions, metaphors, predicates, and so on of language. All these things give us clues and information in understanding the deep structures. Deep structures are the linguistic representations of the sum total of human experience. This is where NLP aids us in understanding the link between verbal and nonverbal communication. As Grinder and Bandler state it:[4]

Humans not only represent their experiences by different representational systems, they also base their communication on their representational systems. Communication occurs in a number of forms, such as natural language, body posture, body movement, or in voice qualities, etc. We call them *output channels*. (p. 12)

YOUR BOSS WILL TELL YOU MORE WHEN YOU TUNE IN TO HIS FAVORITE NLP CHANNEL

How can a person discover which representational system (visual, auditory, kinesthetic) his or her boss prefers? A number of ways exist, but the easiest ways for nonlinguists are to notice predicates and to notice eye movements. Make it your job to listen to your boss's predicates and to read his or her eye movements.

Check Out Your Boss's Predicates to Learn His or Her Channel

Predicates refer to the verbs, adjectives, and adverbs in a sentence. I hope you studied sentence structure in high school. These parts of speech give indications of which representational system a boss uses to map life experiences. If the boss uses the visual system, the words will be words appropriate for describing a visual scene. If the boss uses the auditory system, the words will be appropriate for describing sounds. If the boss uses the kinesthetic system, the words will be appropriate for external feeling or emotion.

For the *visual system*, here are some common sentences:

"I *see* what you mean."
"That's *clear* enough—*crystal* clear."
"That's a horse of a different *color*."
"Can you *picture* that?"
"Please try to *focus* on the subject at hand."
"Now I see the *light*."

The *auditory system* would use sentences like these:

"Be sure to *tell* me how you like it."
"Can we *talk*?"
"Keep your *ear* to the ground."
"It had the *ring* of truth to it."

"That's as *clear* as a *bell*."
"Do you *hear* what I'm saying?"

The *kinesthetic system* would use sentences like this:

"It just *feels* right to me."
"Your speech *moved* me."
"The annual report had a strong *impact* on the board."
"It left a bad *taste* in my mouth."
"I *smell* something fishy."
"I just can't get a *grip* on the problem."

If the boss uses a lot of terms that are nonspecific, then when it comes to the boss's representational systems, one can conclude that the boss prefers using the heightened auditory representational system. Politicians tend to talk in these terms because it is ambiguous and appeals broadly. A few of the sentences used by the *nonspecific system* might be the following:

"That's not appropriate behavior for a person."
"Can you describe what you mean?"
"I want to let you know something."
"I have some questions about that incident."
"I definitely think you know the subject that interested us."
"I bought some nice things today."

Bosses who are nonspecific in indicating their sensory system can sometimes be coaxed by asking them questions. If that is not helpful, you can always use the eye-accessing cues.

Check Out Your Boss's Eye Movements to Learn His or Her NLP Channel

The eye-accessing cues are fascinating. When a person remembers stored data in the mind, the circuits access the information in certain sections of the brain. The eyes move as data are accessed. The eyes move to the same positions for each representational system. Yes, this has something to do with the famous REMs (rapid eye movements) that are connected with sleep and dreaming. The phenomenon is also connected to NLP. The visual data call for one position, the auditory for another, and the kinesthetic yet another. Figure 6.1 is an illustration of these positions. The terms right and left are relative to the person whose eyes we are watching, not our own right or left.

The figure shows eye movements for right-handed people. Left-handed people have some of the positions reversed and maybe all of them reversed. For a left-handed person, a receiver in the communication process must pay closer attention to the eye movements.

Listening and observing to discern the representational systems of a person take skill that comes with practice. Making the process more difficult is the fact that people are not monosystem people. Most people use all the senses to draw maps of experience. It is significant if a person does not use one of the systems. It means that person has shut down that channel of gathering data. Usually, a traumatic experience leads to a shutdown. A professional therapist would be needed to help that person uncork his or her pain, deal with it, and begin developing the use of that channel again, assuming the channel is functional. Nevertheless, people do use several channels to communicate. They do this by rotating through a varied sequence of the representational systems. Michael Brooks explains it this way:[5]

> While it's true that the visual will use her nimble sense of imaging a good deal of the time, and the auditory will rely primarily on her acuity of sound, we must always remember that visuals, auditories, and kinesthetics check their lead representations by scanning their other senses. That's why I call this cascading. We cascade from system to system in an effort to confirm what our primary or lead system has reported to us. (p. 117)

You Can Have Empathy, Sympathy, and Harmony with Your Boss

Another development from studies of nonverbal communication and NLP is a technology called *rapport*. Rapport is a state of empathy, sympathy, and harmony with another person. Rapport takes place when people are in the same communication channel or sequence of channels. A predominantly visual person would be in harmony with another visual person. An auditory person would be in harmony with an auditory person, as would two kinesthetic people. Therefore, a person who understands this and has the skill to switch into another person's channel of communication will experience rapport.

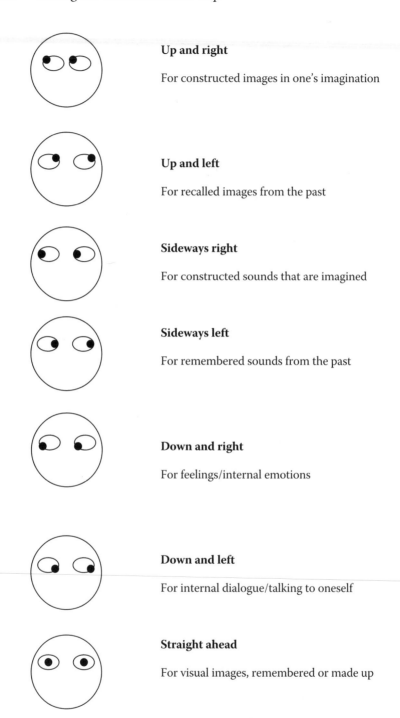

Up and right

For constructed images in one's imagination

Up and left

For recalled images from the past

Sideways right

For constructed sounds that are imagined

Sideways left

For remembered sounds from the past

Down and right

For feelings/internal emotions

Down and left

For internal dialogue/talking to oneself

Straight ahead

For visual images, remembered or made up

FIGURE 6.1
NLP's eye-accessing cues.

CHECK YOUR BOSS'S GESTURES, SIGNALS, AND OTHER TELLTALE ACTIONS

Body gestures vary from culture to culture. The gestures discussed here were developed and studied by middle-class Americans. Research has concluded that some gesturing is inborn and universal. Some is learned and universal. Some are cultural signals and vary from place to place. Remember, caution should be used when interpreting body language. Learn to test and retest messages received. A "dead fish" handshake can mean one thing in a healthy person and a different thing in a person who has arthritis in the finger joints. Also, some messages reflect temporary states of mind and, given time, will be revised or changed.

Some universal gestures are the following:

- Smiling when happy
- Frowning when sad or angry
- Nodding the head up and down when saying yes
- Shaking the head from side to side to say no
- Shrugging the shoulders to show that one does not know or understand

For some time, researchers have known that power or prestige in a person is related to breadth of vocabulary. The higher the position a person holds in management, then the greater the ability possessed by that person to communicate verbally. Furthermore, nonverbal research positively correlates verbal skill and gesticulation. An employee of lower status uses gesticulation more than an employee of higher status.

Proxemics: Give Your Boss His or Her Space

Proxemics is the study of space as it relates to communication. The fact that animals need so much personal space has been known for some time. Lion trainers and animal handlers use this information to control animal behavior. A popular metaphor for this space around an animal is the imaginary air bubble that follows the animal wherever it goes. People have this same need for personal space. The next time you are at an office meeting, observe where people stand and particularly how far they stand from other people. Think of the following factors and look for a common distance related to situations involving the same factors: cultural background, status in the group, position in the company, social relationship, and activity in which the group is engaged.

In suburban, middle-class, white America, the following four space zones have been observed:

1. Intimate zone, 16–18 inches
2. Personal zone, 1.5–4 feet
3. Social zone, 4–12 feet
4. Public zone, over 12 feet[6] (pp. 26–27)

As you could guess, the intimate zone can be entered by a close friend or relative or by someone making a sexual advance. Someone who is belligerent and who is about to attack will also enter it. Definite physiological changes take place in a person whose intimate zone is invaded. Heart rate and respiration speed up. Adrenaline pours into the blood and sends more blood to the brain and muscles.

Sometimes, people are pushed into one another's intimate zone on crowded elevators, buses, or planes. What happens in this situation is interesting and will be recognized by everyone immediately. Allan Pease, an Australian body language expert and co-author of 15 bestsellers, lists the rules that we follow in this situation:[6]

1. You are not permitted to speak to anyone, including a person you know.
2. You must avoid eye contact with others at all times.
3. You are to maintain a "poker face"—no emotion is permitted to be displayed.
4. If you have a book or newspaper, you must appear to be deeply engrossed in it.
5. The bigger the crowd, the less the body movement you are permitted to make.
6. In elevators, you are compelled to watch the floor numbers above your head. (p. 28)

How can you use this information to read the relationships of people in an office? For example, let us say you are sitting in the office of the CEO (chief executive officer) when a person enters. Where does the person stop after entering relative to where the CEO is sitting behind his or her desk?

If the person stops at the door, this tells you that the person is much lower in status than the CEO. If the person walks to the front of the desk, status is higher. If the person walks behind the desk, he or she is either equal in status, an aide, or a close friend or relative. Where would you stop?

Kinesics: Your Boss's Body Movements Have Meaning

Kinesics is the use of the body or body movements in communication. Following are five common movements involving different areas of the body: palm, hands, arms, legs, and eyes.

Palm

The open palm signifies honesty and openness. When a person begins to open up with another person, he or she will show open palms. This gesture should be in alignment with other nonverbal language. When everything in our communication fails to line up in harmony, others can know that we are incongruent and not telling the truth.

While the palm-up position is a submissive gesture, the palm-down position is a position of authority. When you make a request and use this position, a listener will take it as an order. When the palm is closed and the index finger is pointing, the finger is read as a symbolic club used to beat into submission.

Handshakes are also revealing. The handshake with one palm on top and the other on the bottom shows who is in control, who wants to control, or who is submissive. The vice-grip handshake that is vertical shows two equals and communicates respect and rapport. How does your boss shake hands with you?

Hand to Face

Hand-to-face gestures generally signal deceit, doubt, and lying. These gestures are easy to see in children. When a child lies and is caught, usually the hands cover the mouth. As the child grows older, he or she learns to disguise this move. That is especially true of the adult mouth guard move. In this move, the open fingers of the hand cover the mouth while the thumb is pressed against the cheek. This gesture should not be confused with the gesture similar to it that the adult uses when evaluating. The interested evaluation gesture is the hand off the mouth, fingers folded against the cheek, and the index finger extended into the hairline above the temple.

The eye also is covered or rubbed while lying when the person does not want to see the deceit. A man will often rub under the eye and look down. The ears are also covered by a child who lies. Again, the adult is more sophisticated, pulling on the earlobe or rubbing the back of the ear. Sometimes, an adult will bend the entire ear forward.

Another gesture that signals lying is scratching the neck below the earlobe—usually five times. When the boss pulls the collar away from the neck, it signals deceit. Research discovered that when a person lies, it causes the sensitive area on the neck to itch. However, this collar pull also takes place when a person is angry or frustrated.

If a person has his or her head propped up by the hand with one or two fingers in the mouth, it signals pressure. Rubbing the chin with the thumb and index finger shows that a person is making a decision. And, rubbing the palm on the back of the neck while looking down or away from a person is a way of signaling that the person being dealt with is a "pain in the neck."

Folded Arms

Folded-arms gestures or modifications of this gesture symbolize hiding behind a barrier. The need to be behind a barrier indicates a degree of feeling threatened and goes along with a nervous, negative, or defensive attitude. Folded-arms gestures have many modifications that communicate other things: a hostile attitude, a firm stand being taken, a superior attitude, or fear.

Crossed Legs

Crossed-leg gestures send a similar signal as the crossed-arms gestures: a negative or defensive attitude. Crossed arms indicate a more negative attitude than crossed legs. When both the arms and the legs are crossed, a person has withdrawn from the conversation. Of course, you have to be careful when interpreting crossed arms and legs. The boss could be cold or have to go to the bathroom.

Eye Signals

Eye signals do a lot more in communication that tell a listener which channel sequences another person uses to understand the world. The gaze of the eye on the face or body of the person to whom you are talking also speaks. It says "I like you" or "I don't like you." It says you can trust me or you cannot trust me, as pointed out in the section on believability. The length of a gaze can signal fear, courtship, hostility, social encounter, or business encounter. Both intimacy and hostility tend to look straight into the eyes at close range for 10 seconds or more. The business gaze looks a person in the eyes and on the forehead just above the bridge of the nose. The social gaze looks a person in the eyes and in the mouth.

When you are in a business discussion, you can create seriousness by where you gaze. Stare at a spot on the forehead above the bridge of the nose. As long as your gaze does not fall below the other person's eyes, you can control the conversation. Once your gaze drops below the eyes, you have communicated that you are in a social context.

How do you know if the boss is bored with you? She or he uses the eye-block gesture unconsciously. Normally in conversation, a person blinks six to eight times. When a boss closes his or her for a second or longer, the boss is blocking you from sight. If a person feels superior to you, the person will also tilt back the head slightly.

THE BOSS'S ARRANGEMENT OF FURNITURE

Your boss's arrangement of his or her furniture and his or her body angles relative to yours speak volumes. If you have ever gotten the impression that someone you were talking to would rather be somewhere else, your impression came from the way the person pointed his or her torso or feet. The torso or a foot points in the direction we want to go. Say you are standing in the doorway of your office talking to your boss, and his torso is pointed away from your torso, even though he has turned his head toward you and is looking at you. He is signaling that he wants to leave. When people are standing and talking in a small group, one foot will point toward the person who interests each person.

In seated body formations, the arrangements are important for control and communication. The very arrangement of the chairs, desks, tables, and other furniture communicates. Your boss may have given thought to the arrangement of the desk and chairs in his or her office. Aspects of your boss's attitude toward you are revealed in the position the boss takes relative to you. First, the atmosphere and architectural accoutrements of

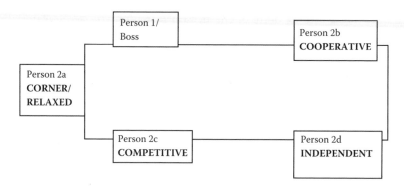

FIGURE 6.2
Seating positions can speak.

a setting can change some of the general rules of seating positions we are about to share.

Generally, in an office environment with standard desks and chairs, person 2 (see Figure 6.2) can take four seating positions in relation to person 1 that convey an attitude:

2a The corner position
2b The cooperative position
2c The competitive or defensive position
2d The independent position

The *corner position* gives a feeling of relaxed conversation. It is the best position for a salesperson trying to sell a product or service to another person. The corner acts as a partial barrier if either person feels a little threatened. It is easy to observe body language and eye movement from this position.

The *cooperative position* says, "I'm on your side." People with the same point of view and same story usually sit in this position. This is a strong position for presenting a case and having it accepted. It also serves a salesperson well if the salesperson must call in a third party, such as a technical expert.

The *competitive* or *defensive position* creates a defensive atmosphere by its very arrangement. The table between the two parties becomes a concrete barrier. This position is also used for encounters between superiors and subordinates.

The *independent position* is the position of a person who is not taking sides with other persons. Perhaps this person is a consultant or a secretary.

A person who understands the effect of seating arrangements has an advantage over those who do not understand. And, no matter what field of business you are in, the purpose in microcommunication is always to see the other person's point of view and to understand before seeking to be understood. The *competitive position* should be used only when that position is absolutely warranted after due consideration of all factors.

When in the *competitive position*, the table or desk is divided in half by each party. Equally between each person on the top of the table depicted in Figure 6.2 is an imaginary line. Whenever the opposing party moves into the space of the other, the other person becomes fidgety and nervous and will usually show physiological signs of nervousness unless something is done to move the other person out of this person's space. A person making a presentation can tell, see, and sense when the other party will allow you into his or her space. If you are using a piece of paper to help with the presentation, lay it on the table in the middle. If the other person leans forward, looks at it, and shoves it back to you, the person has just denied permission for you to enter his or her territory. If the person reaches out to take it and pulls it into his or her space, you can ask verbally for permission to enter the person's space and discuss it. If you fail to get verbal or nonverbal permission to enter another person's space, you put the person off. This is not good communication. Good communication goes with the golden rule: Do unto others as you would have them do unto you. When someone is put off by you and upset, what you have to say better be of such import that it cancels out those feelings. Otherwise, observing territorial rules and using them wisely must be the order of the day.

SUMMARY

About 93% of communication is nonverbal. Only 7% is with the words. To truly hear what your boss is saying, you need to understand your boss's body language.

Body language, or nonverbal communication, tells the truth about what the boss feels toward what he or she is saying. Although verbal content is necessary for clear microcommunication, the full meaning cannot be understood without the nonverbal component. Be careful, though, not to base your actions on nonverbal clues when your boss gives you a directive. You could, after all, guess wrong on his or her meaning.

When receiving a message, you must suspend judgment and take in all the information, verbally and nonverbally, ideally over several conversations, before drawing conclusions. A listener must use the signals and clues from vocal tone and body language as well as understand the preferred and secondary channels of communication used by a person.

Whenever you meet the boss, you must make a good first impression and come across as believable. If you are believable, the boss will tell you more. A sender should use knowledge of NLP to discern the boss's communication channel and switch to that channel. A sender should also use body language to support the verbal message. When the words do not align with the nonverbal message, the truth always lies with the nonverbal message.

> Communications upward need to be adjusted based on the situation the individual is facing at the time the communications takes place.
>
> **—H. James Harrington**

REFERENCES

1. Elgin, Suzette Haden (1989). *The Gentle Art of Verbal Self-Defense for Business Success*, Prentice Hall, Paramus, NJ.
2. Decker, Bert (1992). *You've Got to Be Believed to Be Heard*, St. Martin's Press, New York.
3. Molloy, John T. (1976). *Dress for Success*, Warner Books, New York.
4. Grinder, John and Bandler, Richard (1976). *The Structure of Magic*, Science and Behavior Books, Palo Alto, CA.
5. Brooks, Michael (1989). *Instant Report*, Warner Books, New York.
6. Pease, Allan (1981). *Signals: How to Use Body Language for Power, Success and Love*, Bantam Books, New York.

7

What Do I Say to a Difficult Person or a Bully?

I love humanity. It's people I can't stand.

—Charlie Brown, *Peanuts* comic strip

No one can deal with the hearts of men unless he has the sympathy which is given by love.

—Henry Ward Beecher

Courage is fire, and bullying is smoke.

—Benjamin Disraeli

As soon as a person has clearly demonstrated that they are an energy drain and difficult, confront their behavior. Calmly and clearly describe the behavior and ask for a change.

—R. D. Lewis

INTRODUCTION

The workplace is not always friendly. How do you talk to a person who takes advantage of you at work? Fellow workers can be obstacles to your ability to get your job done. They can harass you. They can sabotage you. They can use and abuse you. A bad boss can affect your career possibilities. Your health and family relationships are also affected, according to a study done by Baylor University. "Employees who experience such incivility at work bring home the stress, negative emotion and perceived ostracism that results from those experiences, which then affects more than their family life—it also creates problems for the partner's life at work,"[1] said Merideth J. Ferguson, PhD, assistant professor of management and entrepreneurship at the Baylor University Hankamer School of Business (Waco, TX) and study author.

The degree of difficulty one has with problematic fellow workers ranges from an annoyance to a difficulty and then, finally, to an impossibility. The least difficult seem bad enough at the time you are dealing with them. The workplace bully, however, is an absolute nightmare come true.

The least-difficult workplace hindrance might be someone who does not get his or her work done or an insecure or incompetent employee who begs and cajoles you to help do their job and thus prevents you from making deadlines. Being helpful is one thing; being taken advantage of is another. It also may be someone who follows the letter of the policy manual instead of being flexible and staying at work an extra 20 minutes to finish a make-or-break project. Nevertheless, when you know that a person has crossed the line and is taking advantage of you, it is time for a talk.

In the middle group lie the so-called difficult people. These are the huge drainers of your emotional energy. They are creators of problems for their work group or team. These middle groups of difficult workmates spread rumors, criticize fellow workers, are uncooperative, say they will do something and do not do it, and hold everyone back. Surely we could add to this list of characteristics, but you get the idea.

The worst type of fellow worker we call *bullies* because they are. The Workplace Bullying Institute (WBI) uses this definition of workplace bullying: "Bullying is a systematic campaign of interpersonal destruction that jeopardizes your health, your career, the job you once loved." It is a problem getting serious attention in the United States. WBI is the first organization to study bullying in the workplace, and the results of their most recent U.S. surveys in 2007 and 2010 are surprising. On its website, www.workplacebullying.org, we find these statistics:

- Of workers, 35% have experienced bullying firsthand (37% in 2007) given the margin of error, essentially equivalent.
- Of bullies, 62% are men; 58% of targets are women.
- Women bullies target women in 80% of cases.
- Bullying is four times more prevalent than illegal harassment (2007).

- The majority (68%) of bullying is same-gender harassment.
- Of the U.S. workforce (an estimated 53.5 million Americans), 35% report being bullied at work.
- An additional 15% of those in the U.S. workforce witness it.
- Half of all Americans have directly experienced it.
- Simultaneously, 50% report neither experiencing nor witnessing bullying.*

This chapter discusses how to communicate with a difficult person in the workplace. This is where good communication takes courage and wisdom. Sometimes, the only good communication is line-in-the-sand, strong talk. This is why it takes some knowledge and skill and a mentally and spiritually healthy person to deal with the most difficult situations. That is why many companies have mental health support.

Communicating with a difficult person requires a mature, well-adjusted person. Your self-esteem, your self-confidence, and your courage must be present and accounted for. You must be able to have an objective view of yourself so that you can look at your situation as though you were a camera on the wall viewing all actors, including yourself, objectively. After all, maybe you are the difficult person, and you do not know it! And, if you cannot be objective, chances are good that you are a contributing factor to the stressful situation. It is always good to have a couple of good friends and maybe someone in the human resources (HR) department give you honest feedback. That said, let us move along to the subject of how to talk to a difficult person or a bully.

DO NOT AVOID OR IGNORE DIFFICULT PEOPLE

Most of us want to avoid or ignore difficult people. We hope that if we pretend they are not present, they will disappear on their own. As experience demonstrates, that is the least likely event to unfold. Usually, difficult people only become more of a problem if they are not confronted. They grow bolder in your silence. However, that is not to say that ignoring them, after they have been confronted, cannot subsequently be used as a technique,

---

* Survey results are © 2010 Workplace Bullying Institute.

especially with some personality types, to actually deal with them. Is that confusing to you? Well, let us shed some light on it by taking a few common personality types and discussing how to deal with them should they belong to a difficult person.

The Dictatorial Personality

Dictatorial personalities are antagonistic, insulting, and unapproachable. They will be right, and you cannot stop them. If you try, you will be attacked. Do not overreact or react too quickly. Give them a chance to expose their supposed reason for objecting and listen for clues regarding what event or statement might have triggered the outburst, other than their personality type. Maintain calm control of the situation and take back the conversation. Do not react in kind. Paraphrase to them what they have just said, describe to them their behavior, their tone of voice, and the way you see features change in their faces. Calmly, firmly state your position and do not argue with them. You will not win, but you can set your boundary, and that is a very important thing to do.

The Know-It-Alls

Know-it-alls seem to have all the answers and appear to know more than anyone else. They use factual information, which makes them feel above others. They crave the spotlight. With a know-it-all in your group, do your homework and know everything they do and more. Use the magic of questions to draw out their knowledge and use them to teach others while controlling the conversation. They will eat it up. And, thank them for their information. Maybe you can make a friend and actually help this personality type.

The Passive–Aggressive Personality

Passive–aggressive personality types use random or incidental criticism against you. They camouflage their attack on your position and undercut your authority in underhanded ways by using sarcasm, often disguised as a joke. Attempt to steer them to the issues. Once they have been exposed as off topic and petty, they usually stop. They do not want center stage or open conflict.

The Whiner

Whiners are negative and see the proverbial glass as half empty. They complain, are judgmental, and act overwhelmed. They feel that others think they are not important, so counteract this from the start by listening to them first. Help them focus on the facts and the positive. Maintain control by bringing up the negatives yourself. Then, dismiss the negatives logically. Direct the person's attention to the more positive aspects of the situation. When the whiner asks a negative question, turn to the rest of the group to answer. Do not give the whiner much eye contact.

The Downers

If whiners could graduate to the next level, they would become the *downers*. These people are ultranegative. The downers have issues with power and project this issue on whoever represents it. They are always right in their eyes because whoever is in power has not seen the "downside" of the issue—but they sure have. Deal with these difficult people by being upbeat but realistic. Forget about meeting them halfway—a good idea, but it never works on this type. Do not totally ignore them but do not argue with them either.

The People Pleaser

The people pleaser personality type is easy to like, yet at times difficult to deal with. These individuals overcommit themselves and their staffs because they cannot say "No." You can see that practice would lead to problems. People pleasers agree to help other persons before examining their own schedule and personal needs. They do not want to hurt anyone's feelings. For this reason, they are often too busy and therefore overly stressed. Of course, that means that their attention also is often divided. With the people pleaser, you must look at their schedule and limit what they commit to do. Help them to say "No" in a positive way that gives them a pat on the back while teaching them that it is not only okay to say "No" but also justified.

The Nonparticipant

Nonparticipants do not reveal their true motives. You can end up in a guessing game with them. The importance of getting them to participate in meetings cannot be overstated. If you do not understand their true objectives, they might undermine your efforts and the efforts of the team. Try the magic of questions on them. Wait them out and do not move on until they answer. Continue asking follow-up questions. Use your deep listening skills (discussed throughout this book) to give you clues regarding what questions to ask.

DO NOT "PASS THE BUCK"

Do not ask someone else to deal with difficult people when it is your responsibility. President Harry S. Truman had a sign on his desk in the White House that read, "The buck stops here." This saying derives from the slang expression "pass the buck." It means passing the responsibility on to someone else. This slang expression "pass the buck" probably originated on the American frontier with the game of poker, in which a marker, often a man's hunting knife that had a "buckhorn handle," was used to indicate the person whose turn it was to deal. If the player did not wish to deal, he could pass the responsibility down the line by passing the "buck," as the buckhorn-handled knife came to be called, to the next player.[2]

When it comes to handling difficult people, you also cannot pass the buck. The person causing difficulty must deal with the situation. To ignore it and not speak or take appropriate action will only cause the problem to grow. In other words, you need to be assertive.

Assertiveness is different from aggressiveness. Assertive behavior discloses one's honest attitudes and feelings to others. This does not mean being rude or offensive. It refers to constructive sharing. You can see how essential this would be to good microcommunication. Many personality types tend to say what the other person wants to hear rather than what they actually think, believe, or feel. Aggressive behavior, on the other hand, refers to action that uses force to accomplish an end. Sometimes, this may be justified by a situation, but generally, aggression is viewed as unacceptable and harmful. In fact, aggression is the trait of a difficult person and a bully. They use aggression in an inappropriate way.

Assertive behavior is intentional, proactive behavior that produces health in the person who uses it as well as the system or organization in which he or she operates. Assertiveness goes hand in hand with emotive behavior. The word *emotive* comes from the word *emotion*. Emotions are feelings. Assertiveness includes the ability to communicate feelings as well as facts or events and behavior. One of the best illustrations of the benefits of talking about our feelings is illustrated by a pressure cooker. It cooks food under pressure and has a pressure release valve to release steam when at a certain pressure point. If this does not happen, then an explosion occurs. When we hide our emotions from ourselves and from others and do not release them, it is the equivalent of a pressure cooker without a release valve. One of two things eventually happens: Our emotions work themselves *out* or they work themselves *in*. They manifest themselves in odd and uncharacteristic behavior, or they work themselves into our bodies and organs in the form of disease and sickness. Business should be interested in preventing sickness in its workforce as well as preventing possible destructive behavior.

The classic story that makes the point of the importance of assertiveness is called *The Abilene Paradox*.[3] This story has been published on video and in book form. It makes many points, but stressed here is its illustration of the need for assertive behavior:

> The story was told of a family sitting on the porch one hot Texas summer evening after dinner. The dad was sweating and casually says something like, "Does anybody want to drive into Abilene to get some ice cream?" After a short pause, the adult son said, "Sure, I guess that's alright." Feeling obligated to say something, the daughter-in-law said, "Ice cream sure would cool us off." Finally, the wife said, "Well, if everybody else wants to go, I guess I'll go, too."
>
> They make the hour long drive in the hot car to Abilene and eat ice cream and drive home again. When they return and are seated on the porch, they began complaining about the long hot drive. The father said, "Well, if ya'll hadn't wanted to go to town to eat ice cream, we wouldn't be so tired and hot."

At that remark the son said, "Well I didn't want to go to Abilene. I only went because you wanted to go, Dad." Each of the women also admitted that they really hadn't wanted to make the trip either. At that the dad admitted he hadn't wanted to go either. He was just making conversation.

Do you see how this story is replayed daily in our lives? If you assume the difficult person understands the damage he or she is doing and you do not verify it, you are living your life based on a fantasy. Remember, it is neurotic to believe someone can read your mind. Learn to pleasantly express your attitudes and feelings to others. It will save a lot of time and money.

USE A PROCEDURE TO HANDLE DIFFICULT PEOPLE

When dealing with the stress and emotion involved in conflict with difficult people in the workplace, one of the best friends you can have is a procedure. A procedure is a thought-out, fixed series of steps used to deal with specific tasks or operations. Here is a suggested procedure for dealing with a difficult person:

Step 1: Confront the difficult person and describe the inappropriate behavior. Be assertive, not aggressive, and factual and fair. Share that the behavior is inappropriate and give the reason or reasons why. If you work out a solution on the spot, then that is good. If not, proceed to step 2. The most likely event will be that you will need to continue the process.

Step 2: Invite the person to a private meeting to solve the issue and set the date of the meeting. Do not miss this step. This is important to nail down at the time you are engaged in conversation about the inappropriate behavior. Set the date for as soon as possible.

   a. Lay ground rules for discussion about the inappropriate behavior.

   b. Mutually endeavor to make a contingent definition of the issues on the spot.

   c. Identify three to five incidents and mutually agree to write incident reports from memory. Agree to share what you have written with one another before the meeting. Also agree not to discuss these with anyone until after the meeting.

Step 3: Conduct the meeting (or meetings if you need more than one) and find the solution.

   a. Identify the common factors in the separate incidents.

   b. Identify your personality type and that of the difficult person.

   c. Identify, as well as you can, the causes of the incidents. Use tools like the Ishikawa diagram to help determine cause.

   d. Produce a definition of the problem.

   e. Arrive at a common agreement on the solution to the problem.

Step 4: Execute the solution. This will require good communication.

Step 5: If the problem cannot be solved by the parties involved, call in the HR department or the boss.

USE GROUP LEARNING TOOLS TO HANDLE DIFFICULT PEOPLE

Businesses today have more resources for employee development and training than at any time in history. Wise employers understand that employee training and education are not optional. Training and education to help employees improve communication are readily available. Group training and group education also can be used for talking to difficult people and for training employees how to talk to difficult people. Education raises awareness. Most harassed and bullied employees think they are the only ones experiencing these things, and that it is their fault, giving the difficult people and the bullies the upper hand. Group learning removes this initial barrier to solving the problem of difficult people and bullies in the workplace.

Also, office bullies and difficult people themselves are often unaware of their over-the-top behavior. That is why they must be confronted and informed by describing their behavior to them in a calm, rational voice. These people could also be helped in group sessions talking about the causes and cures of these behaviors.

Group therapy sessions offered by the HR department can also be arranged. These sessions would help make the workplace happier and more productive for everyone. HR could also arrange for an off-site group learning and therapy session, making it more likely that those who wanted anonymity could have it.

The HR department could also organize small, intimate groups of victims of harassment and difficult people to talk about their experiences and their progress in dealing with their situations. Similar groups for difficult people could be formed to help them deal with the roots of their inclination to treat others the way they do.

We do not all have the same learning styles. In a group or team situation, training that follows a procedure that allows the human brain to learn and retain learning as well as helps to accommodate all the different learning styles is essential. A twentieth century educational psychologist named Robert Gagne (1916–2002), who pioneered the study on how the brain works in the educational process, developed a nine-step procedure in education conducive to learning. He first published these "nine events of instruction" in 1965 in his book, *The Conditions of Learning*, which was reprinted in 1975 and enjoyed one other edition in 1995.[4] The nine-step procedure serves as an important checklist in training teams and teaching groups. These are the nine steps:

1. **Gaining attention** or getting reception from the brain
2. **Informing learners of the objective** or setting expectancy
3. **Stimulating recall of prior learning** or causing the brain to retrieve learned data
4. **Presenting the stimulus**, which is a way of saying giving them the lesson
5. **Provide learning guidance** by giving alternative teaching approaches to aid learning and retention
6. **Eliciting performance** or getting the student to demonstrate understanding
7. **Providing feedback** or giving reinforcement by correcting mistakes or applauding accuracy
8. **Assessing performance** or measuring learning by testing and the like
9. **Enhancing retention and transfer** by helping students take what they have learned and applying it to different situations

USE EARLY WARNING SKILLS AND PREVENTION TO HANDLE DIFFICULT PEOPLE

The best defense is an offense. Training and education of employees will allow them to read the body language and verbal queues that will alert them to a difficult or troubled person. HR performs many temperament and personality tests on employees. There are instruments that identify people likely to fall into this category. Also, as much as the law allows, learn about a person's prior work history. Sometimes, people post these kinds of work experiences on public forums on the World Wide Web or Internet. These ways to help detect a troubled person are currently available. Early detection will enhance good communication in the workplace and lead to higher company profits.

Another method of prevention is the correct social climate and environment of a company and workplace. When a company and the people in it grow and develop in positive ways, a climate in the workplace of mutual trust and respect will begin to grow. This kind of climate makes it harder for difficult people to operate and survive. In an environment of dishonesty, low trust, and little respect, a difficult person's actions are magnified and protected.

If a difficult person makes an outrageous accusation or engages in conduct that hurts the team or a colleague, a climate of mutual trust and respect provides everyone with a clear view regarding whether the accusations have a basis or why certain conduct took place and who did it. The difficult person has fewer places to hide because the tolerance for ambiguity and confusion is extremely low. On the other hand, a difficult person thrives in an environment where the tolerance for ambiguity and confusion is high.

In his book, *Mastering Change: The Power of Mutual Love and Respect in Personal Life, Family Life, Business and Society*,[5] Ichak Adizes postulates that love and mutual respect are mandatory in decision making and management. He reasons that good decisions require the four basic management styles to help one another by lending their expertise and knowledge to a situation. Without the contribution of each of these perspectives, the decision will be a bad one. The problem is that none of these styles can coexist without friction. The only thing that can cause different people to listen to one another's opinions seriously is if those people have love and mutual respect for one another. Only then can the proper balance be brought into management decision making.

We have all known difficult people that we have learned to tolerate because they were valuable to the company. We have also known difficult people with whom most coworkers could not work or they could not understand them, yet because one or two in the work area could handle them, the group allowed the ones who could handle them do it for all the others. And, we have all known a difficult person who, when shown respect and appreciation, suddenly changed and became accommodating and cooperative. The goal of all businesses should be to have a climate that harnesses the assets of the difficult people while helping the whole group to grow. The following story is an example:

> A difficult employee of a large school district in California complained whenever he went into a school office to service the copy machine. He was so gruff and unpleasant that he had everyone scared of him. Principals and secretaries put off calling in a problem with the copy machine as long as possible just to avoid facing this one technician. One secretary, however, refused

to let his gruff exterior intimidate her. She spoke politely to him and always asked about his family.

One day, he was griping about the teachers. "I wish you wouldn't let these teachers touch the copy machine," he said. "They always screw it up."

The secretary immediately responded, "Show me what they do to screw it up, and maybe I can train them."

The man's countenance softened, and he spent an hour explaining exactly what the teachers were doing wrong. That hour of listening made lifelong friends of that man, a real softy on the inside, with the secretary and principal of that school. Now, the secretary and principal always ask for him to come to the school by name. They buy him birthday and Christmas presents. They compliment him on the great job he does, and they write letters to his supervisor for his permanent file commending his services. That employee would do anything for the secretary and principal now. He completely changed his whole disposition. Surely many difficult people would disappear if their gruffness was heard as an invitation to offer a long-range solution to a problem.

USE TECHNIQUES TO HANDLE DIFFICULT PEOPLE

A technique is applying your knowledge of handling difficult people to specific situations. There are two things to remember. First, people can react differently to the same situation. Your technique may work with most situations but not with all of them. Second, the reaction to expect from people in a given situation cannot be known immediately. Some people who receive a challenge for their behavior may show irritation. Others may completely suppress outward emotions all the more. Therefore, obvious calmness from a difficult person who is being called on his or her actions is not always a sign of acceptance of the reprimand. People with hidden anger can explode later at the slightest provocation. Most issues with people are not solved quickly or without effort.

Likewise, think about which specific technique applies to the situation before confronting the difficult person. Read the person's body language and facial expressions while you call them on their conduct toward you. Make adjustments to your technique as you receive feedback from them. You must confront, and you want to help the other person if you can.

Here is a list of suggested techniques for dealing with a difficult person:

- Operate out of integrity and goodwill.
- Confront in a caring way, not in reactive anger or emotion.

- Listen to the person by asking productive questions, describing behavior, and paraphrasing.
- Know the policies and procedures for the job and issue in question.
- Document all incidents and discussions.
- Share your take on the situation or issue and your feelings about it.
- Acknowledge the person's feelings and any legitimate complaints.
- Ask for a commitment to talk about the problem with a view to solve it to the satisfaction of all parties.
- Look for a win/win solution first and foremost.
- Agree on the solution in writing.
- If no agreement on a solution is possible, take it to an arbitrator (e.g., manager, supervisor, etc.).
- Follow the eventual solution with regular meetings to monitor progress.
- Find ways to anticipate future problems and prevent them.
- Have your opening sentences in mind; for example, "Fred, I know you mean well, but when you [describe the inappropriate action or behavior here], it steps over the boundary line. That behavior is not okay. Why did you do it?"

USE FAIRNESS AND CONSISTENCY TO HANDLE DIFFICULT PEOPLE

What two characteristics are needed when dealing with difficult people? Fairness and consistency would be the answer. Confront the behavior, not the person. Be consistently calm and firm. Describe the behavior, exactly what the person did plus his or her reaction to you confronting the person about it, including bulging veins, screaming voice, or shaking hands. Draw your boundary line by informing the person that he or she does not have permission to treat you in the manner. Ask why he or she did it and how you can help. Give the person help, then go about your business. Do not play the person's game by continuing to discuss it, argue, or waste your time.

To greatly lower the incidence of inappropriate behavior from difficult people, why not work on an environment in which fairness and consistency are pillars and practiced by everyone? Then, the contextual force of the corporate social environment would in and of itself both model appropriate behavior and expose incongruous behavior—we mean put it in a spotlight.

Often, a large bureaucracy allows a difficult person to harass a department to the point of uprising and then moves the person to a new department, hoping that the person will tire and leave. This difficult person spends a career fighting the system, causing many great employees to say, "I'm done," and take a job with the competition. Books have been written about how to deal with these vitality-sucking vampires. First, they describe the characteristics of the difficult person. Then, a situation is described with a point-by-point strategy for dealing with the difficult person. These types of books have value, but why not focus on making the corporate environment more conducive to healthy, team-oriented employees rather than a safe haven for people who have a bent to antagonism and anger? Why not build an environment in which the workers who work or, in the case of nonprofit organizations, volunteer there are fair and consistent in their dealings with other people? When the whole environment is one of consistent concern for others, then each employee understands that helping a fellow worker or related division succeed would, over the long haul, ensure his or her own success. One for all and all for one would be the motto.

By way of reminder, sometimes a person is not so much difficult as of a different communication style. Usually, our difficulty with a coworker can be explained by different, conflicting personality types or, as previously discussed, different preferences for collecting and understanding data from our world. In an environment in which the workers and management understand each other and how each person relates to their world, the more initiative workers and managers can take to adapt to their fellow workers' ways of understanding and communicating. Yet, we cannot hope to understand others until we first know ourselves. We can only enter another person's problems and pain to the degree we have faced our own. Also, by establishing rapport through the knowledge gained from NLP and by further understanding of people from the knowledge of personality, we can eliminate most of the contributory factors in ourselves that cause others to seem difficult. We can then develop skills to deal appropriately with people.

One other thing remains to be understood, however. Often, the difficulty between one person and another is caused not by different personality types or different preferences for which sensory channel we use. Many times, the conflict that makes people difficult is the corporate system in which they work. Many systems create conflict situations, and the only remedy is to change the system. Alas, let us leave that subject to people like Peter Senge, the author of the book *The Fifth Discipline*,[6] on the subject of organizational systems and change.

USE THE COMPANY'S COUNSELING AND MENTAL HEALTH SERVICES TO HANDLE DIFFICULT PEOPLE

As you deal with the difficult person in your life, you may come to the conclusion that this person needs professional help. Your HR department will be the starting place to discuss your concern. Take copies of your documentation of your encounters and meetings with the difficult person. When you make your formal report and file a complaint, the company will be able to give psychological help to the difficult person.

According to St. Joseph's Health and St. Joseph's Hospital of Orange, California, counseling may be indicated if a person has major changes in behavior, such as the following, found on the website (www.stjhs.org):

- Withdrawing or refusing to participate in normal, everyday activities
- Being too anxious or panicked to participate in activities
- Displaying sudden outbursts of anger without a good reason
- Hearing or seeing things that are not actually present
- Increasing use of alcohol or drugs
- Having constant feelings of sadness and disappointment
- Wishing to be dead or expressing suicidal ideas

It is difficult to know for certain whether counseling is needed. Only a trained professional can diagnose and determine the need for treatment. Your HR department will be able to encourage the difficult person to schedule an appointment.

USE DIRECTNESS AND POWER TO HANDLE DIFFICULT PEOPLE

When a difficult person or an office bully will not listen to reason, using aggressiveness and power are necessary and appropriate. At times, a verbal confrontation is all that is needed. This can be done one on one between the difficult person and the aggrieved person. Often, this approach affects the desired result; that is, it works. If a difficult employee becomes violent and becomes a danger to others, then physical force likely would be used. By this time, it is evident to everyone that the ability of the company to do its work has been damaged. HR will have been involved in the process already because, to be effective, dealing with difficult people requires a process and procedure.

How does one fire an employee? Most of us have witnessed the wrong way to do it. The wrong way is traumatic for all involved, including the employees witnessing the process. Usually, it is handled in a clumsy, loudly emotional way, like the police often must handle an arrest. Force is used, and no discussion or redemption is involved. This is the wrong way to fire an employee.

By the time it reaches the stage of terminating an employee, a great deal should have already happened. You have gone through a process that has brought you to this point. The objective of the process has to be to help the employee keep his or her job and to grow as a person and employee. When a process like this one is followed, it creates a positive environment of fairness and trust in the department. By this time, you have noticed the process laid out for you in this chapter. It is straightforward:

1. Engage the employee in conversation (do not avoid or ignore the employee and do not pass the buck).
2. Involve the employee in problem solving, self-disclosure, and personal growth (use procedure and group learning tools).
3. If all this fails, terminate the employee with as much dignity for the employee and the department as possible.

Firings that are the culmination of a fair, solution-driven process produce a number of positive outcomes:

- They allow the modeling of appropriate and healthy interaction with difficult people for the benefit of the others in the organization.
- They take into account the well-being of the employees and work teams as well as that of the company.
- They help build a culture of trust and accountability.

SUMMARY

Difficult people and office bullies are realities. Business and not-for-profit organizations must deal with them. Employees and managers can learn to improve their innate abilities in dealing with annoying and aggressive people who cause emotional stress and destroy the work time of other employees. Doing this is part of good communication and will increase the profits of an organization. It will increase the number of productive hours employees log, and it will lower the healthcare costs.

The worst move is to ignore difficult people and bullies. This usually feeds their drive to push further into the lives of fellow workers and to be destructive forces. Difficult people and bullies must be confronted. A person confronting another person must be assertive and not aggressive. The motive must be redemption and not destruction. Having a motive of helping a fellow human being is positive. Having a motive of destroying a fellow human being is negative and would make a person behave like the difficult person or bully.

Process and procedures should be used. Encounters with the difficult person or bully should be documented. Reports should be made. The reports initially are for your private files. Later, they may need to be given to HR or management.

Group training and education about difficult people and about interpersonal skills should be employed. These training opportunities would give knowledge to employees about difficult people and bullies and how to deal with them. It would eliminate the common feeling that the abused person somehow did something wrong to cause the difficult person to react the way he or she did. Also, the training and workshops could help the difficult people and bullies become aware that they themselves have an issue with aggressive or annoying behavior.

An environment that lowers the opportunity for difficult people to abuse employees and hide should be created. An environment of fairness, trust, consistency, and well-being should be created by an organization. Management should make this part of the mission of the organization.

The last step in the process would be termination. In an organization with mechanisms, processes, and procedures in place to deal with difficult people and bullies, this last step should be a positive and value-added experience for the organization.

> The best way to get respect and cooperation is to give respect and cooperation.
>
> **—H. J. Harrington**

REFERENCES

1. Ferguson, Merideth J. (2011). You cannot leave it at the office: Spillover and crossover of coworker incivility, *Journal of Organizational Behavior*, DOI: 10.1002/job.774
2. Mathews, Mitford M., ed. (1951). *A Dictionary of Americanisms on Historical Principles*, University of Chicago Press, Chicago, Vol. 1, pp. 198–199.
3. Harvey, Jerry B. (1988). *The Abilene Paradox and Other Meditations on Management*, Lexington Books, Lanham, MD, pp. 13–36.
4. Gagne, Robert M. (1965). *The Conditions of Learning*, Holt, Reinhart and Winston, New York.
5. Adizes, Ichak (1992). *Mastering Change: The Power of Mutual Love and Respect in Personal Life, Family Life, Business and Society*, Adizes Institute Publications, Santa Monica, CA.
6. Senge, Peter (1990). *The Fifth Discipline: The Art & Practice of the Learning Organization*, Doubleday, New York.

8

How Do I Talk to My Customers?

If you once forfeit the confidence of your fellow citizens, you can never regain their respect and esteem. It is true that you may fool all of the people some of the time; you can even fool some of the people all of the time; but you can't fool all of the people all of the time.

—Abraham Lincoln

There is a time and a place to take a short-cut, but not in the area of developing a personal character of virtue and respect.

—R. D. Lewis

INTRODUCTION

Good communication is a relationship. Good business is about customer relationships. If a business does not have customers, it is not a business. A business having customers is not solely the result of having the best products as far as quality and advanced technology. Neither is it about making many sales. Having customers is about the total population in the universe of your business or nonprofit organization experiencing good communication that results in meeting or exceeding the needs of all.

We view all organizations as having two customers: internal and external. With external customers, the customer is not always right, but the customer is never wrong. The external customers typically pay for the service or products that are delivered to them. In the internal customer case, the output from other employees within the organization has no tangible cost to them. With the external customer, the decision to acquire the product or service is a decision made by the external customer based on the value of the services and the cost of acquisition. With internal customers, there is a different negotiation situation. The service or output is the negotiated value based on value added to the total organization. Good communication is the foundational principal for both the internal customers of an enterprise and the external customers of an enterprise. Happy employees (internal customers) make happy customers (external customers). Following are several definitions in this regard:

Internal Customer: An internal customer can be any participant in the business or company where an employee works. It could be a coworker, a department, a distributor, and so on. While the external customer has a choice of company from which to purchase a product, the internal customer has no control over the departments, coworkers, or suppliers that are in place. Good internal customer service is a requirement for companies desiring to be the best company while creating great external customer satisfaction. High-quality internal customer satisfaction cannot take place without quality communication between coworkers, departments, and divisions.

Internal Service Provider: An internal service provider is the coworker, department, division, or supplier that produces a product used by an internal customer. The internal service provider and the internal customer are the yin and the yang of internal customer relationships. A perfect balance of these creates a healthy business environment and contains a big dose of quality communication.

External Customer: An external customer is the purchaser of a company's product. The external customer buys it. If there are no external customers, there are no internal customers.

Customer: A customer is a person or business that has recently bought a product or regularly buys a product from a company.

Consumer: A consumer is a person or business that actually uses the product created; the consumer is often called the *end user*. A consumer might or might not be the customer who purchased the product.

Although wise people throughout the ages likely have recognized the worth of good relationships between employers, employees, other businesses, and the public, it was Joseph M. Juran who formally introduced and interpreted the idea of the internal customer to the quality management movement. He presented the concept in the fourth edition of the *Quality Control Handbook*.[1]

The examples of the failure to take internal and external customers into account in the building of a profitable business have been highlighted since Juran and his colleagues, including coauthor H. James Harrington, started drawing attention to the unconditional importance of the customer in the fullest meaning of the word. Ancient sayings, like the one of Jesus, "But he that is greatest among you shall be your servant," have been seen to be insightful in the context of fellow employees helping one another succeed by understanding mutual needs through the practice of good communication. To truly help other employees and departments in one's business would fit the definition of the word *servanthood*. This idea was the theme of a business book best seller by Peter Block, *Stewardship: Choosing Service over Self-Interest*.[2] This attitude of service and humility must certainly be present in employees who see the big picture and understand that these attitudes and principles lead to long-term prosperity and happiness for all.

In retrospect, failure to take customers into the equation helps explain why great inventions of the past failed to gain traction in the marketplace and why businesses have failed. Many businesspeople/inventors have had advanced products that were commercial flops even though they were cutting edge. Years later, these products were seen as so advanced for their time that they were considered marvels, like the Lohner-Porsche Mixte-Hybrid invented in 1901 by Ferdinand Porsche, an electric car using two combustion engines to generate electricity to run an electric motor (Figure 8.1). Porsche fortunately had other products that sold well. Yet,

FIGURE 8.1
The 1901 Lohner-Porsche Mixte-Hybrid by Ferdinand Porsche.

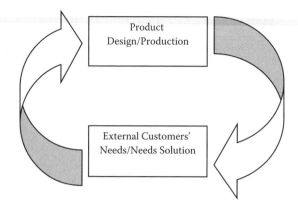

FIGURE 8.2
Circle of external customer good communication profits.

his Lohner-Porsche Mixte-Hybrid, as well as the creations of many other inventors of that era, never became a sustainable commercial success.

Another famous example is Nikola Tesla, the world-famous, early twentieth century inventor of alternating current, radio, wireless technology, neon lamps, and X-rays. He made all the headlines and died penniless. The problem was that these products were ahead of their times and had no application to customers. They were not practical to customers or affordable to customers' wallets. Therefore, the businesspeople/inventors did not have a viable external customer base.

What does a business do to make a profit that sustains business and builds wealth? Think of the process as a circle that begins and ends with the external customers (see Figure 8.2). The circular process begins with the external customers' needs and wants. The circle ends with meeting the customers' needs and wants.

The more complete diagram of this process would be the one seen in Figure 8.3. This is Harrington's interpretation of a process that produces a product or service for any customer. It starts with the negotiation; the requirements of the product or service are mutually agreed between the two parties. There also is agreement reached on how the customer will communicate back to the supplier and how satisfactory the suppliers' output matched the customers' requirements. Once the output requirements are defined, the supplier can design his or her process to produce outputs that are in keeping with the agreed requirements statements. But, in most cases, before the process can produce an output, it will require inputs from some other internal or external parties. At this point, the supplier

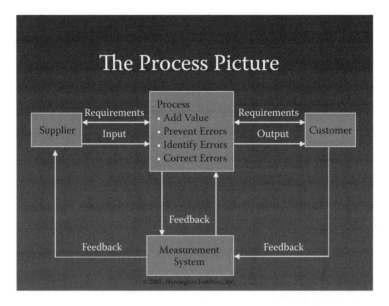

FIGURE 8.3
Harrington's interpretation of a process that produces a product or service for any customer.

to the original customer becomes the customer for the organizations that provide input into the process, which in turn requires a negotiation that defines the requirements related to the inputs that go into the process.

The great inventors of history mentioned would have had to make the discipline of *inventing* a long-range activity of research and development and would have had to put the first money into producing commercial products based on their contemporary customers' needs. Would they have produced a cutting-edge, avant-garde product had they done that? No, but they could have created a simpler product that was the best on the market at the time and included a small innovation that could have been accepted by customers and moved the customer demand forward toward the current avant-garde product. They would have included input from internal customers as well. Why did these cutting-edge inventors not check with their customers? One reason was that they themselves were so enamored with their invention that they could not see anything else. They probably assumed that everyone would be caught up by the pure genius of the machine and technology as they were caught up by it. Another reason was that they did not understand that the external customers were part of their process. Finally, the modern idea of a quality management system was not fully understood in those days.

Seems silly, does it not? Not talking to the targeted end users of a product happens all the time. This chapter addresses how to talk to customers because, among other things, a business needs to know what the external customers and the internal customers need, want, and can afford, whether the cost to them is in currency or in quality working conditions. Talking to customers is about good communication, good relationships, and respect.

TREAT ALL PEOPLE WITH RESPECT

So, why didn't we title this section, "Treat All *Customers* with Respect"? The answer is that customers are *people,* and all people are in the customer-prospect pool; many are bona fide *potential customers.* One never knows. A person could be a potential end user of your product, or a person could be a potential employee of your company. Treating noncustomers rudely can turn into verbal poison for your business. The practice of being rude and condescending can result in the negative public opinion about your company. Word of mouth travels exponentially, and bad word of mouth is said to travel five times as fast as good word of mouth. So, treating people as though they were doormats can cause a loss of a job.

Respect means an attitude of high regard and esteem for another person. If a child is fortunate, his or her parents teach respect for other people. Parents can also teach children to distrust others and take advantage of others, which is to disrespect people. This latter experience is a travesty because respect is a quality that allows us to relate with others. Even if a person is not worthy of respect and we choose to treat the person with respect anyway, then the way we treat the person can cause, over time, a change for the better in the person.

Treating people with respect is a choice that is made. It is a rational choice that may, at times, be in conflict with the emotions. When an angry customer yells at a customer complaint representative, the emotional reaction of the customer complaint representative is fight or flight. In those situations, the attitude of respect is taken by using a process of logical, mental choice. The reasoning might go something like this:

- I made a choice to treat all people with respect.
- To show respect is in my best interest and my company's best interest over the long haul.

- The angry customer in front of me is likely pressured by some factors other than anger about our product's performance, and this customer is better than this behavior.
- The customer's anger is not about me personally since we do not know each other, and because, to the customer, I am just a representative of the company.
- I have an opportunity to defuse the customer's anger and keep the customer's patronage.
- Helping this customer goes beyond good business and enters the realm of being a good person and making the world a better place.

Walt Stasinski, a motivational speaker from Troy, Michigan, has some free articles on his website (http://waltspeaks.com). One is, "You Can Live without Customers But Not for Long." After telling a story about great customer service that went above and beyond the expected, he wrote this:

> Nowadays, the world is extremely competitive and customers have more choices than ever. To develop customer loyalty, you have to distinguish yourself from your competition. This is a challenge because the bar for excellence is constantly being raised and customer expectations go higher and higher. What is the answer? It's the human touch. A sign in the customer service department at Digital Equipment Corporation reads, "Customers don't care what you know, until they know that you care."
>
> How do you show that you care? It all starts with your attitude. Have you ever walked into a business, up to the counter and, within 30 seconds, determined how helpful the customer representative would be? The customer can feel your attitude, can feel how much you care. When the customer shows up, make the customer feel really welcome. Treat the customer as a guest not as a dollar sign. A warm greeting, eye contact, body language and a willingness to help make the customer feel glad he/she is there.[3]

WITHOUT CUSTOMERS, YOU ARE OUT OF BUSINESS

A very old proverb says, "Where no oxen are, the crib is clean: but much increase is by the strength of the ox." We could update that proverb to this: "Where no customers are, the display racks are neat, but much profit comes with untidy customers." Think of how stress free most workplaces would be without customers. Workers could catnap most of the time. But, you would not be in business for long, and you would not get paid. The point being, of course, that we complain about our customers most of the time—our internal customers as well as our end users. It is time for an attitude adjustment, don't you think?

Many businesses as well as not-for-profit organizations are like revolving doors: The customer, employee, member, or volunteer comes in one door, stays a while, and then goes out the other door. The business and not-for-profit organization stay the same size. Organizations cannot grow until they learn to retain customers, members, and volunteers. Other organizations are great at retaining clients but cannot attract new customers. These organizations also do not grow. In fact, they will eventually begin to decline as customers, members, or volunteers die or move away. When it comes to customers, a two-prong approach is needed: retention and addition. Customer relations, which are retention, go hand in hand with the two sides of customer addition, sales (microcommunication level), and marketing (macrocommunication level). Both of these operations rely on good communication for success.

For customer relations, an organization needs good customer relations management software. For marketing, a lot of money is needed because it covers so many things, from advertising on multiple media to being involved in community activity. To show how unwieldy it is, the American Marketing Association (AMA) adopted this definition of marketing in 2007 as seen on the AMA's website (www.marketingpower.com):

> Marketing is the activity, set of institutions, and processes for creating, communicating, delivering, and exchanging offerings that have value for customers, clients, partners, and society at large.

One usually has to read that definition more than once. The reason for that is that marketing takes place on both levels of communication, on the macrocommunication level as well as the microcommunication level. That is why the definition of the AMA is so split level.

LISTEN TO YOUR CUSTOMERS

The first step in talking to your customers is to listen with understanding to your customers. In our experience, nothing insults a man more than to have another person manipulate him. Little else frustrates a woman more than to have a salesclerk try to sidetrack and interrupt her quest. That is the reason why listening to customers is not optional: It is mandatory. Otherwise, lost sales and lost future sales occur.

Internal service providers need to take the initiative of listening to their customers in a more formal way. Service-level agreements (SLAs) are helpful in this regard and need to be used. An SLA defines what the internal customer can expect from the internal service provider. Too often, an internal customer fails to take into account the time needed by internal service providers to respond to a request. Internal service providers, such as the engineering department, respond to many internal customers. Good communication on the part of internal customers and the internal service providers is imperative, and a written document clarifies this.

Listen to your external customers or potential external customers to identify where they fit in the sales process. Are they part of the general pool and not yet potential customers? Have they moved from being potential customers to being prospects? Have they moved from being prospects to being shoppers in your store? Have they bought their first item or service from you? Are they repeat customers? Are they happy customers or disgruntled customers? This information is helpful and even necessary for a salesperson to know.

Sometimes, in a retail store, especially in a downtown area or shopping center, people enter to kill time. They may be waiting for someone and simply want to walk around while waiting. These are part of the general pool, yet the chance of making them a potential customer is better than it was before they walked through the door. The goal should not be to sell them something immediately but to create a pleasant experience. This pleasant experience would be to demonstrate to them that shopping with your establishment would be pleasant. They would undoubtedly overhear your conversations with other customers and how you related to them in a warm and helpful way. You could destroy this opportunity by not talking to the customer and ascertaining the visitor's status.

On the other extreme, how many people have entered a store to buy an item and could not find a salesclerk or manager with whom to talk? At times, these people search, mistake another customer for a salesclerk, and then leave angry, only to go to the competitor. In this case, a person wanted to talk and was prevented from doing so. The unspoken, tacit contract with the community was broken, the contract that said, "We have a store, a sign, an open door, and things to sell, and we want to sell them."

Retail stores are not the only offenders, though. Governments are difficult places to navigate for customers. Which department do I contact for a certain permit or license? In which building would I find the department? What benefits are actually available to me? The reason people persist with governments is that governments collect money with force rather than through commerce, a thing that businesses cannot do. Also, governments are the organizations that make the rules.

We will not stop with retail stores or governments. Let us throw in not-for-profit organizations: religious institutions, universities, community organizations, and hospitals. These institutions need to develop the ability to listen to customers and to be available to the community. A newspaper publisher in a medium-size California town shared that the most difficult professional group with which to obtain an appointment or to find in the office were the pastors and ministers of local churches in town.

Let us say you talk to every customer, potential customer, or internal customer you have. Did you know that the people who do not advance in their organization or who do not make it in the retail sales industry have another problem besides refusing to talk to customers? The other problem is poor communication skills when talking to customers. So, how does one talk to customers? The following discussion provides tips to do so.

Look Them in the Eye

Speaking from the American cultural perspective, eye contact is important. To never make eye contact is considered strange. A shy person might not make eye contact, instead looking at the floor. An intimidated person might do the same. A person who has something to hide would avoid eye contact. On the other hand, a friendly and trustworthy person would be open and engaging, which would include making eye contact.

When greeting a customer, make eye contact long enough to establish contact with the customer's conscious brain. This would be about 4 or 5 seconds of time. Staring longer than that would be done when a person is angrily aggressive or when man and a woman are feeling amorous. So, staring too long with a customer also would be a problem. After the initial contact, look the customer in the eye again from time to time. This will also give you an opportunity to read his or her facial expressions.

When talking to a person on the telephone, smile. The physical act of smiling on the telephone does two things. First, it changes the disposition of the one smiling. Second, the person listening to the smiling person hears the person smiling. On a classic Frank Sinatra standard, you can hear various emotions. I am no expert, but common sense tells me that when we express emotions, it affects the expressions on our faces. When this happens, it is because our muscles contract or relax. This, I surmise, actually changes the tenor of our voice.

Friendly eye contact establishes trust and connection. When a customer is engaged in this way, it is much more difficult for the customer to leave the store or to leave a conversation. And, of course, the customer knows through this important act of nonverbal communication that you are indeed talking to him or her.

Use Friendly Body Language

We discussed body language in previous chapters. Here is more information in the form of a review. The eight elements of body language are as follows:

- Face
- Eyes
- Posture
- Gestures
- Voice
- Movement
- Touch
  - Friendly
  - Professional
  - Social
  - Intimate
- Appearance

When you are expressing friendliness, all of these elements should be in synchronization to express the message of friendship. The words coming out of your mouth should be friendly and sound friendly. Think of one of your great friends who you would love to see come through the door. How would you react to him or her? Focus that feeling on the customer and take it down by half. If you treated a customer like your best friend, the customer would not be comfortable. But, if you took the same feelings and subdued them to the level reserved for someone who gave you your paycheck, you might be about right for your customers.

To be a little bit more specific, to project openness and friendliness, use these body language examples:

- Keep your arms more at your sides and never crossed.
- Keep your palms facing outward without looking awkward.
- Keep your elbows away from the torso, not tucked into it.
- Use straight, good posture (imagine a helium balloon attached to the center of your head and pulling you straight).
- Lean a bit forward, like you are interested in what the person is saying.
- If you are sitting, do not cross your legs and keep them stretched out.

Again, when you use body language to show friendliness and approachability, you are talking to your customer.

Give Feedback and Ask for Feedback

Do you remember the feedback loop? It is simple. When a person tells you something, from time to time, repeat back the meaning as you heard it, and then ask the person if you understood correctly. When you tell another person something, ask the person for feedback. If there is a checklist of things for the customer to do, summarize it before the customer leaves, helping the customer to remember it and reinforcing the idea of its importance. This simple procedure does amazing things for understanding and for minimizing mistakes. Also, it says to your customer that you are a concerned professional doing everything you can to serve him or her.

Conversational feedback with a customer is different from the performance review in which a supervisor gives the employee feedback about the job the employee is doing. Feedback with a customer is to clarify communication, to solve issues the customer is having, and to build relationships so the customer will continue to be the customer.

Sometimes, you have to help your customers talk to you. Here are a few things to prime the pump based on the basic "who, what, when, where, why, and how" method of getting facts and sharing facts:

- Ask who they are buying for or who recommended the store.
- Ask what personal or business needs they have that your business meets with its products and service and ask what about your business they would like to see improved.

- Ask them when they best like to shop and when they plan to come back.
- Ask them where they would like to see a new retail outlet and where in the social media they would like to see your business presence.
- Ask why they buy from you and come to your store.
- Ask them how they make decisions about where to shop and how you could better meet their needs.

Do Not Escalate an Angry Situation

No one enjoys an angry encounter. However, life deals us situations in which we are the ones who are the face of the company for an angry customer. It is an emotionally draining experience, and no alternative exists to handling the situation in the best way possible. Avoiding it is not an option. As the purported Chinese proverb counsels: "If you are patient in one moment of anger, you will escape a hundred days of sorrow."

When a person is angry, the objective is to absorb the negative yelling and the threats and to listen with serious attention. You want to deescalate the situation, not escalate it by yelling back or acting unconcerned and uncaring. Here is a suggested process to gain control of the situation while helping the customer or fellow employee:

- Stop what you are doing, give the customer full attention, and stay calm and respectful.
- Listen deeply for the facts and for any themes or metaphors.
- When the customer slows or starts repeating, firmly and calmly tell the customer you want to help.
- If the customer has not already told you, ask, "What happened?" or say, "Tell me why you are upset."
- Repeat back to the customer the essence of the story, including why he or she is upset, to confirm that you have understood.
- Tell the customer that you apologize for what happened and that you want to help.
- Present a solution and ask if that is satisfactory; if not, ask the customer for his or her solution and give the customer as much of what is wanted as your policies will allow.
- Execute the plan for the solution immediately.
- Follow up to see if the solution was satisfactory.
- Analyze the root cause of what happened and take corrective action.

USE PERSONALITY TYPES TO DETERMINE YOUR COMMUNICATION STRATEGY

Since ancient times, personality styles have been divided into four basic groups. Different teachers have given different names to each group, yet they remain essentially the same. Learning these four types and their most noticeable characteristics will help you to identify a person's dominant traits and what kind of communication style best fits the person. If your company does training for employees, training in personality types and communication with various communication types is readily available.

Here is one summary of the four basic personality types:

- Drivers, controllers: most chief executive officers (CEOs) (assertive to aggressive, emotionally challenged); key motivators are achievement and compensation.
- Promoters: easy to read; most salespeople and marketers (more assertive, comfortable with emotions); key motivators are independence, originality.
- Analyzers: practically all of those in engineering and accounting (less assertive, low in emotion); key motivators are comprehending, know-how, and competency.
- Supporters: amiable; most secretaries and counselors (less assertive, more emotional); key motivators are allegiance, connection.

What communication strategy would get through to a controller who is challenged emotionally? Do not talk about your feelings, how much you care about the company, or how hard you work. Just give the controller the results of your research and a plan to reach and accomplish the goals, hit the numbers, and succeed. Do not expect much sympathy or listening to your ideas unless it helps the person achieve his or her goals. If you need something for yourself, find a way to tie it to aiding the controller personality type in accomplishing his or her goals.

How would you communicate with a promoter? You should respond enthusiastically, sharing how you feel about a project and how it would result in more market share and bottom-line profits. Ask the person how he or she would go about doing a project or solving a problem. Listen and then ask questions. Suggest changes that move it in your direction.

What strategy works with analyzers? Give the analyzers the facts, just the facts. Give them data that support what you want to do. Let them look at the data for a few days and make notes. Then, read their notes and their questions. Take their questions and go do your homework. Come back with your answers and reasons. In time, they will give you a firm yes or no.

The communication strategy that works well with supporters is the one that shows them how they can help someone, build a stronger relationship, and remain loyal to their team and their boss. These people need ideas that will help them show their love and support. Connecting what you need to communicate to them with these personality strengths will certainly result in a strong connection.

Two reasons exist for needing to peg a person's personality type. The first reason is to truly understand what is being communicated to you by them. The second reason is for you to know the best approach in how to influence them in a direction that you would want them to go. In a world where businesses need to make sales, this is important.

Customers need your product. You have done the research before you ever produced the product; you have put a lot of time, resources, and energy into producing it. Now that you know from your research and through listening to your customers that there is a market for your product, you need to help your customer see that the product you produced actually meets their need. You need to influence them, and here is where understanding personality type aids in influencing people. The approach that influences one personality type will not influence another personality type. For example, with driver/CEO types, you would use an approach that shows quickly how your product can help them achieve their current objectives and increase their bottom line. For promoter types, you would stress how the product helps them in their quest for independence and being original by standing out as the first to lead the way. For analyzer types, you would give a detailed presentation that would help them analyze the product in comparison to what they currently have and how it would increase their competency. For the supporters, you would stress how it would help them better help others and how much others would appreciate them because of what the product allows them to do.

SUMMARY

The bottom line is no customers, no business. Good communication is a relationship. Good business is about a customer relationship, with both internal and external customers. Having customers is not just about having the best products as far as quality and advanced technology. It is about having the best products that customers want. It is also about having happy employees who are willing and able to engage in quality internal communication.

To make this happen takes a company that understands the importance of the virtue of respect. Respect within the company for colleagues, respect for other businesses, and respect for customers is a hallmark of a great company. Good customer service cannot be divorced from respect for and to customers.

A very old proverb says, "Where no oxen are, the crib is clean: but much increase is by the strength of the ox." We could update that proverb to this: "Where no customers are, the display racks are neat, but much profit comes with untidy customers." Getting customers, retaining customers, and servicing customers costs a lot of money and takes a lot of time. The alternative is no business. These points of good microcommunication are covered:

- Listen to your customers.
- Look the customer in the eye.
- Use friendly body language.
- Give feedback and ask for feedback.
- Do not escalate an angry situation.

Finally, train your business in the art of body language. Use simple body language training to help your people become aware of the true communication taking place. Here are the four basic, classic personality types:

- Drivers, controllers: most CEOs (assertive to aggressive, emotionally challenged); key motivators are achievement and compensation.
- Promoters: easy to read; most salespeople and marketers (more assertive, comfortable with emotions); key motivators are independence, originality.
- Analyzers: practically all individuals in engineering and accounting (less assertive, low in emotion); key motivators are comprehending, know-how, and competency.
- Supporters: amiable; most secretaries and counselors (less assertive, more emotional); key motivators are allegiance, connection.

The best salesman sells himself or herself as being interested in his or her customer before trying to sell the product.

—H. James Harrington

REFERENCES

1. Juran, Joseph M. (1988). *Quality Control Handbook*, McGraw-Hill, New York.
2. Block, Peter (May 1993). *Stewardship: Choosing Service over Self-Interest*, Berrett-Koehler, San Francisco.
3. Stasinski, Walt (2009). You Can Live without Customers But Not for Long, http://www.waltspeaks.com/story/12/03/09/you_can_live_without_customers_not_long

9

How Do I Communicate to a Corporation from the Outside?

Talking to a corporation takes a good plan and a lot of time, a lot of luck, and a lot of money.

—R. D. Lewis

INTRODUCTION

Communication with people is challenging; communication with a corporation or other kind of organization is more challenging and more complex. And, it takes time, know-how, and money. In this chapter, we look at how to communicate to a corporation by those outside the corporation, for example, how a city, a church, a community group, or another business can communicate with a corporation.

We are not saying that individuals do not have needs from time to time to talk to a corporation. It is simply much more difficult for an individual to communicate with a corporation. Usually, the expense and complexity would prevent an individual from receiving an audience. After all, think of the thousands of individuals who want to sit down with executives of a big corporation and talk. It is not feasible. And, from the corporation's standpoint, it is not a good use of the executive's time.

As it stands, most individual communication with a corporation concerns a product that has been purchased from the corporation. For this kind of communication, corporations have toll-free numbers and call centers. Just pick up the phone, call the listed telephone number, and ask the question. As long as one asks questions for which the help desk has a script, things should work out. However, you do have to get through the recorded messages, push the right buttons, and, if the help desk is outsourced to a foreign country, understand the foreign accent. These phone calls to a corporation are such unpleasant and frustrating experiences that they have become material for comedians.

What if you, as an individual, have something to discuss with the company that is not scripted for the help desk? What if you need to talk to a manager or C-level manager? How can this be accomplished? You will need a phone number for this person or at least a phone number with an extension that goes directly to the desk of the person with whom you wish to talk. Finding this telephone number usually is a small project in and of itself. If you do find this telephone number, you had better know what to say and how to say it.

Now, here is a key point we want to make. One common mistake when communicating with a corporation is to communicate with the corporation as though talking to a person. In a small business, this might be true since often a small business is an individual person. A corporation, on the other hand, is not an individual person but a plurality of persons united by a mission and organized into teams, departments, divisions, and countries. They each work in one small part of a huge corporation with employees numbering to the size of small to large cities. One most certainly could not talk to the chief executive officer (CEO) or board of directors without having something the company really wanted or needed. Even if one talked to the CEO or board of directors, that person could not expect an immediate response or answer to a question since so many groups, contracts, patents, and legal matters have to be reviewed and interpreted by many people before any decision is made. That person's question would have to get in queue behind many other questions being answered. And, answering one question would take not only much time but also much money. So, even if one were to be paired in a foursome at a country club with the CEO and ask a question, obtaining an answer just cannot happen easily or quickly, if at all.

The movie *Erin Brockovich* is about a city talking through a law clerk, Erin Brockovich, to a large Northern California utility about a polluting problem at one of its substations that was causing cancer in the population of Hinkley, California. Since the corporation was trying to quietly cover up the problem, Brockovich could not very well get a conversation going with the CEO. The only way to talk to the utility was with a lawsuit brought by the firm where she was employed.

Using the courts is one way to talk to a corporation, but what if no grounds for a lawsuit exist, and you have other reasons to talk to a corporation? Here are a few reasons you might want to talk to a corporation: What if you are hired as a consultant to the corporation and you need to communicate your recommendations to the corporation? What if you are a community leader and need to talk to the corporation in your community about community issues? Or, what if you are a corporation and want to talk to another corporation about a strategic alliance or merger? All of these are good reasons to want to know how to communicate with a corporation.

A party wishing access to a corporation could, and perhaps should, send the corporation a formal letter. Do you want our frank understanding of the usefulness of writing a letter? Unless you are a powerful person, a famous person, or another CEO, this almost never opens the door to good communication, even though it is the logical place to start.

It takes a lot more than a letter to open dialogue with top management of big corporations. It takes a strategic communication plan and good implementation of the plan. For example, coauthor Robert Lewis's daughter, Tiffany, shared an example of how one publication in San Diego, California, opened the door to dialogue and interaction with the CEOs, chief financial officers (CFOs), and other top corporate and business leaders in San Diego. Each year, the publication has a contest for nominating the top business leaders and C-level managers in the greater San Diego area. Then, there is a banquet where all the nominees are invited to eat and mingle with their colleagues and other businesses, including the sponsoring publication's staff. Lewis's daughter, at that time working in the accounting department with the San Diego chapter of the American Red Cross, attended the banquet with her CFO. At the banquet, she said that she and her CFO got to meet the top leaders of business, education, government, and nonprofit organizations. The announcements of the winners of the awards were made after attendees mingled and ate together. Later, the publication publishes the results with pictures. Now, that is a great strategy for a publication on several levels, is it not?

How would your organization go about meeting the corporate leaders who are potential clients or strategic partners of your organization? Let us explore that question by looking at various elements your firm would need to take into account to communicate effectively to another corporation.

UNDERSTAND AND RESPECT THE CORPORATION'S CULTURE

To talk to a corporation, one must understand the culture of the corporation. Yes, corporations are made of people and exist in a country with a language and history, so corporations have a culture that differentiates the corporation from other corporations and entities.

What is culture? As you might expect, definitions differ a little from one sociologist and textbook to another, but most agree that it consists of intangible beliefs and ideas. It is not the tools, businesses, architecture, and so on of a group or society per se that are the culture, but the feelings, symbolic meanings, and attitudes toward the tangible things in the society that are the culture. There are shared patterns of behaviors that identify the members of a group and distinguish them from other groups, but they rest on intangible beliefs and ideas.

Nations have cultures and common languages; the cities within the nations have distinctions of culture. And, corporations have cultures. Corporate culture is expressed in the way things are done; their preferred vocabulary; and the common history and the stories that are told and passed down about the founders and history of the corporation.

Nothing offends or pushes away a person more than disrespecting his or her cultural values. Good communication does not push away. By not understanding a person's culture, miscommunication can easily happen. By saying something that does not fit the culture, a person trying to communicate with the corporation could risk not being heard at all.

Savvy corporations determine and shape the company's culture. Google's Eric Schmidt has talked about how Google's culture is one made up of a certain type of person who fits the desired culture. From listening to the information Schmidt has shared, the Google culture includes motivated, self-actualized, creative people. Google's philosophy of shaping and maintaining its company's culture is to hire people who fit the company's cultural profile at every level. Schmidt said in a video interview posted on the website of the consulting firm Corporate Culture Pros (http://www.corporate-culturepros.com) that Google interviews prospective new hires up to eight times, but not less than five times. Google does this to determine if the interviewees are people who will fit and continue to shape the Google culture.

Even if a company is unaware that it has a culture, the company still has a culture. To communicate with a company, one certainly needs to respect its culture and not insult it during the communication process. Learning about a corporation's culture is basic to communicating with a corporation. The entity wishing to communicate can find points of agreement in the culture and connect with the target of communication by using that as a discussion bridge. What are the key elements of culture that need to be studied and understood?

- *Artifacts*: Visible items that symbolize culture
- *Values*: What an organization views as significant
- *Assumptions*: Deep-rooted beliefs that are unexpressed yet guide behavior
- *Characteristics*: The organization's customary way of interacting, dressing, working, resolving conflict, and so on

If the corporation exists in a different country from your country, then you need to do some study in cross-cultural communication. Courses and books have been written about nation-to-nation communication. One should not underestimate the need to be trained in this area when communicating with a corporation or government agency from a foreign country.

UNDERSTAND THE CORPORATION'S PERSONALITY

If your organization were a person, what kind of personality would it have? The first time I asked that question, I was doing organizational consulting and meeting with a group of about 85 persons. I was shocked with the barrage of words and phrases that were immediately thrown at me describing the personality of the organization. The most emotional and frustrated "shout-out" was the word *schizophrenic*. The pertinent thing for our current topic is the fact that the people in that group had absolutely no problem with my question. They had no problem visualizing their organization as an individual person with a personality.

Organizations have a personality. William Bridges, who adapted the *Myers-Briggs Type Indicator* to use with corporations and organizations, decided to use the term *character* rather than the term *personality* when referring to organizations. Because we had noticed that different organizations exhibited characteristics like persons, we grabbed the book by Bridges[1] when it first appeared in 1992. I am sure anyone working in various organizations, especially in a consulting capacity, has noticed that organizations exhibit characteristics like individual persons. That assumption being true, study the 16 types of personality that are possible in the Myers-Briggs Type Indicator. It will help identify the kind of organization and the personality of that organization and how it communicates.

Have you found it more difficult to communicate with certain individuals than others? It could very well be a personality-type conflict. William Bridges wrote,[1] "And just as type conflict can undermine and even destroy a personal relationship, character conflicts within or between organizations can lead to breakdowns in communication and collaboration" (p. 7). Knowing the personality of your own corporation and the one with whom you want to communicate is important.

The four foundational dichotomies of personality based on the work of Swiss psychologist Carl Jung and the development of it by Katherine Cook Briggs and Isabel Briggs Myers, are the following:

- Extroversion or introversion (outwardly or inwardly orientated). This means that the organization derives its energy from either focusing on markets and customers or focusing on technology, mission, vision, strategic plans, and its own history and culture.
- Sensing or intuition (how it perceives and gathers information). This lets you know how the organization gathers information. It lets you know if it is future oriented or interested in the present and the details of running the organization.
- Thinking or feeling (how it processes information). How does this company make its decisions? How does it process the information you will feed it? This lets you know if it majors on consistency, competence, and efficiency, or if it majors on personal processes related to individuality, the common good, or creativity.
- Judging or perceiving (how it tends to deal with its external world). How does an organization handle the external world? Does it tend toward one of the judging functions or one of the perceiving functions? This lets you know if it likes things in little boxes and firm decisions with closure or whether it likes things loose and its choices open.

Knowing the personality of the corporation you want to communicate with prevents destroying the relationship and killing any opportunity for communication. When you know the personality type, simply account for the way that corporation receives and processes information as you plan your discussion.

UNDERSTAND THE CORPORATION'S FORMAL COMMUNICATION SYSTEM

A formal communication system relates to the structure of the organization. The organization communicates from team to team, from team to department, and from departments to divisions to C-level managers. The organization also communicates with customers and the public. Formal corporate communication uses forms, reports, charts, records, memos, processes and procedures, newsletters, websites, media commercials, media interviews, magazine articles, annual reports, press releases, certain types of smartphone, and certain computer software. The corporation's buildings and their shapes and configurations, the information technology (IT) system, and the culture and personality of the organization all work together to determine the way communication takes place within the corporation. It is necessary to understand how a system operates if effective communication within a corporate system is to take place.

Layered on top of these factors are the personal preferences for using the corporation's formal communication system. If people have options within the formal system, which preferences do they have? Do they return telephone calls and ignore e-mails or vice versa? Do they respond to memos more quickly than to a telephone message? Do they want to read a white paper on a proposal or see a PowerPoint presentation on their computer screen?

In communicating from outside an organization, information about the formal communication system must be understood and used when appropriate and if it is accessible to an outsider. Requesting information that might be needed from the organization will usually require a correct form, or the request will not be processed. Experience with a government agency certainly illustrates this. Have you ever used the wrong form to request something or to submit information? Then, you know what happens. The wrong form is automatically rejected and sent back to you. The worst-case scenario is that the wrong form is rejected without a word of communication regarding what has happened to your form. Of course,

188 • *Closing the Communication Gap*

the form is returned via the cheapest method, which means slowly. This is the nature of a formal communication system. It can be frustrating if you think you are communicating with a person. If, however, you regard the formal system as an inanimate machine, and you learn how the machine works, you can communicate and perhaps start a consulting business helping others to communicate with the large organization.

How does one on the outside learn to use the formal communication system of a large corporation?

- Debrief others who have been successful at communication with the targeted organization.
- Ask a current employee or a former employee how he or she would do it. (If you do not know an employee, hang out at a place where current employees go and use your charm to meet and make a friend of one of them like the private detectives do in the movies.)
- Use trial and error.
- Do research. Research sounds glamorous, but it is not. It is hard work. You have to be part detective, part scholar, and part street-smart gang member. Here are some suggestions regarding how to approach research work:
  - Confirm how the business is organized and set up (sole propri-etorship, partnership, LLC [limited liability company], nonprofit corporation, C corporation, etc.) by checking with the secretary of state in the state where the company is domiciled, which can often be done online;
  - Check the capitalization of the company online if a publically traded company;
  - Determine the age of the company;
  - Study the company website;
  - Get a copy of the annual report and read it;
  - Read articles, newsletters, and books about the company and its CEO and the like;
  - Ask the receptionist of the targeted company for brochures and other literature and then ask who the receptionist knows that could answer your questions;
  - Check out authors of books and articles about the company, call them, and debrief them about how to communicate with the company;

- Check with the business professors in various universities who might have information for you or might tell you where to go to get information;
- Contact the local newspaper business editor and ask for information on how to communicate with the targeted organization;
- Call other business editors from large newspapers or business publications who might be able to give you information;
- Obtain a personnel manual from the targeted company and study it;
- Obtain an operations manual from the targeted company and study it;
- Talk to former employees or retirees of the company and ask questions about working at the targeted company and its formal communication system;
- Study the vendor that provides the IT system for the company and study how it works;
- Attend a company picnic;
- Talk to the company's competitors about the differences;
- Talk to vendors who sell and service machines to the target organization;
- Meet other persons who are successful at communication with the targeted company and learn from them;
- Interview plaintiffs and their lawyers who have sued the company and collect information on how to communicate with the company from them; read the transcript of any trial to see if it holds any information.

UNDERSTAND THE CORPORATION'S SHADOW COMMUNICATION SYSTEM

The shadow communication system is our word for the informal communication system of the corporation or organization. People who work at the corporation talk to one another. They become friends. They celebrate birthdays. And, they have knowledge of what has happened and what might happen at the corporation. The shadow communication system runs inconspicuously alongside the formal communication system and plays an important role in the communication of the company. It is like the lymphatic system that runs alongside the blood circulatory system. The people of the shadow communication system can grease the wheels of the formal communication system and help a friend get a foot in the door.

When Robert Lewis worked at a midsize organization in his years after postgraduate studies, he learned to make friends with the secretaries, partly because the bosses treated him with less seriousness than they did the secretaries. Because he was low in the hierarchy, it was common for him to be in the same break room with the secretaries at the morning and afternoon breaks. It was amazing what saying hello and learning a few names of grandchildren could do in gaining acceptance as a safe person. After a few months, Lewis was allowed to be involved in the conversations with the secretaries at break time. He always knew about changes or events at the organization before his boss knew. He knew who was sick, and he knew who was on the hot seat. Sometimes, he shared the information with his boss. Sometimes, he sat on the information if it served his purposes. After a couple of years, whenever he needed something, he knew just the secretary to ask. That is the shadow communication system.

If you want to communicate with the corporation from the outside, you might want to find a way to meet some of the people of the shadow communication system. Make friends with the custodial staff, the secretaries, the mailroom clerk, and the junior executives who work at the corporation. Where do they hang after work? Which of the Little League teams contain their children? These people are easier to get to know than the bosses, of course. When you have a relationship, they can coach you and even help you communicate with the right people in the right way.

You can also drop information into the shadow communication system through your friends at the corporation. If you are skilled at suggestion and packaging an idea, it might get some legs. Be careful, though, to omit enough information so that you will be needed to supply the rest.

UNDERSTAND THE CORPORATION'S ENVIRONMENT AND ITS PRESSURE/STRESS POINTS

The corporate environment is the influence produced on the people in the corporation by the blended effect of the physical setting, the legal organizational type, the stage of the corporate life cycle, the organization's personality, and the social and cultural circumstances of the people making up that organization. The environment influences the manner and degree of communication of the corporation. Also, environments can be conducive to quality work or conducive to poor-quality work. Environments can be a pleasant or, on the opposite extreme, an unbearable place that produces physical and mental illness in employees. Each of these environmental characteristics influences the manner in which an outsider communicates to an organization.

What are factors in the corporate environment that can be used to facilitate outside communication with an organization? We have already discussed the personality of a corporation related to good communication. The legal type of an organization determines some of the character of an organization but is not pervasive in common, day-to-day communication. The social and cultural circumstances of the corporation have been introduced in this chapter as well. So, let us spend some time thinking about the corporate life cycle and how it influences the environment of an organization and thus how to slant your communication with the organization to make it good communication.

Ichak Adizes's book, *Corporate Lifecycles: How and Why Corporations Grow and Die and What to Do About It*,[2] revealed how corporations are born, grow, reach their prime, and then start aging toward death. At each of the 10 stages of the life cycle, an organization exhibits telling characteristics, much like the life of a person. The corporation either successfully negotiates each stage or else gets stuck in each stage in what Adizes terms a *pathology of the organization*. Also, in each stage in the growth of an organization, the organization is learning essential practices for success in business. Our observation, as we relate this to good communication, is that an entity outside the organization endeavoring to communicate with the organization must slant the conversation to the organization's stage of development in the life cycle. The same is true of a mature organization that is in decline. Each stage of growing old as an organization has *white noise*, a constant background noise drowning out other sounds, which must be factored into good communication.

Here are the 10 stages of the organizational life cycle as named by Adizes:

1. Courtship: Building commitment to the concept.
2. Infancy: Launching the business.
3. Go-go: Success has arrived and the business takes on too much and risks pathology by growing too fast.

4. Adolescence: Coming of age and being reborn apart from the founder.
5. Prime: Excellence in the process of doing business while maintaining the perfect balance of self-control and flexibility.
6. Stable: The company begins to lose the spirit of creativity, innovation, and encouragement of change.
7. Aristocracy: Money goes to control systems, benefits, and facilities rather than to marketing and sales.
8. Early bureaucracy: The blame game starts with conflict, backstabbing, and infighting.
9. Bureaucracy: A disorganized system that looks good on the outside but produces nothing and lives on its reputation and accumulated assets.
10. Death.[2]

At each stage, the opportunity for communication is to slant the message to relate to the dominant characteristics of that stage of development. For example, in stage 3, the go-go stage, acknowledge the great opportunities that have come the way of the company and ask questions about them and how they are affecting the employee morale. When a natural opening comes, show how your service, product, or strategic alliance not only can leverage and enhance the business but also can streamline by narrowing the activity to fit the mission, vision, and core competencies of the company. Emphasize that the services you offer can solve the problem of overextending and ensure even higher profits in the future. By pitching your message to the front-burner issues of the target organization, you ensure that you will be heard.

PLAN A COMMUNICATION STRATEGY

A formal communication strategy with a corporation will keep the focus on what you are doing and help you to keep the main thing as *the main thing*. It aids in discussions and coordination with partners or teammates who are working together. Effective communication requires a strategy.

That being said, making contact and having some level of communication with upper management of a large corporation happens more as serendipity to an author, supplier, or service company than a result of any strategy-planning activity. We heard about a bakery in Seattle frequented by the chairman of a large company that sold coffee beverages.

He came into this shop two or three times and ordered donuts and other pastries. Workers recognized him and were flattered that he liked their shop. Shortly, the bakery was offered a contract to supply baked goods to the coffee company's shops in an area of Seattle. A reporter interviewing the workers asked them what strategy they used to make contact with the big company. They replied that they did not have a strategy and did not initiate contact; the company had contacted them. Usually, this is the way it happens.

Nevertheless, this bakery did have a shop, a sign, and a great product. It also obviously had a location that was traveled by an influential businessman. In addition to having a quality product and a good location, having a strategy for targeting selected corporations as customers or clients and working the strategy is also important. As with most endeavors or projects, the incidental consequences are often worth the effort. The effect of developing a strategy and a plan for reaching a target organization has side benefits. It focuses the unconscious mind of the management and employees on the objective of communication with a target corporation. This brings awareness to casual life events outside the workplace that have a connection with the targeted organization. One never knows the weird or unusual ways contact can be made with key persons in the target organization when the senses are alert. When opportunity does appear, thought and effort have already been directed at communicating with another business or corporation, and certain things are already in place.

As your organization prepares a strategy, keep the principles that we have previously discussed in mind:

1. Corporations do not react to the marketplace and business environment as seen by your organization but as seen by their organization.
2. The secret of communication lies with the receiver (the target corporation). Until your "message" is understood by the target corporation, it is just elevator music. Effective communication begins with hearing and understanding rather than talking and selling. Remember the feedback loop and use it to confirm your understanding of what the target corporation is saying. Remember habit 5 in *The Seven Habits of Highly Effective People:*[3] Seek first to understand, then to be understood. It also works with organizations.
3. No magical solutions exist for communicating with a target corporation. No single message connects with every corporation or organization.

What is a communication strategy? Your organization can hire management and business consultants to help you with this, but a strategy is the thinking part of a plan. Here are basic characteristics of a strategy:

- A strategy expresses, explains, and supports a vision with its attendant set of distinct goals. What is your vision, and how does the targeted organization play into the fulfillment of that vision?
- A strategy produces an unchanging, unified "voice" for the organization that joins different activities and goals in a way that appeals to your organization and stakeholders. Everyone knows why and how you plan to contact the target organization.
- A strategy differs from a plan with its tactics and techniques used in the carrying out of goals. A tactical plan is actually based on a preexisting strategy. Working with your company on specific steps to contact the target organization gives momentum and synergy to your effort.

Many approaches can be made in putting together a strategy. Here are some key elements that must be included in a strategic plan:

- Objectives (these are the key to success and should be organizationally driven, not communications driven).
- Target organizations (organizations with whom you need to communicate to reach your organizational objectives).
- Messages (summarize the core message of your organization and repeat it to your target organization regularly and creatively in multiple communication vehicles).
- Communication vehicles and activities (match your communication vehicles—TV, radio, print, e-mail, brochures, telephone, workshop activities, etc.—to the target organization).
- Resources (never overtax your resources to deliver what you have agreed to deliver; know your limitations and be forthright).
- Delivery timetables (deliver when you say you will deliver and call when something interrupts delivery).
- Improvement (evaluate your performance and continually improve).

Using these strategies, put together a step-by-step plan to reach goals and objectives.

IMPLEMENT THE PLAN

Implementing or executing the plan seems like an easy thing to do. After all, the hard work is done, right? The strategic plan and the Gantt chart are in place. So, what is the problem? The problem is implementing the plan. Most strategies are worked on for months and then filed in a manager's drawer. The plan is never executed.

What prevents most plans from implementation? Here are some commonly named corporate conditions that block execution of a strategic plan:

- A culture of status quo
- The seniority system
- Impermeable functional silos in the system
- Poor change management skills in an environment resistant to change

Do you notice anything about these corporate conditions? Where do they fall in the life cycle of a corporation? They fall in the area of an aging corporation after prime. To be implemented, the corporation will need to be brought back to prime, not a small task in itself. An organization needs flexibility to implement a good strategic plan. A good strategic plan responds to the marketplace and environment, which is changing, or else there would be no need for a strategic plan. Change is a fact of life. When an organization can no longer be flexible, it cannot change, and flawless and effective implementation of the strategic plan becomes impossible.

Corporations in the life-cycle stages of prime, adolescence, and go-go have an environment that is conducive to change. Implementing a strategic plan in prime and adolescence would be comfortable. However, in go-go, even though the environment is conducive to change and implementation of a strategic plan, there is another problem. In the go-go stage, the people are running so fast after opportunities that look like low-hanging fruit they do not take time to strategize and plan.

Lots of good books have been written about planning. More books and manuals are being written about execution and implementation of plans. The technical aspects of execution need to be studied. Project managers need to be consulted about tricks of the trade. Your education in this area is a given. However, we want to make one more statement about implementation that might not appear in the books to which we referred. Top

C-level management might adopt an attitude that being directly involved in the process of strategy implementation is beneath their pay grade. Here is the truth: Strategy implementation cannot be successful without the intelligent, vocal, passionate, and visible support of the corporation.

EVALUATE AND IMPROVE THE PROCEDURE

After implementation, the job is not complete. The continuous improvement process requires that a thorough evaluation be made. Participants should be debriefed. Suggestions on how the strategic plan and its implementation could have been improved should be elicited and recorded. These findings should be put in a report and distributed to corporate management and the persons involved in the process of strategy planning and implementation. A file should be kept for the next strategy-planning project.

Here are some suggested key elements to consider in detail in the evaluation of a strategic plan and its implementation:

- Was the strategic plan in alignment with the corporation's mission and vision?
- How accurate was the strategy in reading the direction of the marketplace and business climate?
- How integrated was the plan related to the logical flow of the steps toward reaching the goals and objectives?
- How well did the plan's implementation requirements match the in-house talents and skills and the physical, technical, and financial resources of the corporation?
- How adequate was the time it took to implement the plan?
- Was the overall quality of the implementation excellent?
- Did the strategic plan accomplish its objective?
- What would you do differently?

SUMMARY

How does an outside firm or vendor talk to a corporation? It takes a well-thought-out strategic plan and good execution. Research must be done about the corporation to which one would want to communicate. The corporation to which one would want to talk is called the *target organization*.

First, the culture of the organization needs to be researched and understood. Culture is a factor in communication that can negate communication. Another factor to be understood is the personality of the corporation. This will give clues regarding how to effectively connect with the corporation in the arena of communication.

Take into account the formal and informal communication systems of the corporation. Know how they work and seek to use them in your communication with the corporation.

Finally, understand the corporate environment of the target organization. This is made up of the coalescing of the national culture; the corporate culture and personality; the structure and system of the organization; and the history and people of the corporation. Of key interest is the stage of the target organization's corporate life cycle and its effect on the environment of the organization.

When all your research is done, put together your strategic plan and implement it. Do not forget the important activity of continuous improvement: evaluation and improvement of the strategic plan and implementation of the plan. Store the evaluation results in a place for the next round of strategy planning.

> The key to open the door to any corporation is understanding what is important to the corporation.

—H. James Harrington

REFERENCES

1. Bridges, William (2000). *The Character of Organizations: Using Jungian Type in Organizational Development*, updated edition, Davies-Black, Palo Alto, CA.
2. Adizes, Ichak (1988). *Corporate Lifecycles: How and Why Corporations Grow and Die and What to Do About It*, Prentice Hall, Englewood Cliffs, NJ, pp. 11–109.
3. Covey, Stephen R. (2004). *The Seven Habits of Highly Effective People,* Free Press.

10

How Do I Communicate to a Corporation from the Inside?

Today's problems come from yesterday's solutions.

—Peter M. Senge, *The Fifth Discipline*, 1990

Being heard by an impersonal corporation means being counter-intuitive; or put another way, it means learning to understand and manipulate the organization's systems that are right in front of your face, yet as unseen as a magician's trick.

—R. D. Lewis

INTRODUCTION

Let us begin this chapter with a story.

> Fred had 25 years as an employee of a large nonprofit corporation. Lately, Fred was alarmed. The signs of a serious slowdown in its activity and contributions were apparent to him. He had just attained his 55th birthday and, frankly, was worried about his retirement should his organization's slowdown turn into a decline.
>
> The response of the nonprofit corporation was to redouble efforts at growth and contributions. The newest and best training for reversing decline and restoring growth was brought in to the employees by the executive director and her staff. New programs for increasing membership were offered, but the growth did not come. What did come were further decline and a glossing over the fact that the old and glorious nonprofit was declin-

ing. Long-time employees were fired. The death spiral had started. Could it be reversed?

Fred, a midlevel executive, hoped that it could. He had become a student of organizations. He studied everything, from marketing principles to business process improvement methods. He even figured out what Six Sigma meant and wondered if it fit a nonprofit situation. He studied the life cycles of corporations. He studied cross-cultural communication and capital stewardship campaigns. And then, he read a book about systems thinking (ST). This information was the information Fred had needed. It was the answer to the question: "Why is my organization declining?" Fred learned that the decline was not because his organization's services were no longer needed or wanted. Rather, it was because the organization was in a *reinforcing loop* that had become a *vicious cycle,* and that his nonprofit fit the systems archetype called *shifting the burden.*

When he began to share his information with his colleagues, he received a disconcerting reaction: hostility. Instead of embracing this information that could save the nonprofit, they pushed it aside along with Fred. Upper management would not allow training about ST to take place. They would not allow the conclusions that Fred had reached to be shared even though the figures and facts used in the analysis Fred had done were the nonprofit's facts—facts that they had published in reports and magazines of the nonprofit. It was as though they were afraid of the truth. So, they began to say that Fred was negative and not a team player. Even though this rejection hurt Fred, he was able to cope because he knew from his studies what he was experiencing. In ST, it is called *compensating feedback.* The existing system was protecting itself from change. In the end, Fred took early retirement, became a consultant to other nonprofit organizations, and continued to witness from his fishing boat the slow death of a once-dynamic nonprofit organization.

Now that you have read the story, I have a question: Why couldn't Fred talk to his nonprofit organization? Would not a dying and troubled organization welcome an employee who claimed to have suggestions to solving major problems and challenges? We wish we could say yes. However, talking to corporations is not like talking to individuals. While talking to a troubled individual is challenging and scary, talking to corporations takes longer and a more sophisticated strategy for getting to the table. First, communicating with large corporations requires capturing the attention of top management and sometimes the board of directors. Also, communication to a corporation is done through training programs, the continued education of leadership, value-added books, symposiums, and sometimes important leaders in the business world obtaining the ear of C-level management. On top of all that, it must take place at the right time in the life cycle of a corporation—before the corporation becomes too old to hear, talk, walk, and think. However, when the people with the authority to make changes to the corporation are awakened and informed, and when they learn the way to change the structure, then true change can take place. And, when that happens, you have communicated with a corporation. Does it sound complicated? Well, it is. But, everyone loves a challenge, and this challenge is worth it.

INTRODUCING SYSTEMS THINKING AND THE LEARNING ORGANIZATION

This chapter assumes expertise in the use of the media and tools of microcommunication, which you will remember is defined as interpersonal communication theory and skills. Therefore, our topic of discussion in this chapter focuses on a function of macrocommunication. *Macrocommunication* refers to the system and processes in which microcommunication is nested. Macrocommunication is characterized by two-way communication from an impersonal system, culture, or environment with large groups of people.

A corporation is not an individual person. Although legally considered a person, a corporation is nothing like an individual person when it comes to communication. Communication with a corporation requires an understanding of ST.

What is a system, and what is ST? First, a system is a set of connected things or parts forming a complex whole. In Western civilization and in the United States, we think in pieces, parts, and snapshots. We divide our corporation into divisions, departments, and teams because we have divided up the whole process of building a complex product, like an airplane, into hundreds of parts; there is nothing wrong with this except one really big thing: One department has no idea what another department is doing or thinking. Each individual department working on the whole airplane understands only one part of the airplane. A department in a factory has little-to-no understanding of how its actions and decisions affect the other departments working on the same airplane. To truly *commune* with an impersonal organization, one needs to see it as a whole and understand how the parts fit together and affect one another. The best learning takes place through experience. A child does something and then receives immediate results. The child learns from the feedback process. The same process works when an adult learns, and the same process works when a department in a corporation learns. The problem for the department is that it does not see the results of its actions. The results take place over time and space. For a department in a corporation to understand how its actions effect the corporation is part of corporate communication and corporate learning. Simply stated, doing this is called ST, and ST is necessary for a corporation to learn.

ST requires a change in the way most of us have been taught to think. Instead of understanding the corporation with linear thinking, we need to see it more like a connected circle where what we do in our part of the circle not only affects our division but also affects the whole organizational circle, in both directions, and our related suppliers and strategic partners. Peter M. Senge said,[1] "Business and other human endeavors are also systems. They, too, are bound by invisible fabrics of interrelated actions, which often take years to fully play out their effects on each other" (p. 7). Using ST is at the heart of being a learning organization and a communicating organization.

To exist in the modern business environment with its rapid change, organizations must learn from their work. Teams are the basic unit of learning in a learning organization. Teams must fundamentally understand two things to be in position to be the learning unit of the organization.

First, teams must understand ST to learn. Why is this true? It is true because of the delusion of learning from experience, as Peter M. Senge pointed out in his landmark work, *The Fifth Discipline: The Art and Practice of the Learning Organization.*[1] As alluded to previously, when the consequences of actions are never witnessed or seen, learning from experience can never take place. In a modern corporation, where things are broken into parts and where different companies build certain components used in the final product, no one ever sees the consequences of his or her actions. The consequences are removed to the distant future or to the distant part of a huge system. ST takes into account the consequences of actions in a complex system and analyzes the results of the actions of the various components. ST simplifies the system to a coded language of circles, arrows, parallel lines, and notes into the lowest denominator so it can be grasped and studied. Then, teams can learn from their actions and the actions of other teams. A truly high-performance team must understand ST.

Second, learning teams must understand dialogue, which is different from discussion. Discussion has one idea or opinion that wins. Dialogue has a team of individuals who suspend assumptions and think together, arriving at a group consensus or agreement. Dialogue *is* quality communication. High-performance teams work as one person because they have become as one person through mutual love, respect, and the discipline of dialogue.

Communication, then, is about learning. This learning targets not only our friends and family but also our world. More profoundly, learning is about creating our future. Learning organizations create the future, and we are part of that process as we have a dialogue with our organization on a meta-level of communication called ST.

UNDERSTAND THAT A CORPORATION IS A SYSTEM

We all have heard of a weather system. A weather system is a group of related weather conditions that combine to produce various air movements in the atmosphere that affect a region for a period of time. The effect of a weather system could be a thunderstorm. It could be a hurricane. It could also be the cause of serious soil erosion during a 100-year period, changing the topography of the region. It is called a system because none of the separate events within the system alone could produce the weather that we experience. Several separate things must happen in sequence over a period of time to produce the weather or the results of weather that we experience. A corporation is also a complex system. It is a network of actions that can take years to play out. It remains invisible, however, to most workers in the system. People in a large corporate system can become the person who does one job, and this can become their personal identity for their lifetime. They do not know who they are apart from the work that they do. This is why in the twentieth century so many people died 18 months after retirement. They ceased to have significance in their minds apart from their job.

Nonetheless, over the years these workers did see patterns in their corporate environment and talked about them. They described what they saw with terms that have become part of the vocabulary of folk wisdom:

- Momentum is everything.
- The rats are jumping the ship.
- There was a snowball effect.

- The rich get richer and poor get poorer.
- Unless you are the lead dog, the view never changes.
- Take the bull by the horns.
- If you want a job done right, do it yourself.

These folk sayings show that we bump up against corporate systems even though we do not have the conscious awareness and understanding that systems exist. The sayings reveal that we do notice the effects produced by systems. Systems can produce momentum that is *like a snowball effect*. Systems can produce slowdowns in business, and when slowdowns happen, top leaders and key workers know they will be blamed, so they begin to quit, *like rats jumping the ship*. When systems put up resistance to the accomplishment of a newly assigned company goal, workers responsible for accomplishing the goal can apply pressure to the system to reach the goal by *taking the bull by the horns*, but later, the system will push back with force, making conditions worse than before the goal was set. When we do not know that it is the system at work, we cast blame on others and punish them.

Every human endeavor is made up of a system of influences and events that are invisible to us. Identifying the system in which we work and understanding it is a requirement for a truly high-performing team. To do this is called ST.

UNDERSTAND THAT A SYSTEM HAS CHARACTERISTICS

Enough research has taken place over the course of the twentieth century that we now have an awareness of some basic characteristics of systems. First, one characteristic of systems is that they have a structure, a set arrangement and relationship between the parts or elements, and these structures influence behavior. The amazing thing is that people in the same structure produce similar results. So, if a system needs different results, then the structure must be understood and modified. Structure influences behavior. This is an important characteristic of a system.

In ST, structure does not mean the logical structure of an organizational chart. Systemic structure deals with many factors in the situation of a corporation that influence personal and organizational behavior. Some examples of factors in the corporate situation influencing organizational behavior would be the population demographics, the availability of natural resources, and the ability of a country to produce food and provide infrastructure. Other factors could be the product ideas of the engineering department, the operating policies of the decision makers, or the managerial know-how of a high-tech company.

Another characteristic of a system is that it is circular rather than linear. American and Greek thought is linear and logical. One thing leads to the next. However, the discipline of ST is circular. One event not only is the cause but also the effect. The illustration used in Senge's book[1] is the simple act of filling a glass of water:

> As we fill the glass, we are watching the water level rise. We monitor the "gap" between the level and our goal, the "desired water level." As the water approaches the desired level, we adjust the faucet position to slow the flow of water, until it is turned off when the glass is full. In fact, when we fill a glass of water, we operate in a "water-regulation" system involving five variables: our desired water level, the glass's current water level, the gap between the two, the faucet position, and the water flow. These variables are organized in a circle or loop of cause-effect relationships. (p. 74)

It is a loop because it is a continual process of knowing the desired level, seeing the current level of water, and adjusting the flow of water. This is a picture of a system at work. It is not linear, but circular.

Because of the circular nature of a system, the idea of causality is changed. For example, in the process of filling a glass of water, is the person filling the glass of water or is the level of water controlling the hand that manipulates the faucet that controls the flow of water? Long story short, we are influencing our reality, and at the same time, we are influenced by our reality.

This leads to another characteristic of a system: No one person is to blame when problems arise in a system; everyone shares the blame. Remember this: Linear thinking has its place, just not regarding problems of dynamic complexity like systems. These situations call for ST. In linear thinking, someone is always to blame. In ST, no one person is to blame; everyone shares the blame.

A language has been developed for ST. The written language looks like diagrams with the circle as the principal character. The language has these basic ideas:

- A *reinforcing* loop that signals accelerating growth or decline

- A *balancing* loop that limits growth or decline whenever there is goal-oriented behavior
- A *delay* or interruption in the flow of influence causing a delay in results

These are the basics of the language. This language and the resulting diagrams from it can help high-performance teams communicate with others about the system in which they operate and the leverage points for change.

Another characteristic of systems taken as a whole is that some systems occur repeatedly. They are so universal that they are identified as archetypes. Two of the system archetypes that are common are the *limits-to-growth* archetype and the *shifting-the-burden* archetype. These archetypes are discussed more fully in this chapter.

UNDERSTAND THAT AN INDIVIDUAL WITHIN A SYSTEM MUST DEVELOP A SYSTEM MINDSET

What is a system mindset? It is the practice of the ability to identify a system and to recognize that organizational behaviors and individual behaviors within a corporation are caused by a system. How does one develop this kind of mindset? Studying ST would be a place to start. One can find a business school offering courses on ST and take the courses. One can network with others who are system thinkers. One can hire a consulting firm like the Harrington Institute to come to train teams in ST. Of course, practice makes perfect.

To possess the systems mindset also means to teach others in the corporation about ST and how it complements and differs from other management approaches to problem solving and process improvement. To be a teacher means not to give up on the student who rejects learning. The system is producing that person's bent to reject the teaching about systems. It is the system pushing back and rejecting change. Of course, some people come out of the public education system thinking that they cannot learn, so maybe some heart-to-heart talks will help some team members overcome old scars.

Why is it important for everyone to understand ST? The reason is that the journey is the reward. The reason is that the process is the end and not the means. That is because we are not involved in linear thinking in a complex system. We are involved in more of a circular thinking pattern in which each activity or station is both cause and effect. ST is dramatically different from linear thinking and the normal pattern of thinking in most of the corporate world. Therefore, unless everyone understands ST, some manager will continue to use linear thinking. This would be like the proverbial fly in the ointment.

Here are principles of a system that should be taught and understood:

- Nonsystemic solutions to problems are temporary.
- When you fight the system, it fights back.
- Nonsystemic solutions often make things worse than they were before the fix.
- A system has an optimal rate of growing, so when you speed it up, ultimately you only slow it down.
- Systemic changes take a long time to happen.
- Systemic changes can be made using the principle of leverage.

SYSTEM ARCHETYPES HAVE BEEN IDENTIFIED THAT PEOPLE WHO COMMUNICATE WITHIN SYSTEMS MUST UNDERSTAND

Although the term *systems thinking* (ST) was coined by Senge, Dr. Jay Forrester, the Germeshausen Professor Emeritus of Management at the Massachusetts Institute of Technology's (MIT's) Sloan School of Management (Cambridge, MA), taught Senge about complex systems. Senge popularized the study of complex systems with his book *The Fifth Discipline*.[1] He took the teachings of Forrester's *system dynamics* and renamed them ST. Senge endeavored to teach business leaders and others to use a set language made up of diagrams of circles, arrows, and hash marks to symbolize different complex systems and to try to understand them and how they would play out in a particular business situation without using the complex mathematical computer software that was developed by Forrester. This, by the way, is a point of disagreement between Forrester and his former student. Forrester feels that systems in many settings are far too complicated to understand without the aid of a computer. Senge, who understands his former professor's point, feels that it is more important to make leaders aware of the existence of complex systems. We can thank Senge for letting us get a grasp of a world that most of us would never have seen without his attempt to make it fathomable to the masses.

One of the tools Senge gave was to teach about system archetypes. Forrester and his students had identified a set of system archetypes. Archetypes are the common system patterns. These model patterns occur repeatedly in a variety of systems.

Why are archetypes useful? Here is a list of some of the more common archetypes:

- Limits to growth (or limits to success)
- Shifting the burden
- Tragedy of the commons
- Eroding goals
- Success to the successful
- Escalation
- Accidental adversaries
- Fixes that fail
- Growth and underinvestment
- Attractiveness principle

Senge produced the language to share system archetypes in a way that was easy to understand for the layperson. The purpose of this language was to help leaders see the hidden structures of a system to distinguish high- from low-leverage points. Low-leverage points are the areas that are the easiest places to change an entire system.

To help learn this language, let us use the arms race between the United States and the former Soviet Union as an example. After World War II, the Soviet Union greatly expanded its borders and made no secret that it wanted to expand more and end the dominance of the United States. This set off an arms race. You know the story. The USSR began to build up their military. It took time for U.S. intelligence to discover the buildup. When the United States discovered it, it began to build its military greater than the Soviet Union. There was a lag time between the U.S. buildup and its discovery by the USSR. When the USSR discovered the U.S. military was larger, then it began a buildup. Next, new and bigger weapons were built by the United States in response to the Soviet buildup. When the Soviets discovered that the United States had new and bigger weapons, then they began to develop and build bigger and better weapons. So on and so on went the arms buildup, accelerating as it built. This can be diagrammed in

FIGURE 10.1
The Soviet diagram for the arms race.

FIGURE 10.2
The U.S. diagram for the arms race.

a linear way. The Soviets would diagram it like Figure 10.1. and the United States would diagram it like Figure 10.2.

The two nations saw the issue only from their own individual viewpoint. Neither saw the whole and identified it as a complex system. To understand it as a system, it helps to diagram it in a circular form, which shows the interrelatedness of the arms race. All one needs to do is put the two linear diagrams of Figures 10.1 and 10.2 together in a circular diagram (see Figure 10.3).

Figure 10.3 shows the continuous cycle of the arms race. Both sides were trying to be more secure. The unintended result was that both sides and

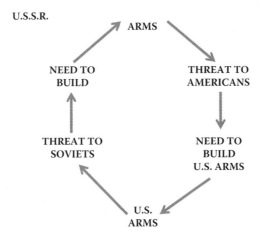

FIGURE 10.3
Arms race viewed as a system.

the whole world became more at risk for nuclear holocaust should aggression on either side erupt.

Notice that doing the obvious does not produce the desired results in a complex system. Often, doing the counterintuitive produces the wanted outcome, and the only way to know is to identify the system, study it, and find the place of lowest leverage. Then, use the place in the system of lowest leverage to change the whole system. Senge points out that when the same action produces very different effects in the short term than it does in the long term, you are in dynamic complexity. Detail complexity is different in that it deals with a complexity of details and variables. Dynamic complexity means that cause and effect are hard to detect and recognize; they may be separated so far in time and space that they are not readily discerned.

Now, let us use the circular format to diagram our description of filling the cup (Figure 10.4) that was discussed previously. Think of circles as flows of influence. By tracing the flows of influence, you discover a pattern that repeats itself over and over. The repetition of the flow of influence might make things better and better, or it might make things worse and worse. When you trace the circle, follow the direction indicated by the arrows. Start with the "perceived gap" between the desired water level and the glass's current water level. The mind has a desired level. The mind watches and calculates the gap between the "current water level" and the "desired water level" constantly. The "faucet position" determines the "water flow." The water flow determines the current water level. The perceived gap influences the faucet position. In a linear view of the world, we say, "I am filling the glass." In a circular view of the world, we have a reciprocal flow of influence in which every influence is both cause and

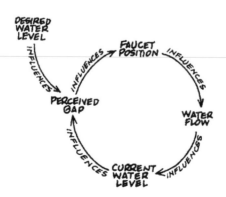

FIGURE 10.4
Filling-the-cup diagram.

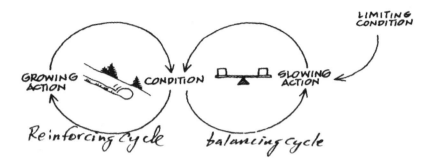

FIGURE 10.5
Limits-to-growth system archetype.

effect. We say in this ST world, "My hand on the faucet is controlling the rate of flow of water into the glass." We can also say, "The rate of the flow of water into the glass is controlling my hand." We could also talk about our "intent" to create a system that causes the glass to be filled.

Let us look at two diagrams from the list to learn how to read them. The first one is the archetype of generic limits to growth system (Figure 10.5). The limits-to-growth archetype was introduced by Donella Meadows, Dennis Meadows, Jorgen Randers, and William Behrens in 1972 in their book of the same name.[2] Basically, what this model teaches is that something always pushes back. Something always stops growth. An ensuing management principal of this model is do not force growth; deal with the limiting factors in the system instead. The hypothesis is that in an expansion of a business, there is always a process that balances growth as the limits to growth are approached.

Also, a corporation's efforts at growth will produce diminishing returns as one enters the zone near the absolute limit. When the limit is hit, which it will be, continued efforts at growth are fruitless. At some point in time, the rate of growth stops, and then it reverses. An excellent example in the Internet age is America Online, or AOL. Originally, it charged a fee for each minute that its Internet service was used. Then, competition came that offered a flat fee for service. AOL's market share began to shrink, so to recapture it AOL began an aggressive marketing campaign. It flooded the market with CDs designed to make connecting to their service and the Internet easy. They were so successful at subscribing new customers, that the flood of new customers overwhelmed their capacity to deliver what was promised. The end result was that they lost more market share than before the effort because of angry customers. Their efforts at growth pushed back on them and caused them to get the opposite effect that they were seeking.

To read the limits-to-growth diagram (Figure 10.5), begin with the circle on the left and start with the "condition." A condition, such as a product that has high demand, is produced. That leads clockwise around the circle to a "growing action." The growing action results in a change in the condition, namely, in our example, an increase in production of the product that has high demand. Now, let us look to the circle on the right, the balancing cycle. Eventually, the growth in sales of the product that has high demand slows because of some "limiting condition," seen on the extreme right of the diagram box. This limiting condition for our example might be competition. Therefore, the condition, which connects each circle in the diagram, changes to one of the competitive production of the product. Now, follow the balancing cycle counterclockwise to "slowing action." The slowing action would be loss of market share because of the competition. This would lead back to the condition, which would change again to another cutback in production because of the competition causing a greater loss of market share. This cycle would continue until the company intervened. To do the logical thing without looking at the total system would result in something similar to the story about AOL.

The correct response to reverse the slowing action would be to find the place in the system of lowest leverage. Leverage consistently lies in the balancing loop and never in the reinforcing loop. To change behavior in a system, one must identify and change the limiting factor, which, in our example, is causing a slowing action that reduces market share. Changing the limiting factor and reducing competition produce more growth. Apple computer would be an example of success in doing this with the iPod, the digital device that was small and portable and held hundreds of digital music recordings. Whenever competition started, Apple improved it so that it was smaller and easier to use and would hold thousands of songs. This continued as long as possible, and then Apple combined the capacity of the iPod in the new iPhone, along with many other features, and repeated the process of spectacular improvements. Next came the iPad. This was the leverage that was applied to the balancing loop against the limiting condition of aggressive competition.

The second system archetype diagram that we examine is called shifting the burden. This system generates symptoms that are of a serious nature, yet the permanent and best solution to the problem is either hard to detect or the cost of confronting it is prohibitive. Therefore, the fix is in some manner to shift the burden of the problem to other solutions that seem to do the job. The solutions treat the symptoms rather than the problem. Over time, however, the substitute solutions only mask the symptoms produced by the real problem while the real problem grows steadily worse. Eventually, the organization loses the ability to solve the primary problem. The management principle in shifting the burden is not to solve the symptoms but to solve the problem.

The diagram for the shifting-the-burden system archetype has two balancing (stabilizing) processes that often produce a reinforcing (amplifying) process from the side effects of the symptomatic solution. Think of the side effects of certain medicines that are unintended consequences of taking the medicine for curing a malady. Real solutions for the shifting-the-burden archetype require a coordinated effort at enhancing the fundamental response while diminishing the symptomatic response that might have been made.

Notice the diagram of Figure 10.6 has two balancing circles stacked on top of one another. Begin reading the diagram from the center where the two circles connect where it reads "problem symptom." Follow the arrows on the top circle to where it reads "symptomatic 'solution.'" The symptomatic solution causes more symptoms, indicated by the arrow pointing to problem symptom. Now, follow the arrow on the bottom circle from problem symptom to "fundamental solution." Notice the "delay." The delay in seeing the fundamental solution is what causes the problem of treating the wrong thing. Symptoms are treated rather than the primary cause. Treating the symptoms often produces side effects. That is what the

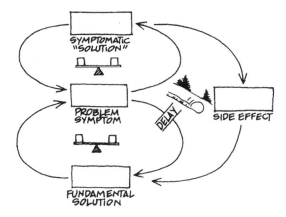

FIGURE 10.6
Shifting-the-burden generic system archetype.

reinforcing circle to the right side of the two stacked circles says to us. The "side effect" augments the primary problem underlying the fundamental solution, which exacerbates the problem symptom, which causes more symptomatic solutions, which cause more side effects, which makes the problem more entrenched and more invisible.

HOW DO YOU COMMUNICATE WELL IN A SYSTEM?

To communicate well in a system, all people in the system must be trained about the characteristics of a system. Much literature has been produced about ST. Corporate management must study this subject to truly communicate with a corporation from the inside. Using universities and colleges to train corporate personnel or using on-site training and consulting from the Harrington Institute is also recommended.

The reason for study and training is obvious. Complex systems and ST are subjects that are outside the realm of our thinking patterns. Also, when a Harrington Institute consultant comes and analyzes your corporation for solutions, the consultant needs a group of managers and decision makers who understand the concepts and terminology of ST. Training and study are the way to attain this understanding.

Our language structures our brain. Our brain determines how we view the world. Therefore, language has a dominant effect on how we view the world. The English language and most other Western languages are linear. A linear way of thinking is one of cause and effect, in which the cause and the effect are different entities. This biases the managers making the decisions in a corporation to the linear view. This bias results in looking for an obvious cause that is producing an effect. The language of ST, on the other hand, is circular in nature; the problem is both cause and effect. This goes against everything Westerners have been taught.

Therefore, to communicate with a corporation from the inside, people in the system must be trained to understand the system's characteristics. Actually, they first need to be made aware that a corporation is a system. This takes training and education. The hurdle to training linear thinkers in a system, which behaves in a nonlinear fashion, is developing a language for systems. This has been done using drawings of circles and arrows that draw a diagram of the influences moving in a complex system.

So, the language simplifies the complicated system so that it can be easily grasped and visualized.

This language, developed at MIT by Senge and associates, is called ST. Some of the elements of this language are the following:

- It uses closed mutual dependencies that circle around on each other: a influences b, b influences c, c influences a.
- It uses pictures of circles and arrows that create a strong visual component, which aids learning.
- It emphasizes the whole rather than the parts.

To learn any foreign language, it must be studied. Any foreign language must be practiced to master it. This is true with ST.

Language is a tool, however, to help the people in a corporate environment work together. ST needs to be put to work. Understanding a system archetype is important for training, yet understanding an identified system in a classroom setting is very different from discerning and analyzing an existing system to which you are connected and in which you live. That takes understanding and perhaps the help of an outside consultant who comes to you with new eyes. Your final training takes place in ST when you work with a consultant to understand (i.e., to communicate) with your corporation while being a part of it.

SUMMARY

If you think this chapter is about how to write a memo or an e-mail with clarity and good grammar, you will be disappointed. However, if you would like to explore the world of how to communicate with a nonpersonal system called a corporation in the broadest sense that the word *communication* can give, then you will like this chapter about complex systems. As we learned in other chapters, *microcommunication* is person-to-person communication, either spoken or written. *Macrocommunication*, on the other hand, deals with the system and processes in which microcommunication is nested. Macrocommunication is characterized by two-way communication to or from an impersonal system, culture, or environment containing large groups of people.

To communicate with a corporation, we must first understand ST. Systems exist everywhere in life. We are familiar with weather systems. A corporation is a complex system. A complex system is a network of functions, events, processes, and people. A corporation is also a complex system. It is a network of actions that can take years to play out. It remains invisible, however, to most workers in the system. To truly *commune* with an impersonal organization, one needs to see it as a whole and understand how the parts fit together and affect one another.

A corporate system has characteristics:

- A system has a structure, a set arrangement and relationship between the parts or elements, and this structure influences behavior.
- A system is understood with a circular worldview rather than a linear worldview.
- In a system, everyone shares the blame and the credit.
- A system needs a language to be understood, and ST is a language.
- Systems have repeating patterns, and system archetypes have been identified.

People who desire to understand and communicate with a system in which they work must develop a systems mindset. Having a systems mindset means that a person is aware of the existence of systems and is able to identify systems by the effects that are seen and felt in a corporate environment. A person with a systems mindset will appreciate and use the pictorial language developed to describe the structures of systems. The systems language helps both to study and to understand systems.

Leaders in a corporation, who are the decision makers, must commit themselves to study and implement ST. A corporation is a system with a structure. The need to understand ST and to communicate with other decision makers about ST is imperative to make good decisions related to the corporation.

Too many people fight the system instead of using their energy to correct the system.

—H. James Harrington

REFERENCES

1. Senge, Peter M. (1990). *The Fifth Discipline: The Art and Practice of the Learning Organization*, Doubleday Currency, New York.
2. Meadows, Donella; Meadows, Dennis; Randers, Jorgen; and Behrens, William (1972). *Limits to Growth*, New American Library, New York.

11

How Does a Corporation Use Social Media to Communicate?

The ancient story in the Bible about the Tower of Babel was that the whole earth had one language and was united. God came down to check it out and said, "Now nothing that they propose to do will be withheld from them," and God created many languages, dividing the people of earth. With the Internet and the ease of translation of language and the rise of social media, it looks like we are coming back full circle.

—R. D. Lewis

social media: noun (usually used with a plural verb). Computers, Web sites and other online means of communication that are used by large groups of people to share information and to develop social and professional contacts: Many businesses are utilizing social media to generate sales.

—dictionary.com

social media: forms of electronic communication (as Web sites for social networking and microblogging) through which users create online communities to share information, ideas, personal messages, and other content (as videos).

merriam-webster.com

First known use of *social media,* 2004

What is Social Media? It's any medium of communication or conversation that gets all of its value from the people—your customers—who participate in it.

—Christopher S. Penn, lead subject matter expert,
SanFranonline.com, Advanced Social Media Certificate
Program, University of San Francisco, California (2012)

INTRODUCTION

Communication implies the exchange of information, feelings, and ideas that can ultimately lead to a relationship at some level. A single customer can now communicate online with a corporation in the world of social media and build a relationship with a corporate brand. That is how a corporation communicates using social media: by building relationships with customers one by one. The phenomenon of the Internet is that a corporation can have *individual* relationships with customers en masse.

Social media take place on the World Wide Web, known as the Internet or "being online." Social media are the use of technological communication tools that facilitate and allow continual online social interaction and communication of any and all who choose to participate. Social media have changed the traditional media of print and broadcast from a monologue to a social dialogue. They almost put traditional media out of business. Today, traditional media are quickly making up for lost time and adapting to the social media model, and they have a lot of ground to make up. Social media currently dominate the classifieds (e.g., craigslist) and dictate the headlines of traditional media (e.g., the Drudge Report). They cover traditional social news (e.g., Reddit, Slashdot, Fark, Delicious, Newsvine, etc.) and dish out sports (ESPN and Yahoo!).

But, if you think that social media are only about newspapers, radio, and television, you would be wrong. They are about corporate brands; corporate public relations and marketing; corporate sales; and corporate production and customer service. In fact, the evidence at the printing of this book was that the corporations that do not log on to social media will go out of business.

Things have moved so fast in the area of social media that at first it seemed like a tsunami in the marketplace; now, we know that social media are becoming the marketplace. Social media are a megashift in society. A single person can now blog and influence the world.

So, where does that leave most businesses and twentieth century corporations? It leaves them on the edge of a paradigm shift looking in and wondering what to do. As an aside, here is a word of advice: If you are in a decision-making position at a traditional corporation and have lived your life there—not in the "dot-com" world—then do not try to make the changes on your own. Hire the best, and we are not talking about weird Freddy down the street who knows everything about the Internet and computers and nothing about business. The best would be a person with a foot in both worlds. The way to sidestep blunders is to hire professionals who not only know social media but also understand the corporate world and its interrelatedness. That way, they understand the broad effects of decisions and can avoid costly unintended results of their decisions and actions in launching your social media presence. Hiring the best is the place to start because business blunders can be expensive and sometimes lethal, but please, finish reading the rest of this chapter before you do anything.

THE RAPID PROMINENCE OF SOCIAL MEDIA

Social media have been continually expanding through advances made in technology and in modern electronic communications. Computers and the World Wide Web have created a form of communication that is quickly becoming available to all. It is revolutionary in that it connects everyone in a way that the telephone, newspapers, and postal service could not. One not only talks to people through the World Wide Web, but one can also see them while talking to them. One can use the computer or one can use a traditional telephone to talk to them through the computer. One can send pictures and videos. It is possible to watch movies from the World Wide Web or to upload movies to the World Wide Web. One can even publish books or articles online. You know all of this, of course, yet someone reading this might be totally new to the World Wide Web and the world of computers, so bear with the discussion.

In the United States, the public libraries are now hot spots where computers are available to the public. It is actually difficult to find a spot in many libraries when just a decade ago it was difficult to find people in the public libraries. Restaurants, bus stations, coffee shops, cities, and airplane flights are providing access to the Internet just to draw customers. The developing countries also are involved in the Internet and social media in growing numbers. Just as a hut in the jungle of Africa or in Central America has sported television antennas, now the World Wide Web with social media is moving to the villages of the world.

Usually, the term *social media* congers up thoughts of certain well-known websites that connect people, like Myspace, Facebook, Twitter, Plaxo, and LinkedIn. These companies were built on the idea of social interaction and sharing everyday life with one another. However, social media have also expanded to many other websites. Interaction of people and their opinions can now take place on a website sponsored by a traditional newspaper. People can comment on editorials or stories at the end of the stories. On television shows like *American Idol,* people vote by texting from a smartphone. These smart mobile phones are plugged into not only the telephone networks but also the World Wide Web, including social network sites.

Shopping online is also a growing trend. Some shop online because it is fun and usually cheaper. Busy people shop online because they cannot get to a store themselves. People who live far from a commercial center can shop online because the big delivery companies or the postal service will deliver. And, the people who shop online can go to a company's website and post. They can also go to consumer websites and complain. Some of the websites where they can complain are the following:

- RipoffReport.com
- Shamscam.com
- ComplaintsBoard.com
- PissedConsumer.com
- PlanetFeedback.com
- MeasuredUp.com
- Complaints.com

Have you heard of these? A good human resources (HR) department monitors them for damage control on a company's brand.

Several books have been written about social media. Here is a list of some of the first ones to be written about this new and sudden reality of communication:

- *Groundswell: Winning in a World Transformed by Social Technologies,* by Josh Bernoff and Charlene Li (2011) Harvard Business School Publishing, Boston, MA
- *Trust Agents: Using the Web to Build Influence, Improve Reputation, and Earn Trust,* by Chris Brogan and Julien Smith (2010) John Wiley & Sons, Hoboken, NJ
- *The New Community Rules: Marketing on the Social Web,* by Tamar Weinberg (2009) O'Reilly Media, Sebastopol, CA
- *Engage: The Complete Guide for Brands and Businesses to Build, Cultivate, and Measure Success in the New Web,* by Brian Solis (2011) John Wiley & Sons, Hoboken, NJ

Also, universities are now offering classes in social media, as are business schools. There is a quotation from Christopher S. Penn at the beginning of this chapter; at the time this chapter was researched, he did and perhaps still is involved with an online class at the University of San Francisco (these things change quickly). Penn was the lead subject matter specialist for the class, and he also worked at companies that help corporations and businesses with the tools of social media for sales and marketing. Here is a copy of the course schedule found at the University of San Francisco's website by doing a search as this chapter was written. This outline was from a course listed in 2012 on the Web site of the University of San Francisco for an online certificate in social media:[1]

Introduction to Social Media
    Introduction to Advanced Social Media Techniques
    Key Ways that Brand Informs Social Media
    Best Practices in PR, Customer Service, Monetization and Executive
        Strategy Prior to Social Media
    Essential Social Media Tools and Services
Listening and Monitoring
    Expert Advice on Monitoring Your Brand and Reputation
    Listening for a Crisis Before It Happens
    Identifying Money-Making Opportunities
    Listening for the Next Big Idea
Content Creation
    Identifying Which Content Is Best Marketed With Social Media
    How Content Can Help You Reach More People

Successfully Monetizing Your Content
Best Social Media Tools and Services for Content Creation
Communication
How Social Media Is Changing Communications
Solving Private Problems in a Public Way
Monetizing Communication Tools and Methods
Managing Social Media Communications
Metrics and Science
Measuring Brand Presence and Influence in Social Media
Measuring Customer Satisfaction and ROI in Social Media
Evaluating Your Social Media Efforts
Proven Social Media Metrics Tools
Legal and Ethical Considerations
Key Legal Issues and Danger Zones in Social Media
Practical Tips for Legal Issues in Social Media
Must-Know Social Media Policies
Essential Contracts and Related Enforceability Issues
Adopting Social Media
Selling the "Purple Cow"
Case Studies: Adoption of Social Media by a Marketing Firm, PR
    Firm and Fortune 500 Organization
Profitable Social Media Experiments
Piloting Social Media Projects
Social Media Case Studies
Social Media Deployment in a Campaign
Didiom
Predicting Election Results Using Social Media
Podcasts and Social Media
Social Media Success Stories
Communications Decency Act
Effective Use of Social Media by Businesses

Is it possible to obtain an advanced degree in Social Media? As we researched this chapter in the year 2012, it was difficult to find any universities that offered classes, much less degrees. A few institutions of higher learning were found (we discovered them mentioned on Internet comment pages) that were rumored to offer a degree—nothing solid though. And, of course, we found the certificate in Social Media offered at the University of San Francisco that we produced above. By the summer of

2013 it was a different story. The Google search page lit up with links to colleges offering degrees in Social Media. These usually were online Master's degree programs. There were so many Social Media degrees suddenly appearing online that we found the beginning of a discussion about the degrees. One link (http://bslashc.com/2013/01/21/why-social-media-degrees-are-like-throwing-money-out-the-window.aspx) reflected a backlash to Social Media degrees with the title "Why Social Media Degrees Are Like Throwing Money Out the Window." The author, Arnold Tijerina, had 11 years in the auto industry and claimed to have personal experience in digital marketing and social media, which we have no reason to doubt that he did.

Those readers familiar with institutions of higher learning will likely be impressed by how quickly these institutions have responded to Social Media as an academic discipline. Usually it takes years, and in earlier centuries it took decades for a new discipline to be accepted in higher education. For higher education, having a degree in Social Media offered at this early date must seem like moving at the speed of light. To get faculty, alumni, board members, accrediting agencies, state legislatures, and the local communities to agree to award a degree for study in any new discipline has taken, historically, much longer. That we see these degrees already in place speaks to the way Social Media has changed the world of communication.

THE CHARACTERISTICS OF SOCIAL MEDIA

In these early years of the birth of the social media, some characteristics of social media are evident. Here is a list that pulls together some of the things we notice about the characteristics of social media at this writing:

- **Social media are the marketplace,** and that changes everything. One of this book's coauthors, Robert Lewis, has a daughter, Kimberly Page, with a skin care and therapeutic massage business in Sacramento, California, that is just turning 3 years old as a startup business. It was started during the "Great Recession." She reports that all of her customers book online. All new customers find her on Yelp.com or find her website through a search engine. All of her new customers came from the services of social media marketing companies like Groupon.com, LivingSocial.com, AmazonLocal.com. She says that the best site to be on is Yelp.com, but a business owner has to monitor it for customer complaints and respond pleasantly and truthfully immediately, giving a defense of the business or a heartfelt apology. Had she not used social media, she would be closing her doors.

- **The business use of social media is not cheaper.** It is expensive because all divisions and departments must be trained in the use of social media and given the means to engage in social media. This takes someone with expertise who must be hired; employees who must be trained and assigned to use social media as part of their work; and state-of-the-art equipment and productions. When you add up the cost, it is not cheap.

- **Social media cannot be controlled; they must be engaged (dealt with).** Complaining customers will post negative and angry comments on a blog, a microblog, or a website of the company so that other customers can read the comments. When a company receives bad word of mouth from an unhappy customer posting on the Internet, the company must respond. The response must be timely, friendly, as brief as possible and give either an apology or explanation, making clear what the company's policy is regarding customer service.

- **Social media spread information widely and quickly.** The word *diffuse* is used when discussing the way information spreads on the Internet through social media. Diffuse means "not concentrated or confined." Applied to a person, it means that the person talks a lot in a scattered, unorganized sort of way, leaping from one subject to another. On the Internet, in the social media world, information can spread quickly to many people on Twitter and Facebook, yet the information is not laid out in a thorough, logical discussion. It is about one thing, one thought, and one point of view. It is as much about attitude and emotion as it is about content. It can also be a video clip or a song. On youtube.com, when a video goes viral, that means in a short time a link to it was sent to tens of thousands or hundreds of thousands, and sometimes even millions, of people who clicked on the link and viewed the video. When this explosion of clicks and views happens, the video often is mentioned in the traditional media.

- **Social media are a level playing field and have been dubbed the democratization of the media.** The media are no longer the domain of the few, controlled by a few corporations or governments. Everyone is now a publisher as well as a consumer of the media. Online newspapers allow reader comments to be made at the end of each article. Some of these responders engage in a conversation with one another about the subject. Even the publishing of books has gone online for anyone and everyone. A person can sign up with Barnes & Nobles's e-publishing entity, PubIt! (now NOOK Press), publish a book, and then sell it. The same can be done at Amazon.com. It can even be done at other lesser-known websites, like BookRix.com. The Society for New Communications Research (SNCR.org) has done research on the "volunteer" business model phenomenon. It studied several volunteer enterprises as compared to traditional enterprises, for example, Yelp versus *Consumer Reports* and Wikipedia versus encyclopedias. So, now traditional encyclopedias and famous magazine publications are being bested by the masses of the World Wide Web.

• **Online marketing is not about selling or advertising.** It is first and foremost about building relationships that ultimately lead to the client choosing to buy and to recommend the brand to friends. The recommendations to companies are to designate real people in the company—people with a name and a face—to be the spokespersons for the company brand. These people engage other people in the social media world and build relationships with them. When a company constantly engages in selling and marketing on social media sites, it repels people and is a "turnoff." People soon skip this company's tweets, postings on Facebook, or updates on LinkedIn and other social media sites when they are a constant barrage of sales and marketing. On the other hand, building genuine relationships is not offensive. In fact, it builds a bond between the person and the company that later translates into business. But, the consumer is in the driver's seat, not the salesperson. At the least, good relationships help prevent and minimize bad word of mouth for the brand.

THE TOOLS OF SOCIAL MEDIA AND THEIR USES

A wide range of social tools exists. These tools help businesses become more interactive with customers. These tools have become game changers in the social media world. Savvy businesses see them as required tools for doing business in the new sales and marketing climate. Do a search to find an updated list of social media tools. Here are a few of the current prominent categories of social web tools used in social media:

- Blogs—commentary and opinion in chronological order on a website
- Microblogs—a form of blogging for more frequent, brief updates, like Twitter
- RSS—a running feed of information on the computer web page like a ticker tape that syndicates current and updated information and streams it
- Photo sharing—allows photo uploads and sharing
- Podcast—digital audio that is distributed via the Internet
- Social news and bookmarking—the ability to save, organize, and share "bookmarked" web pages with others or to upload recipes, craft ideas, and the like and share
- Social networking—provides the ability to connect and share information with other online users
- Video sharing—provides the ability to upload and share videos
- Wikis—collaborative websites that allow users to contribute and edit the content (*wiki* is a Hawaiian word meaning "fast")

(For a complete social media tools list for brands and marketers, visit http://dailytekk.com/.)

The SNCR has done interesting social media research and will be a good source of scientific research on social media. One study, "Higher Ed Documents Social Media ROI: New Communications Tools Are a Game Changer,"[2] discovered that U.S. colleges and universities use Facebook, Twitter, YouTube, and downloadable mobile apps (short for the word *applications*) to recruit new students. Colleges are decreasing their use of traditional media as tools of recruitment. In another study, "The 2011 Inc. 500 Social Media Update: Blogging Declines as Newer Tools Rule,"[3] the SNCR reported a 37% drop in blogging among the 500 corporations studied beginning in the year 2010. It found that corporate blogging was being rapidly replaced in 2011 by the use of YouTube, Twitter, Facebook, LinkedIn, and texting on cellular phones.

Other tools being developed are the tools that crawl the World Wide Web and the social media world in search of information. These tools cover the major players in social media, like Myspace, Facebook, Twitter, LinkedIn, and others and are adding other social media sites as rapidly as possible. A company can now data mine the World Wide Web, including

YouTube, Twitter, Facebook, LinkedIn, and many other newer social media sites. Tools have the capacity to aggregate, filter, and moderate data from the World Wide Web and place the data on a selected company site. The company might choose to put the data it mined and edited from the World Wide Web in any number of places. For example, it might choose to program these tools to put the edited information on its website, on a Facebook tab, in a company blog spot, in a software widget on a third-party site, or in a branded Facebook app. Social media tools can be used to monitor a corporation's brand for damage control, to manage multiple conversations on social media sites, to publish and schedule updates across all the social media channels, and then to perform analysis and reporting.

The website Socialnomics.net studied the comprehensive list of social media tools listed at dailytekk.com and chose 30 tools that it really liked. Here is the list from Socialnomics.net:

1. Percolate: Turns brands into curators; creates content for the social web.
2. HubSpot: Inbound marketing, a marketing hub for small biz.
3. Awe.sm: Analytics for social media.
4. TweetReach: How far did your tweet travel?
5. Contaxio: Contact management for your social networks.
6. PostPost: Awesome stuff becomes lost on Twitter; strip search your timeline.
7. SocialScope: A mobile inbox for your social networks.
8. NutshellMail: Delivers a social media summary to your e-mail inbox.
9. Amplicate: Finds out what people love and hate on social media.
10. Bottlenose: A smarter way to surf the stream.
11. AddShoppers: Reward sharing, measures results, adds shoppers.
12. GroupTweet: Creates a more dynamic Twitter account with multiple authors.
13. HowSociable: Measures your brand magnitude.
14. NorthSocial: Quickly creates and manages Facebook pages.
15. BrandMyMail: Includes live social content in your Gmail e-mails.
16. CardMunch: LinkedIn app scans business cards to your contacts.
17. SocialMention: Real-time social media search and analysis.
18. FeedMagnet: Social curation for websites and events.
19. TabJuice: Ultimate e-commerce solution for Facebook (100% free).
20. Conversocial: Delivers great customer service in Facebook and Twitter.
21. BitlyEnterprise: Short URL branding, real-time alerts, monitoring, and more.

22. PeopleBrowsr: Social analytics for marketers.
23. Needium: Social media lead generation.
24. Crowdspoke: Finds relevant content to share with customers, fans.
25. TheArchivist: Saves and analyzes tweets.
26. MyLikes: Publishers promote your content through social networks.
27. Postling: Provides small businesses with social media tools.
28. bre.ad: URL shortener like bit.ly with customizable billboards.
29. Evernote: Never lose a random thought again—all stored in the cloud.
30. Eventbrite: Online tool for events and selling tickets.

THE STEPS TO A CORPORATE VOICE IN THE SOCIAL MEDIA ARENA

Do not make the mistake of thinking your corporation does not need a strategy plan for its launch into—and debut in—the social media world. The need for a media/communication strategy is as real as ever. It must fit the overall corporate mission and vision. It must answer the relevant questions, such as the following:

- Who is our market?
- What social sites are being used by our target market?
- What priority will we give this endeavor to establish a presence in the social media world?
- What are we presently doing as a company in this area, and who is doing it?
- Who in our company will be the lead person/department in developing and utilizing social media?
- How many employee hours will be needed to interact with the targeted social community?
- How will social media be integrated and implemented enterprise-wide?
- How much will it cost, and are we willing to fully fund it?
- How will we measure return on investment?

Do not wait, however, for your strategic plan to be in place before registering on the various social media sites. Do that immediately.

Once the strategy is in place, the work begins. Executing the strategy will require policy changes, selection of the social media implementation team, the training of the team and the employees, the identification and purchase of needed equipment and software, and the launch. It would be wise to hire consultants during the implementation process who can bring expertise and objectivity to the process.

- First, let the chief executive officer (CEO) call the company together to introduce the strategy. Let the CEO be the evangelist for the use of social media tools and communication. Do we have to tell you that if the CEO is not onboard, it will not be as successful—and usually not successful at all?
- Next, let the CEO introduce the implementation team and formally turn the process over to the team.
- Next, give training to the people of the corporation on social media: what it will mean to them and their department and how it will be implemented.
- Start implementing the plan. A comprehensive plan will use social media in these four areas of corporate life:
  1. Internally across business functions
  2. Externally in recruiting new employees
  3. Externally in business-to-business communication
  4. Externally in building relationships and communicating with the end users of the company's products.

The work is slow at first. You must build up a following. On Facebook, it is called a fan base. Before opening your fan base on Facebook, be sure you have some fans. Facebook caters to businesses, as does Twitter and Google. They each have features that allow businesses to join as businesses, and this feature is tailored to fit business rather than an individual.

By the way, a fan and a follower are consumers or businesses who choose of their own volition to sign up on your account at Facebook or Twitter. Do not decide to sign up an individual or business yourself; let the individual or business decide to do it and then sign up. Once you have a fan base or a large following, you can begin to do many things to build relationships and obtain references from them to other consumers. Of course, you can spend a lot of money in campaigns for people informing and inviting the public and your customers of an opportunity to join you on the social media networks. This will likely speed the process with those who are already committed customers and loyal fans.

The next component will be to "wow" or to be attractive to your customers and potential customers. If your company has a fantastic product that is popular and your company is already a superstar company, then you will have lots of fans quickly. Another hook to obtain fans is to have just fantastically interesting and attractive little messages on your posts and tweets that add value to the lives of people. Again, experience shows in the United States that trying to sell or market in an obvious way drives customers and potential customers away from your posts and tweets. They may not unsubscribe from your group, but they will no longer read the posts or tweets. Giving them something valuable in your posts and tweets will build your relationship with them and make them read the next one in anticipation. Do not try to hit a home run; just get on base with your tweets and posts. Of course, occasionally having a giveaway by way of a contest, drawing, or the like will drive new people to your social media family. Coupons are also big draws.

Encourage your people in your social media group to share about your company and product with friends and family. People need reasons to share. They need value added from the posts, tweets, and information given from the company. It could be a valuable coupon that they receive when a friend signs up or just a fabulous piece of information that will make the life of their family safer, richer, or happier, something that they can forward. Corporate social media sites need to give people a reason to share the corporate brand with others.

THE USE OF SOCIAL MEDIA WITH HIGH-PERFORMANCE TEAMS

Social media do collaboration well. Such was one of the findings of a research study by the American Society for Training and Development (http://www.astd.org) and reported in a paper, "The Rise of Social Media: Enhancing Collaboration and Productivity Across Generations" (http://store.astd.org/Default.aspx?tabid=167&ProductId=21139):[4]

> High-performing organizations are more likely to use shared workspaces and wikis than low-performing firms. Workers at high-performing

organizations are also more likely to say that social media boosts collaboration and improves knowledge sharing.

According to an online article by one of us (H.J.H.), in QualityDigest.com:[5]

The disadvantage with teams is that they are inwardly focused. They are small groups that, if functioning correctly, strive to better other teams. Teams, by nature, are competitive. A team in the Pop Warner baseball league competes against all of the other teams in its league. We don't train people on a team to cooperate with other teams if doing so detracts from the team's performance. Just think how long a San Francisco Giants pitcher would last if he started throwing nice, easy pitches to the Los Angeles Dodgers batters so they could improve their batting averages.

Although teams are so necessary in low-performing organizations and in organizations that have problems with management trust, they're much less effective when the organization is well-managed. In well-managed organizations, trust runs high and people are empowered to make decisions on their own. These organizations focus on promoting teamwork between individuals. Teamwork can be pictured as a series of boxes connected together by outputs, much like a process (see Figure 11.1). Each individual (represented by a box) knows what the interface person needs, and adjusts his or her work to fulfill these needs. It is an attitude of "How can I help?" "What can I do to make your job easier?" and "How can we work together to produce more value for the whole organization?"

In an organization that establishes an environment supportive of empowerment and teamwork, connecting lines between individuals are formed and dissolved continuously as the individual's needs change. An organization that builds teamwork is a fluid organization, quick to react

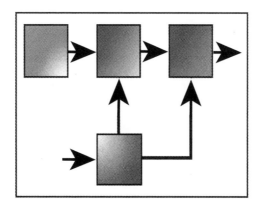

FIGURE 11.1
Teamwork network.

to business opportunities and personal requirements. These are organizations whose people feel that they make a difference. They are organizations that people are excited to work for, where team boundaries become dotted and individuals feel challenged.

Add to this insight recorded in 1999 to one made by Sharlyn Lauby on April 15, 2012, in her online article, "What Creates a High Performing Organization,"[6] and you will get the idea that using social media with high-performance teams as well as using them enterprise-wise is important to an environment supportive of empowerment and teamwork:

> Basically high-performing companies share more knowledge. Having more knowledge makes the company smarter and therefore, perform better. When you add social media tools enhancing the sharing of information … well, everything seems to just fall into place.

What about those low-performing organizations? Well, they still need teams and enterprise-wide social media, or they will bankrupt sooner rather than later. The hunch is that adding social media with training and solid implementation will aid these low-performance companies in becoming high-performing companies if they are in the early-to-prime stages of the life cycle of corporations.

SUMMARY

Social media take place on the World Wide Web, known as the Internet. Social media use technological communication tools that facilitate and allow continual online social interaction and communication of any and all that choose to participate. Social media have been continually expanding through advances made in the technology of modern electronic communications. Computers and the World Wide Web have created a form of communication that is quickly becoming available to all. It is revolutionary in that it connects everyone in a way that the telephone, newspapers, and postal service could not do.

The characteristics of social media are the following:

- Social media are the marketplace.

- The business use of social media is not cheaper.
- Social media cannot be controlled; they must be engaged (dealt with).
- Social media spread information widely and quickly.
- Social media are a level playing field and have been dubbed the democratization of the media.
- Online marketing is not about selling or advertising; it is first and foremost about building relationships that ultimately lead to the client choosing to buy and to recommend the brand to friends.

An array of new tools to help corporations produce social media content and to mine data from social media is now available. Here are a few of the current prominent categories of social web tools used in social media:

- Blogs—commentary and opinion in chronological order on a website
- Microblogs—a form of blogging for more frequent, brief updates, like Twitter
- RSS—a running feed of information on the computer web page like a ticker tape that syndicates current and updated information and streams it
- Photo sharing—allows photo uploads and sharing
- Podcast—digital audio that is distributed via the Internet
- Social news and bookmarking—the ability to save, organize, and share "bookmarked" web pages with others or to upload recipes, craft ideas, and the like and share
- Social networking—provides the ability to connect and share information with other online users
- Video sharing—provides the ability to upload and share videos
- Wikis—collaborative websites that allow users to contribute and edit the content (*wiki* is a Hawaiian word meaning "fast")

For a corporation or business to enter the social media for business purposes, such as marketing, a strategic plan is required. Even before the marketing plan is executed, a business should register or sign up with the major social media sites. The company must be totally committed to using social media, from the CEO down the line. Giving adequate training is mandatory. The approach in social media to the end user is nothing like the traditional approaches of sales and marketing. Some "unlearning" will be necessary to make the shift in paradigm. Direct and high-pressure selling and marketing in social media blow up in a corporation's face and create the opposite effect than the one intended. In social media, the corporation's objective is to connect and build relationships with other people and businesses on the World Wide Web. Sales come eventually, and the end user is in the driver's seat.

Social media enhance the work of high-performance teams. High-performing companies have less need for teams and benefit greatly from social media. Low-performing organizations need social media, but they also need to continue to use and develop teams.

Embrace something new and different for it will keep you young and vibrant.

—H. James Harrington

REFERENCES

1. University of San Francisco (n.d.). Internet Marketing. Advanced Social Media. http://www.usanfranonline.com/online-courses/social-media-training.aspx
2. Barnes, Nora G. and Lescault, Ava M. (2013). Higher Ed Documents Social Media ROI: New Communications Tools Are a Game Changer. http://www.umassd.edu/cmr/socialmedia/socialmediagamechanger/
3. Barnes, Nora G. and Lescault, Ava M. (2011). The 2011 Inc. 500 Social Media Update: Blogging Declines as Newer Tools Rule. http://www.umassd.edu/cmr/studiesandresearch/2011inc500socialmediaupdate/
4. American Society for Training and Development (2010). The Rise of Social Media: Enhancing Collaboration and Productivity across Generations. http://store.astd.org/Default.aspx?tabid=167&ProductId=21139
5. Harrington, H. James (1999). Beyond Teams: Teamwork. http://www.qualitydigest.com/aug99/html/body_perfrmnce.html
6. Lauby, Sharlyn (April 15, 2012). What Creates a High Performing Organization. http://www.hrbartender.com/2012/strategic/what-creates-a-high-performing-organization/

12

Social Communication
in the Workplace

Being sociable on the job is not wasting time; it's creating time.
Sociable colleagues produce more.

—R. D. Lewis

INTRODUCTION

It is often said that promotions are based more on who you know than on
what you know. The truth of the matter is, it is not who you know but who
likes you. Many deals that could not be closed in the conference room
are closed on the golf course. People who are technically competent are
signed to technical jobs. People who are interesting and engaging, who
handle casual conversation confidently, are the ones who are selected to
become managers and to lead the organization. These are the people who
develop friendships that lead to good cooperation from the people with
whom they work. Too many excellent people are technically competent
but are social outcasts because they cannot carry on casual conversations.
They go to the annual company Christmas party and hang around in the
corner because they have nothing to say that is of interest. Their social
conversation is completely exhausted once they talk about the weather. All
too often, we ignore the importance of the social side of the organizational
environment. This is a major mistake as it greatly limits the growth potential of many excellent people.

Do your colleagues like you? How much do they like you? How would
you know? Well, you might know if their faces brighten up when you

walk into the room or if they choose to sit by you at lunch or at meetings. Another indication would be if they tell you when they have a loved one who is sick or a family member is graduating from college. Do you know the name of their spouse? Do they say happy birthday to you on your birthday? If so, then they have a certain level of rapport with you.

Do you think these things are unimportant? If so, you would be wrong. These things are very important. For one thing, people who are social receive pay raises and increased responsibilities. Surprisingly, they also have a happier, longer life and better overall health.

Just do a search on the World Wide Web for the phrase "social interaction in the office" or a variation. You will discover significant references to the research relating to health and happiness attributed to social interaction at the workplace. In one search, the article "Low Social Interaction Harms Lifespan on a Par with Obesity, Smoking, Inactivity" was found on the website medicalnewstoday.com. It was a study done at Brigham Young University in Provo, Utah. It cited a 50% improvement in odds of survival with social interaction.[1] And on About.com, the piece "Study: Lack of Workplace Social Interaction Poses Health Risk" cited a 20-year study by Tel Aviv University researchers. The article, written by Michael Desmond, About.com guide, on October 4, 2011, quoted the study abstract from Tel Aviv University: "Only one main effect was found: the risk of mortality was significantly lower for those reporting high levels of peer social support."[2] We found an article on naturalnews.com, "New Research in Mind-Body Medicine Shows that Social Interaction Accelerates Healing." It was written by Mike Adams, the Health Ranger, NaturalNews editor. This study was done at Ohio State University and published in the journal *Psychoneuroendocrinology*. According to just one sentence fragment from this article: "Social interaction makes wounds heal faster."[3]

In one more of the 7.9 million hits received using the search phrase "social interaction in the office," an article was found on cnn.com, "Workplace Happiness: What's the Secret?" The article was written by Amanda Enayati and was special to CNN, published July 10, 2012. It states that a company can increase productivity by as much as 25% by doing simple things that do not involve a total reorganization:[4]

- Larger lunch tables to aid in increasing a worker's network led to higher performance over time.
- A tight-knit group that can help workers commiserate and cope with stress was a factor in increased performance.

- Diversity within the network with people who are not similar to who you are as a person was also a factor; the article suggested that one take time to walk around and explore the workplace.
- Reducing the amount of e-mail a worker receives was a factor; too much reduced productivity.

This research was done by Waber Research, which began when a man named Waber was a doctoral student at the Massachusetts Institute of Technology (MIT) Media Lab's Human Dynamics Laboratory. Waber founded his own company in 2011 and continued his research on workplace happiness.

So, let us provide a definition. What is social communication? It is the practice of friendly relations. Yes, that is it. Very basic and not very titillating is it? At least it does not appear too exciting or important on the surface, which is why it has been overlooked in the corporate planning and strategizing arena for so long. What is the truth about a practitioner of friendly relations? A friendly person, in the true sense of the word *friend*, is hard to find. A genuinely friendly person has a highly developed understanding of life, of people, and the need of a long-range view of life. They are practitioners of wisdom whether they know it or not. What enterprise would not want truly wise employees and leaders?

Social communication skills are also critical for every executive and manager for other reasons besides happiness and health. The authentically successful chief executive officers (CEOs) have mastered these skills. The level 5 leader as described by Jim Collins in the book *Good to Great*[5] is described this way: Builds enduring greatness through a "paradoxical blend of personal humility plus professional will" p. 13. And, those who read *Good to Great* know that the research showed that these leaders and CEOs were not afraid to mingle with employees and managers and be so much blended into the crowd they were unrecognized as the CEO and leaders of the company as they engaged the employees in conversation. These executives were not necessarily gregarious, but they interacted socially with the others in the company: listening, feeling, observing. Taking time to take time is a social skill, and it is important. Small talk is bigger than you think.

It is our experience that the weakness of many technical people is not related to management or technical skills but social communication, that is, friendly relations. More often than not, the person who moves ahead in the company is the individual who can carry on nontechnical conversations that develop personal relationships with other people in the company.

Take as an example our imaginary technical person, Sid:

> Sid works in the laboratory of Consolidated Medical Arts, Incorporated (a fictitious company, like Sid) and is brilliant as a lab technician. This man knows his chemistry and his tools. He works hard and stays abreast of developments and advancements in his field. Nevertheless, his reputation among his colleagues is that he is unfriendly and stuck-up. Sid would like to move into management. He is perennially passed up for promotions. The reason, unknown to Sid, is the lack of people skills. Sid is not social. Sid is not likeable.
>
> Sid's view of his situation is that he is the luckiest man in the world to be living his dream. He loves the state-of-the-art laboratory where he works, and he loves the challenges of his work. Even though he is the "go-to guy" when the boss needs something really important or difficult handled, he feels that no one appreciates what he does or likes him. He has some great ideas for improving the workflow and expanding operations and wishes he could have some input or be in the position of manager so he could implement them.

How can Sid change his situation? Sid needs to disengage from his test tubes long enough to study his fellow workers. He needs to disengage to the point of seeing them not in their roles in the laboratory but as people in his social network with things on their minds other than work at Consolidated Medical Arts. He needs to become social. And, he needs to do it in a natural, easy sort of way. Do you remember the iconic cop, Joe Friday, on the early TV show *Dragnet*, who told the lady who witnessed a crime to give him, "Just the facts, ma'am, just the facts"? To be social, it is, "Just say hello, Sid, just say hello"—and mean it. It is just focusing on the person you are greeting and then listening to what the person says back to you—or should say back to you but delete it. It is just being low key and relaxed, just being you without your work role dangling from every word, and just being genuinely friendly and cordial.

Let us say that you are like Sid. What should you do to engage in social interaction or to improve your social interaction? Let us explore some basics.

DECIDE TO BECOME SOCIAL

Deciding to make friends or expand your circle of friends with your workplace colleagues takes more courage for an introvert than for an extrovert, but nevertheless, it takes a definite decision. Extroverts want to connect, yet in a business situation, especially a new one, they might act differently than at home, school, or the civic club. Also, extroverts still need to think through the best way to "become social" at work. What we are saying is that you need to make a conscious decision to be socially interactive. For some, this will be easy. For people like Sid, this will take time, energy, and focus. Making life-changing decisions can be hard, especially for someone who has been in the workplace for some years and has a degree of success and comfort with the current setup.

Have you ever had to make a big decision? Was it easy? Did you have to go through a time of understanding and defining the decision, a time of listing the options, a time of prioritizing the options, and a time of deciding on the approach to take with your selected option? Of course you did. The same process happens with easier decisions. It goes unnoticed because an easy decision is one in which you have predetermined and predecided the answers to many of the steps in the decision-making process.

A good decision is eliminating everything that you do not want to do and committing to the one thing that you want to do. A good decision is as much about eliminating what one does not want to choose as it is about selecting what one wants to choose. A good decision makes a firm commitment to a desired outcome and then puts energy into accomplishing the objectives and goals that will lead to the outcome. A good decision contains an element of risk. The outcome in Sid's case is to first become aware of how fellow workers see him and feel about him and then to decide to change that situation by becoming known as a friendly person who is liked in the workplace. The objectives and goals are the steps taken to reach the outcome. Once reached, the new reality of being friendly in the workplace needs to be maintained and, of course, improved. As the brand Nike reminds us, "Just do it." In other words, you must jump out of your comfort zone and take the first step, then the second step, and then the third step. You will not be perfect when you start. You will stumble and make mistakes—no mistakes, no learning. Just do it. In no time at all, you should feel encouraged and comfortable about getting social in the workplace.

Here are some practical suggestions to help you start:

- Make a plan and write it out with your stated desired outcome and the objectives and goals for reaching it. This is helpful to most people, and taking time to write it out helps to think, especially in societies and cultures that favor written communication over oral communication, such as the United States. Also, talk to trusted persons about your desire to improve your social communication at work and ask for advice and ideas on formulating a plan.

- Start simple by engaging people in a social way. In Western culture, that means making eye contact and taking the initiative to say hello to people when they return your eye contact. This practice will be necessary in any plan to become social, so start on it immediately, even while formulating your plan. If you have some distracting mannerisms, like eye flutter or the closing of your eyes for several seconds while talking, practice not doing these things.

- In the Western world where we (the authors of this book) live, the handshake is the way of greeting. Be sure to have a firm and confident handshake. In other parts of the world, where other ways of greeting are used, do it appropriately and do it with ease and confidence.

- Practice breaking your concentration on work at regular intervals to study your work environment. Who is there? What are they doing? How are they dressed? What pictures do they display on their desks or in their cubicles? What expressions are on their faces? How do their desktops or workplaces look? Are these cluttered or organized? Are they eating while they work? To whom do they talk? Who calls them? Do they waste time, or are they workaholics? Are they basically positive persons or negative persons? When do they take their break? What are some of the habitual routines of the people around you? Use your own method of analyzing your fellow workers and the work environment. Ask yourself how you can use this information to be a friendlier, more helpful, and genuinely likable person in the workplace.

- When you are waiting for something, like the copy machine, take time to walk around a neighboring work area or department, watch the individuals at work, and introduce yourself to one new person, even if it is the mail clerk. Knowing a mail clerk can sometimes come in handy.

- C-level managers (the chiefs) should also walk around and meet a few mail clerks. Go incognito, that is, without your suit and Rolex on, and see if anyone knows or cares who you are. Learn about the people and departments that are affected by your decisions. Sure, it is a bit scary, but that is why you are paid the big bucks. Besides, research shows it could ultimately result in making your company so great that you might get your picture on the cover of *Forbes* magazine.

- Study how others interact with their colleagues and how they meet new people. What words and sentences do they use to open conversations? When do they choose to approach a new person? What tone of voice and body language do they use? Ask yourself if you could adapt and use any of these techniques and methods?
- In fact, take the previous practice a bit further. Find someone more skilled at being social in the workplace and make them your template and model. Watch what they do not do as well as what they do, and ask, "Why do they sometimes approach a person and sometimes give a person space?" You will find that friendship is as much about respecting a friend's privacy and space as it is about reaching out to the friend. Understanding the appropriate times to give space to a person or to interact with a person is a matter of experience and the wisdom gained from understanding yourself and others. When corporations or companies practice copying the industry best practice, it is called *benchmarking*. That is what you would be doing if you followed this suggestion.

BECOME OBJECTIVE ABOUT YOURSELF

A person like Sid must have the ability to be objective to have relationships with people. We have learned this fact by working with people, using psychological inventories, and by being human and making our own share of mistakes in personal relationships. It is an interesting fact that in some of the psychological testing instruments, like the Taylor-Johnson Temperament Analysis, a prediction can be made that a couple will fail in a relationship. This prediction is made when a person scores high in the trait of *subjectivity*, which indicates an absence of objectivity. To be subjective means that one cannot see things from another person's point of view. It means that one can only see the world and other persons as an extension of oneself. A person who cannot exercise objectivity cannot have quality relationships, in marriage or any other venue of life, and will increasingly be alone. In Sid's case, as in most of our situations, it is not that we cannot be objective. Rather, it is an underdeveloped use of the trait of *objectivity*.

What is objectivity? To be objective means that we can identify mentally and emotionally with an object outside ourselves and in our minds see things as though we were that object. That object, in the current discussion, would be a fellow worker. Sid could not see his fellow workers objectively, even though Sid did not have that problem with his dog, Frisco. He attended to Frisco's every need. Sometimes, we can be objective in one setting but not another. In some situations, we are highly subjective, and it takes an event that is painful to make us aware that we are being selfish. This can be true when a dad is dealing with his teenage son or a mother her teenage daughter. We want our children to be what we were not able to be or what we want them to be to impress our friends and family, and it takes a painful event to break us out of our subjectivity and into an objective frame of mind regarding our children. The same situation can happen in the workplace when we are highly invested in our position through years of training and experience or when our self-identity is tightly bound in our work.

An engineer and manager at a company that was involved in the aerospace industry, among other things, during the twentieth century, Rockwell International Corporation, told one of us (R.L.) an interesting statistic from that company. This conversation happened early in the 1990s when defined benefit pensions were still the standard retirement plan for large corporations. This manager was also used by his human resources (HR) department as a seminar leader for employees who were preparing to retire from Rockwell. He said that Rockwell's statistics showed that when a man retired, his average life expectancy was 1.5 years. When asked for the reason for this short average for life expectancy after retirement from Rockwell, the answer was that men's identities were their job. They did not know who they were when they retired. They had no reason to live. Therefore, he incorporated a section in his seminar urging men to develop outside hobbies and pursuits that would fill their lives after retirement.

This story illustrates how easily we can lose perspective on our lives. We can think that our work is the totality of who we are as a person instead of our work being simply a component of who we are as a person. We can sacrifice the other things of life that are equally important, or possibly more important, on the altar of our pursuit of our profession or job. By an objective view of ourselves, that is, by becoming aware of ourselves as though we were standing outside ourselves watching our lives and seeing ourselves as others see us, we can analyze ourselves in a detached, unemotional, logical way. We pointed out previously in this book that the ancient Greek philosophers taught the world that the beginning of knowledge was to know ourselves. "Know thyself" was the basic tenet. Today, we tell people in a less-classic, less-direct way, and in a way influenced more by twentieth-century psychobabble, that they have to be objective. Either way, the message is the same.

Communication was defined in this sweeping way in Chapter 1 of this book:

> The root word of communication is *common,* from which we derive the word *commune.* To have true communion, a group must respect, trust, and in the best-case scenario, care for one another. People must have virtue and be trustworthy people who keep their word. Good people make good communication, and good people commune with one another in a lasting way.

Once you decide to become objective and have spent time thinking about yourself, here is an exercise. Ask your colleagues how you can help them do their jobs more effectively. This is a nonthreatening way to phrase the question, "How would you like to see me change?" If your colleagues feel safe with you, they will give you the honest answer to this question. Thank them for their answers. They just gave you what corporations pay consultants thousands of dollars to discover: the truth about what employees think about their company and what is really going on in the workplace. Even if they hedge on their answer, they have still given you a clue to how they see you. They have helped you become objective. They have helped you to know who you are. And, you have made a bigger statement to them that will make them think about themselves. Every improvement effort has to have a starting point based in facts, and every improvement effort has to know the destination.

DISCOVER YOUR REASON FOR BEING

Why are you here? We do not think animals ask that question, but humans have always asked it. Animals seem to know why they are here; human beings have the capacity to decide on a purpose for life that gives an overall meaning to all we do and all that happens in life. What gives meaning to your life?

For some people, it is what they do for a living or a profession that gives them a sense of value in life. Recently, a friend, who had taken medical retirement as a policeman told about a man he met in his post-law-enforcement profession. In talking to this new client, it was revealed that he also was retired from law enforcement. This new client had spent his life as a deputy sheriff. When the client learned that the friend had also been in law enforcement, he reached down to the briefcase he was carrying and retrieved the plaque he had received on retirement and showed it to this friend. Then, he retrieved the policy manual from his former sheriff's department and began showing my friend the revisions he had made on the policy manual and the forms that he had revised or created. The client was really energized by sharing what he had done to the office policy manual, thinking that my friend was equally interested. However, my friend viewed it as a strange and uncomfortable experience and asked, "Do you think this man had an identity problem?"

Some mothers have this same identity problem because they do not have a reason for being that transcends being a mother. These moms want to be as involved in their adult children's lives as they were when they were children. As wonderful as family and children are to us, perhaps we need a larger reason for being that includes family while transcending it. In fact, a noble and lifelong reason for being should include our job, our family, our education, our recreation while transcending these components. The word *transcend* means to outdo or to exceed in excellence or extent (http://www.dictionary.com).

When we have a reason for being that transcends these components of our lives, it gives all the components of life a higher meaning. The correlative of this effect is that the misfortunes and disappointments of life assume a reduced meaning. Our identities should not be what we do. What we do should have meaning because of who we are and what we hold as ultimately important.

We cannot give you a reason for being. You should take responsibility for your own reason for being. Some think that a reason for being is entirely a personal decision open to change. Others believe it is preassigned to humanity, and our job is to discover it. We are not writing a philosophy or a religious book, yet maybe you should read what others have said about this subject. Our point is this: To be a friendly person in the workplace, you must overlook many of the shortcomings of others and forgive the wrongs against you that cannot be fixed. One cannot ultimately succeed if the reason for being on this earth is to work for your company, receive promotions, receive a plaque, and make more money than everyone else. What have you gained if you become CEO and you discover in the end that you are not an authentic person? Ultimately, you are just a lonely individual living in the past.

KNOW WHEN TO SHUT UP

Have you been present when a colleague embarrassed you because she revealed too much personal information? You instinctively knew that she had crossed an invisible line. You cringed for her because she had entered an unmentioned danger zone. She had found the outlying forbidden ground where extreme emotion and private information would cause her to be hurt, penalized, personally humiliated, or blackballed in the future. Men also do it, revealing too much information and then reacting, often, by riding the emotions of anger and control. Sharing too much about one's personal life to the wrong people, including political, religious, or philosophical convictions, can boomerang at the most inopportune moments. What are some other examples of subjects that likely should be avoided or mitigated and toned down?

- Your bad health condition, unless it is affecting your work and your supervisor needs to know in a private conversation
- Your pregnancy or the fact that you are trying to become pregnant
- Your personal family matters unless they are *not* private but celebratory, like your 30-year-old son getting a job and moving out
- Your job-hunting efforts
- Your second job
- The details of your divorce
- Your office love affairs

Basically, assume that anything you share will be repeated to bosses, fellow workers, the local television news, your family, and friends. Make sure you would not be embarrassed or hurt later by what you say in the office.

May we say one word here? The word is *e-mail*. E-mails never disappear. At least memos can be burned. E-mails can become like the scarlet letter of classic literature; you could end up wearing what you send in an e-mail for the rest of your life. Do not discuss private or sensitive information on your office e-mail system. Be careful about pictures and words posted on the social media you may use. Usually, we include some people from our workplace in our connections in our social media world.

On the other side of the coin, what should you do with private, potentially hurtful or embarrassing information that you are told by your fellow employees? May we suggest that you are to treat it like you would want to be treated if the situation were reversed? Be a good steward of the private information you are given by your colleagues at work.

Do you work in the beauty and hair-cutting industry? Then, you have seen the sharing of too much personal information disrupt lives repeatedly. Do you work in a school district or a school? You also have seen it. Do you work in the corporate world? Oh, yes, you have seen it, and they write feature films about it. Truth be told, not even a monastery that features the rule of total silence can avoid this problem because the monks would have become masters of using body language, hand signals, and written notes. We are afraid we have to give you the news that the only cure is TCB— taking care of business. Develop wisdom and self-control. Never cross the line into that forbidden ground yourself and never use sensitive information given to you as a knife to stab a colleague in the back.

When our friend Sid mastered social communication in the workplace, he learned that he could extend it to other areas of his work. Social communication is not just for interpersonal talk. It should be used in groups and teams as well as in public speaking.

USE SOCIAL COMMUNICATION IN A GROUP OR TEAM SETTING

Social communication is an essential part of becoming a high-performance team. Often, solutions and insights sought in a team setting come when the team is relaxed and informal, including times when the team members are talking about non-work-related subjects like the local sports team. Failure to build in times to allow the flow of social conversation in a team meeting would be a mistake. Sometimes, when the team moves off task, it is the unconscious, collective mind of the group trying to reveal a solution. Deliberately planning social times for the group when discussion of business is not the purpose of the meeting often leads to the production of great results and solutions. Also, team members who see each other regularly between formal team meetings often get ideas and solutions while casually talking.

Have you been introduced to the five stages of a team? Let's review:

1. Forming
2. Storming

3. Norming
4. Performing
5. Adjourning

The Harrington Institute and Dr. H. James Harrington (an author of this book) have provided much literature and training on high-performance teams and the breakdown of what quality communication in a team setting should include. What we are emphasizing here is that throughout these stages and sprinkled through the formal communication channels that are set up for teams, social communication should not be avoided or eliminated but embraced and seen as a lubricator of the other formal communication structures.

The team leader would do well to watch the body language and be aware of the emotional component of the team. Sometimes, doing a check of the subjective side of the team (i.e., the emotional side) helps clear personal feelings of team members out of the way, thus aiding the objective side of the team to more efficiently and effectively deal with the facts.

To do a check of the emotional status of team members, the leader could say something like, "Let's stop a moment and take a check on how we are feeling about our status and where we are in the process. Let's start with John and move clockwise. John, how do you feel?" If someone is highly emotional, do not be afraid. Even emotions that are being expressed physically, like a slightly raised voice or a tear in the eye, should not alarm the team unless the physical expressions turn to violence against a team member and become a danger to others. If someone loses control, giving the person a little shake on the arm and a word or two, like, "Okay, regain control," and then persisting in being in their personal space until they calm down will usually do the trick. Then, get the person to use words to describe what he or she is feeling and why.

The other way to sprinkle social communication throughout the team process is to introduce and allow humor during serious communication as a form of emotional release or a way to make a difficult point in a non-threatening way. Poking a little fun at one another or the issue at hand gives some distance to the subject, which helps the reasoning functions receive a different view. Not everyone has developed a sense of humor or has a knack for it, but it is such an important thing to have and use in communication, at least in the culture of the West, and perhaps in all cultures. Things that would cause division and hostility when said bluntly and seriously can be said using humor and be accepted. When we can laugh at ourselves or our situation, then it puts everything in perspective. Making ourselves the brunt of the joke can let people know that we are approachable and human.

USE SOCIAL COMMUNICATION IN PUBLIC SPEAKING

In a work situation, occasions often require the use of a speech or a talk. Presentations are used often in the workplace. The one technique in public speaking that makes the speaker interesting and that engages an audience is to interact with the audience. We call this becoming social during a public address or a speech. This is social communication in the midst of a monologue. To be sure, times to be formal do exist in public-speaking venues. Usually, these are used when addressing an audience that is prestigious or a formal part of a government, such as a court or legislature. However, even in these settings a touch of social interaction can be used to engage and endear.

When beginning the speech, if you know people in the group, as you might in a workplace setting, you break the ice by taking time to acknowledge the audience and specific persons. We call this activity *mutuality*. Mutualities would include saying, "Hello, how are you," when you first meet. It is the sharing of sentiments and establishing the rapport needed to become "mutual" to communicate. The introduction stage of a speech is not only to introduce the subject but also to engage the audience and gain their attention for the purpose of listening.

Taking time at the beginning to acknowledge key persons, or perhaps to say thank you to those who made the arrangements, will endear these people to you and help quiet the crowd and shift attention from talking to the people next to them to listening to you. During the talk or presentation, asking the audience to participate in some way to what you are saying will keep them engaged. Using humor directed at a person in the audience, walking among the audience and making eye contact, and asking rhetorical questions or asking for answers to questions from the audience are ways to use social interaction in public speaking. Sometimes, a speaker or presenter uses visual or auditory props to aid in the speech or presentation. If pictures or sound bites from people actually sitting in the audience or personally known by members of the audience can be used, then this technique of social interaction is doubly powerful.

Another way to use social interaction in a presentation or talk is to enlist audience members to participate in a role-play or short skit. This can be arranged ahead of time or done on the spot by enlisting volunteers. This connects with the audience and uses a powerful medium of communication at the same time.

Here are a few other ideas to add to the ones provided to engage an audience during a presentation:

- Ask a question of the audience and do not let silence scare you. Give them a few seconds to think. Someone will say something. If not, move on to the next question and come back to the first one later. You can make a joke over the fact that the audience was afraid of this unanswered question the first time.
- For long presentations, you might break the audience into small groups to work on a problem. Ask the groups to appoint a team reporter to report to the whole group.
- Come up with a totally original setup for your presentation rather than the usual, which is around tables or sitting in chairs facing front. This will loosen up the audience and get them wondering what you are going to do, a way of focusing attention.
- Use the whiteboard or flip chart instead of or in addition to using PowerPoint to present. PowerPoint is set and the slides cannot be changed during a presentation. By incorporating the use of a flip chart or whiteboard to record data or information from the audience, you will give the audience some control of the content.
- Insert times for taking questions throughout the session instead of waiting until the end. Also, allow people to write questions and send them to the front at any time. Be sure to read through these questions and answer them at some time during the training.
- If you have an expert in the audience, invite the expert to come to the podium for an interview. Interview the expert on the spot about a point you are making in your presentation.
- Based on the four basic personality types and the different learning styles, craft your questions and activities to each of the individual styles. Divide the style-specific questions or activities evenly throughout the total number of groups during each exercise. At the same time, rotate these style-specific questions and activities styles within each individual group over the course of your presentation so that each group gets to use each of the four styles during the day.

In closing, do not "say a speech"; converse with your audience. Do not "give a presentation"; guide your audience on an exploration of the subject. Social interaction has a place in public speaking.

WHAT HAPPENED TO SID?

Sid decided to become social, and he came up with a plan. Long story short, Sid is a graduate of the Dale Carnegie Leadership Training course, he is a member of Toastmasters, and he has learned to say hello at work and show up in the break room to celebrate birthdays. He joined a civic club and became involved in the church youth group with his children. He attends his kids' soccer games, which, as fate would have it, includes children of several people from his work, including his CEO. Sid is now manager of the laboratory.

SUMMARY

Social communication belongs in the workplace as well as in one's home life and private life. Social communication is the practice of friendly relations, and its use in the workplace is not optional for those who desire to go as far as they can go. Employees and management who are friendly and sociable receive more promotions and more pay and enjoy better health while being more productive.

If a person is not social in the workplace, this chapter will help with motivation to become social by explaining the benefits of doing so while discussing the major adjustments that the person will need to make in his or her inner self to become more sociable. Here are the strategic changes that need to be made in a person to allow more social interaction in relationships at work:

- **Deciding to become social.** Committing to the decision to change into a more social person requires leaving one's comfort zone and taking a risk of failure. All great decisions eliminate every other course of action while becoming married to just one.

- **Becoming objective about oneself.** This chapter discusses the difference between subjectivity and objectivity. A person who has too much subjectivity cannot become social. A person capable of being objective needs to use that ability to see him- or herself as their coworkers see him or her. Without this ability, no change is possible. Once a person becomes objective about the situation, then change is possible because the person discovers and clearly sees the starting point of change.
- **Discovering your reason for being.** Everyone needs a reason for living that transcends work, family, friends, or hobbies. Your reason for being answers the questions, "Who am I?" and "Why am I here?" To be social in the workplace, one has to see the importance, not only of oneself, but also of the people around oneself, including family and friends. Knowing one's reason for being aids in valuing other workers and keeping work for oneself in perspective. Without a transcendent reason for being, work can easily become the reason for being. Should this happen, then people can be seen as tools to be used for one's own selfish purpose. The end of this kind of life is lonely because the person is incapable of relating normally to people. The statistics show that two common results for this kind of person are a less-productive work life followed by a very short retirement life span.
- **Knowing when to shut up.** Sharing too much personal information in the workplace comes back to bite you. Do not do it. The litmus test would be to ask oneself, "Would I, my family, my boss, or my friends be embarrassed or hurt if what I shared was the lead story on the nightly news?" Share at your workplace with your fellow workers yet do not share highly personal and sensitive information.

In addition to these strategic qualities and practices in a person's inner life and daily practice, two other applications for social communication in the workplace are discussed:

- Using social communication in a group or team setting, and
- Using social communication in public speaking

REFERENCES

1. Brigham Young University, Provo, UT (28 July 2010). Low Social Interaction Harms Lifespan on a Par with Obesity, Smoking, Inactivity. http://www.medicalnews.today.com/articles/196056.php
2. Desmond, Michael (4 Oct 2011). Study: Lack of Workplace Social Interaction Poses Health Risk. http://homeoffice.about.com/b/2011/10/04/study-lack-of-workplace-social-interaction-poses-health-risk.htm
3. Adams, Mike (06 Aug. 2004). New Research Mind-Body Medicine Shows That Social Interaction Accelerates Healing. http://www.naturalnews.com/001619.html
4. Enayati, Amanda (10 July 2012). Workplace Happiness: What's the Secret? http://www.cnn.com/2012/07/09/living/secret-to-workplace-happiness
5. Collins, Jim (2001). *Good to Great: Why Some Companies Make the Leap … and Others Don't*, HarperCollins, New York.

13

Interviewing Guidelines

Everyone thinks they're good interviewers—very few are.

—H. J. Harrington

A job interview is like a dance with a stranger. Someone leads; someone follows; and both have to tell their friends how they thought it went. Sometimes it leads to marriage, but most of the time it doesn't.

—R. D. Lewis

INTRODUCTION

Every manager and most of the staff personnel need the ability to gather highly accurate and detailed information. This ability is critical to the success of the organization on every level and inside every function. It is particularly important when interviewing potential staff members, interviewing people to gain information related to a critical business problem, and when collecting customer-related information. These data-gathering techniques require knowledge on how to get individuals to share detailed information about themselves or the situation being investigated. A commonly used method of gathering information is the one-on-one, interactive interview.

Interviews are used to collect information from potential employees, internal and external process customers, people who execute the process at the task level, process owners and managers, and suppliers to the process. They are also used in benchmarking to acquire information on best industry practices. Customer market research is based on one-on-one interviews as well as telephone surveys and focus groups, all of which demand effective interviewing skills. One of the most important interviews is the interview with a potential staff member.

The purpose of this chapter is to provide the professional, manager, or process team member with the specific skills needed for successful interviewing. The focus will be on the one-on-one, face-to-face interview directed at obtaining information necessary to address organizational performance problems. However, most of the concepts covered will be relevant to telephone surveys, focus groups, job interviews, and direct-mail questionnaires.

PLANNING THE INTERVIEW

Information gathering occurs as an activity or step within a process. The objective of information gathering is to provide the data required to successfully execute that process of which it is a part. Within the context of this book, the objective of the process is generally to improve the quality—the effectiveness and efficiency—of the business processes. Processes include functions such as billing, inventory, marketing, payroll, accounting, planning, and hiring.

As with any process or activity, the first step in interviewing is to identify the customer: the individual who will use the information to be gathered. The next step is to determine the customer's requirements, including what information is needed and at what level of detail, in what format, and when.

The best approach for gathering that information should be selected. Methods include one-on-one interviews, focus groups, telephone surveys, and questionnaires, either direct-mail questionnaires or online questionnaires. With the advent of local and remote computing networks, interactive websites, and social media, surveys can be conducted electronically and online.

The information required and the collection method will be determined, to some extent, by the specific improvement process being used. For example, the process analysis technique (PAT) requires the use of one-on-one interviews, while benchmarking uses almost every approach mentioned.

Interview Guide Preparation

The next step is to create an interview guide. Key to the success of the interview, the guide serves several functions. It includes an introduction designed to cover all the preliminary information needed by the interviewee. It provides a logical and orderly sequence to the interview and ensures that questions are phrased in an easy-to-understand and consistent manner. It may also include a glossary of industry or process-specific terms for use during the interview. Most important, it provides a structure to ensure consistency across all the interviews.

The introduction will be read or paraphrased by the interviewer at the beginning of the interview. Some items that may be included in the introduction are as follows:

1. Why is the interview being conducted?
2. Who authorized the interview?
3. Who else is being interviewed (by title, job type, etc.)?
4. How was the interviewee selected and by whom?
5. How will the information be used?
6. Will the person be anonymous?
7. Will the person be quoted in the summary findings?
8. Will feedback of any kind be given to the person?
9. How might the person participate in the outcome of the process?
10. What is in it for the interviewee?
11. Why is highly detailed, accurate information important to the success of the interview?
12. How does the person play a key role in an important process?
13. Will the interviewee grant permission to tape-record the interview?
14. Does the interviewee know that it he or she is invited to ask questions about the interview process itself?

Generally, informational questions are located next in the guide, although some interviewers prefer to put them at the end of the guide. These questions include requests for information, such as the interviewee's name, job title, time in the job, time in the business, and department name and number.

The third section consists of the questions related to the subject of the interview. In constructing these questions, keep in mind the educational level and cultural background of the interviewees and use words and sentences at a level that they can easily understand and with which they are comfortable. If a series of interviews covers many levels in an organization, consider the use of multiple guides, each tailored to fit a specific level.

Avoid the use of jargon, if possible. If industry-specific or process-specific terms are necessary, be sure that the interviewee understands the accepted definitions. Include the definitions in an appendix to the guide for reference during the interview.

When the guide is complete, it may be appropriate to conduct a few pilot interviews. Two to four such interviews should be sufficient to determine how well the guide flows and how long the interviews will take. Additional topics may be identified and redundant questions eliminated. After the pilot interviews are completed, the interview guide can be revised and put in final form.

Selecting the People to Interview

Selecting the appropriate people to interview is key to the success of the improvement process. Specifically how to go about the selection of the appropriate people will depend on the improvement process employed. For example, if the interviews are in support of PAT, selecting candidates is relatively easy. Find out from the process managers who are best at doing the process. Consider who has been doing it longest and who is considered by the task-level people to be the most knowledgeable.

If the interviews are for market research purposes, selecting the appropriate interviewees becomes more difficult. Look for the people in the customer organization who make the buying decision, those who influence the buying decision, and those who use the product. All may have information appropriate to the interview.

Locating good interview candidates for benchmarking is challenging. Robert Camp devotes a large part of his book *Benchmarking*[1] to the process of identifying companies to contact and interview.

Scheduling the Interview

Scheduling interviews well in advance will give the interviewees the opportunity to fit the interviews into their calendars and to prepare adequately. When you are carrying out process analysis, it is best to do the interviews in the sequence in which the process is executed.

Individual interviews can run from 30 minutes to 2 hours or more. Experience will tell you how much time to allow for each interview.

Generally, interviewing managers takes more time than interviewing task-level people, and interviewing executives takes more time yet.

If you are unsure how much time will be required, plan more than you think will be needed. It is better to finish early than to run over the allotted time. After all, the interviewee may have to return to his or her regular assignment or may have another commitment.

Schedule only the number of interviews within a day that can be comfortably completed. Allow adequate time between interviews to make notes and relax for a few minutes. Interviewing takes a great deal of energy. Planning eight 1-hour interviews in a day will result in an interviewer exhausted by noon and ineffective in the afternoon sessions.

Location of the Interview

Select an interview site away from the subject's place of work, if possible. This helps eliminate interruptions and puts the interview on neutral ground. Hold the interview in a location where the person feels at ease. A third-shift shipping clerk will feel more comfortable, and probably not distracted, in a meeting room or office near the work area than he or she would in a walnut-paneled boardroom.

Avoid holding interviews in the interviewer's own office. This is particularly true if a manager is interviewing his or her own employees. Being interviewed in their manager's office tends to put the employees on the defensive and makes them more guarded in their responses.

A critical part of the interview is firsthand observation of the activity being performed. As a result, at least part of the interview will often be conducted in the work area.

Can interviews be conducted through electronic computing devices such as iPads, tablets, laptops, or smartphones by using FaceTime or web cameras and microphones? The younger generation will probably prefer the use of these virtual interview techniques, and some situations may require using this virtual method. However, nothing can replace being in the work setting in person. The more critical and important the interview, the more the in-person interview becomes mandatory.

Inviting the Interviewees

The next step is to inform the interviewees and invite them to participate. This can be done by the person's manager directly, by e-mail, or by letter. It can also be done in an informational meeting that includes the managers and the people to be interviewed. Ideally, a senior member of the management team will be involved in the invitation process. This may be done by an e-mail or a letter to the interviewees or through participation at the announcement meeting. Involvement by a senior manager demonstrates that top management supports the improvement process and the interviewee's participation in it.

However they are informed, the invitees need to understand the purpose of the interviews, when they will begin and end, where they are to be held, and what preparation is required of them.

What Is in It for the Interviewee?

If the interview is for a job, the benefits are obvious. The person either gets the job or loses it. If the interview is related to improving the process that involves the employee, it is a different matter. The people interviewed are making a significant contribution to the improvement process in which they are involved. Be sure they understand that they are providing valuable information and insight. They need to understand the benefit to them to make this effort.

If the interviewees are people who work within a business process, the opportunity to improve the process and be recognized for it may be enough. If they are customers of the process, the chance to improve their supplier's product or service may be sufficient. If they are suppliers, the opportunity to shape the process and to ensure that they can provide the appropriate input is of value.

In some cases, something more tangible may be needed. If the results of the interviews are not confidential, the participants may receive a copy of the final report. This may be in the form of a summary of the complete findings.

In the case of customer market research interviews and focus groups, the people interviewed often receive payment for their time. They may also receive gift certificates or merchandise. If the interviews are around mealtime, a free meal may be provided.

APPEARANCE IN THE INTERVIEW

Dress and personal appearance in an interview are important. Clothing in an interview for the interviewer should be similar to that of the subject of the interview or slightly more formal. For example, do not interview the chief executive officer in casual attire, or even a sports coat and slacks, unless that is the way he or she dresses.

On the other hand, do not appear on the plant floor during the third shift wearing a dark blue, pinstripe, three-piece business suit. Your interview subjects will probably be overpowered by the clothing and will not be willing to open up to you.

RECORDING THE INTERVIEW

Recording interviews is useful. It allows the interviewer to devote attention to what is being said without having to take extensive notes. In addition, other people can listen to the interview later.

Digital recorders are useful. They are small and easy to carry and handle during an interview. The storage capacity of these digital recorders will likely handle all the interviews you will care to do. Also, smartphones are now equipped with digital recorders and video recorders.

May we suggest your recording devise be black? We suggest this color because within a few minutes after the interview begins, the interviewee will be unaware of the presence of your recording device. (This is why professional photographers use cameras with black cases rather than polished metal.)

This may sound basic, but be sure to learn how to use the recording device thoroughly before starting interviews. Almost every professional interviewer has lost valuable information by becoming confused regarding which direction to move the pause control or the voice-activated switch.

Take a backup recording device and batteries to the interviews. Remember Murphy's law: If anything can go wrong, it will go wrong.

THE INTERVIEW

The first step in a successful interview is to arrive on time and to be prepared to start on time. A late arrival creates a negative impression and wastes valuable interview time. Promptness is particularly important with internal executives and customers. If at all possible, try to arrange for all phone calls and other interruptions to be held.

When meeting an interviewee, greet him or her warmly and with a smile and then invite the person to sit down, relax, and feel comfortable. The objective is to gain rapport and the person's trust and confidence.

When the interviewee is seated and comfortable, begin with a discussion of the interview guide and how you are going to use it. Then, read or paraphrase the introduction. Give the subject the opportunity to ask any questions about how the interview process works, how the information will be used, and the like. Doing this allows the interviewer to know the person better and begin to build stronger rapport.

Be sure to point out that it is important that you fully communicate with each other. Ask the interviewee to interrupt and request clarification if you use industry terminology or jargon that the subject does not understand.

If the interview is to be taped, this is an appropriate time to ask permission. Explain that the recording device will be used so that you can pay complete attention and not need to take detailed notes. Show the interviewee the tape recorder, turn it on, and then place it aside. Incidentally, in more than 12 years of interviewing, a request to record an interview has never been turned down. If the interviewee is uncomfortable and asks that the tape not be used or be turned off during the interview, do so immediately. Put the recorder away and take many good notes.

Now, begin questioning following the sequence called for in the interview guide. Remember, however, that the guide is just that. It does not necessarily have to be followed step by step. If the interviewee moves off the track but the information is useful, go along with the discussion. The guide is there as an aid to ensure that all the required points have been covered in the interview.

Keep in mind that the objective is to gather information as the interviewee perceives it, not as it really is or as the interviewer perceives it. There is always a temptation to correct an interviewee who responds with information the interviewer knows to be incorrect. The interviewer must resist the temptation to correct the person and must remember to keep gathering information.

If the interviewee has incorrect information, the interviewer should wait until the interview is over and then turn off the recorder to provide the correct information. At this point, you can recognize the person's perception and then ask a question like the following:

> I understand that you don't believe the firm provides good service. What
> are some examples of good service? What if you found that the firm did

provide that service? How would you like to have discovered that the service was available?

If the subject says something that is not entirely clear, stop and ask for clarification. It may be an important point or something on which future questions may be based.

Give your full attention to the subject. Deal with the subject as an equal. This will require flexibility since you may be interviewing first-line production and administrative employees as well as executives.

In addition to starting on schedule, make every effort to end the interview within the scheduled time. If the meeting cannot be completed on time, ask permission to continue or schedule another meeting to complete the interview later.

When the interview is complete, summarize the key points and give the interviewee an opportunity to make any closing comments. Be sure to tell the interviewee what happens next. Thank the interviewee for his or her time and the information that has been provided.

INTERVIEW FOLLOW-UP

At this point, you have a recording and possibly some written documentation and flowcharts. Follow up with a thank you letter to the interviewee and, if appropriate, to the person's manager or to the person who set up the interview.

This last point is key. Like any other skill, interviewing takes practice. Do it over and over again. Watch to see the results you obtain as you phrase questions in different ways. Be sensitive to the reaction to everything you do. Continue to improve your skills by observing results, changing your technique, and doing it again.

GAINING RAPPORT DURING THE INTERVIEW

High-quality communication begins by establishing rapport between the parties involved. Most sales texts suggest gaining rapport with a potential customer as the first step in an effective sales call. Establishing rapport is an equally important skill in the interview process.

Rapport is defined by the *New Webster's Dictionary* as "harmony" or "affinity." People who have rapport with one another feel comfortable together and tend to be open and honest in their communications. This is certainly a desirable situation in the interview process.

The question then becomes how the interviewer can gain a state of profound rapport with the interviewee in a very short period of time. The traditional approach is to try to get to know someone, to find a common ground. It entails asking questions such as, "Where are you from?" "What do you do for a living?" "What are your hobbies?" and even, "What is your astrological sign?" Although, given enough time and some common ground, this will sometimes work, it is not the fastest and most elegant approach.

Think of a time when you saw someone, or when you just exchanged a few words with someone, and immediately felt comfortable with that person. You might even have felt as if you had known the person for a long time. Did you ever wonder what it was that created this feeling of rapport so quickly?

John Grinder and Richard Bandler developed a communications model called *neurolinguistic programming (NLP)*. They did this by studying several prominent therapists and communicators. Some NLP concepts explain how a high level of rapport can be established quickly. Grinder and Bandler also described NLP in such a way that it can be easily learned and applied.

The first concept is called *matching and mirroring*. The idea is to help the interviewee to feel comfortable by matching his or her posture and breathing patterns. We have already discussed the idea of dressing at approximately the same level as the subject. This is a form of matching.

Observe the interviewee's posture. Is it erect, relaxed, or slouched? Is the person sitting with arms crossed or open? At what rate is he or she breathing? Does the person use his or her arms and hands expressively? It is not necessary to mirror the person exactly, just pick some specific characteristics and match them.

For practice, watch people at the next meeting or party you attend. People match and mirror unconsciously. They are not even aware of what they are doing. Practice it yourself and notice the difference in rapport.

Next, let us look at speech patterns. People represent their outside world by creating a map or model inside their brain. This model of the world is represented by pictures, sounds, words, and feelings. However, people generally favor one of the three methods of representation and are less aware of the other two. They have a favored *representational system* that is visual, auditory, or kinesthetic.

There are several ways to determine a person's favorite representational system. The easiest is to listen to the predicates they use most frequently. Visual people will say things like, "I see your point" or "I've got a big picture of that." Auditory people will say, "I hear you," "That really clicks with me," or "It sounds good to me." Kinesthetic people will use feeling-related words and will say things like, "I am comfortable with that," or "I really need to get a handle on that."

Another indicator of a person's favored representational system is his or her rate of speech. Visual people speak rapidly since they are describing pictures in their head. Auditory people speak in a more measured pace. Kinesthetic people tend to speak slowly.

People are most comfortable with people who are like them. Therefore, if you are interviewing someone who is visual, you will be better received if you speak quickly and use visual predicates. If your subject is auditory, use auditory predicates and speak clearly, distinctly, and at a medium pace; if the interviewee is kinesthetic, speak slowly and use predicates that relate to feelings.

Using physical and language matching will help build rapport with the interviewee quickly and help obtain the best information.

INTERVIEW TECHNIQUES FOR GAINING HIGHEST-QUALITY INFORMATION

In addition to the rapport-building skills already discussed, NLP describes questioning techniques that can be used to elicit the highly detailed and accurate information needed for quality improvement. These techniques are based on a model that Bandler and Grinder call the *meta model.*

To understand these skills, it is important to understand that the language we use is only a model of what is represented in the human brain. The representation in the human brain is made up of pictures, sounds, and feelings that represent a person's experience of the real world.

As questions are asked during an interview, these pictures, sounds, and feelings are described by the interviewee in words. Of course, the words alone do not provide a complete representation. It is up to the interviewer to know whether the words represent enough of the interviewer's model to be sufficient for the purposes of the interview.

If the words are not sufficient, the interviewer must know how to ask additional questions to create a richer description. This description will be about the needed customer requirements, internal business process, supplier's ability to provide the required input, executive's need for management data, or the employee's need for feedback.

The following examples demonstrate how the meta modeling technique can be used to gather additional information. Of course, in many of the examples other questions could be asked as well. Also, for ease of comprehension, the phrasing of the questions in these examples is simple and direct. The questions may be softened in a real interview.

Omissions

Often, interviewees omit information from their responses. For the interviewer to make sense of a sentence, he or she either must supply the omitted information inside his or her brain or must recognize that something is missing and ask for more information.

Here are some examples of omissions and the interview question designed to elicit the omitted material. (In the following examples, Qs are the interviewer's questions, and Rs are the interviewee's responses.)

Q: What is the biggest problem regarding the billing process?
R: The process costs too much.
Q: Too much compared to what?

Q: What prevents us from responding to the customer's request for additional information on the invoice?
R: The information is too expensive to provide.
Q: Too expensive compared to what?

Q: What prevents the customer invoices from getting out on time?
R: The computer system was down too often.
Q: How often was the system down? What is an acceptable level of downtime?

Notice that in each example, useful information was missing from the interviewee's response, and an additional question was asked to get that information. In a real situation, it might be necessary to ask several questions to obtain the level of detail required.

Unspecified Nouns

Interviewees frequently use nouns that are not specific enough. The word *vehicle* is less specific than *car;* the word *car* is less specific than *Ford;* the word *Ford* is less specific than *Taurus*. Less specific yet are words like *this, it,* and *they*. Here are examples of typical interview responses and the questions designed to obtain the additional information required:

Q: What is the biggest problem in the department?
R: The monthly report is out late again.
Q: Specifically, which monthly report is out late?

Q: What prevents the department from making its budget?
R: The workers are just not productive.
Q: Specifically, which workers are not productive?

Q: What is the next step in this process?
R: They bring the invoices to the data entry clerks.
Q: Who, specifically, brings the invoices?

Unspecific Verbs

Interviewees often use relatively unspecific verbs, although some may be more specific than others. *Move* is less specific, for example, than *carry*. To obtain more detail on unspecific verbs, simply ask "How?":

Q: What is the first thing that happens in the billing process?
R: The shipping notices come to the billing department.
Q: Specifically, how do the shipping notices come to the department?

Q: How are delivery schedules established?
R: Manufacturing forces us to conform to their build schedule.
Q: Specifically, how do they force you to conform?

Q: How do you know when a product ships?
R: Shipping and receiving lets us know.
Q: Specifically, how do they let you know?

Words Implying Necessity

Interviewees often use words that imply judgments, such as *should, should not, cannot,* and *must.* These imply a lack of choice. It is often useful to obtain additional information to understand what is behind these words and phrases. This understanding will help expand the number of choices available. Here are some examples of interventions that can be used to expand the interviewee's thinking and possibly generate additional options for process improvement:

Q: Can your department do the commission rate check function as part of the revised sales' payroll process?
R: No, we can't do that here.
Q: What prevents you from doing it?

Q: The customer needs to know the shipping date within 1 week of order submission. Can you provide it?
R: We should not give them that information.
Q: What would happen if you did? What keeps you from doing it?

Q: Checking part numbers against the master file is now done by computer. Can you stop doing it in this department?
R: We really should continue to do it.
Q: What would happen if you stopped?

Universal Quantifiers

Words such as *never, always, all,* and *everybody* are universal quantifiers and are usually broad generalizations. There are exceptions in almost every process or customer requirement. When an interviewer hears one of these universals, a flag should be raised. Here are suggested interventions to obtain the additional information required:

Q: Do you check the salesperson's employee number on each order to ensure correct commission payment?
R: No. The employee number is always on the order form.
Q: Always? Without checking, how are you certain?

Q: Mr. Customer, what is your requirement for color-coding on the packaging?

R: We will never have a need for that.

Q: Can you think of a time in the past when it might have been convenient to have color coding?

Q: How do the employees feel about implementing the new process?

R: They are all enthusiastically in favor of it.

Q: All? Who might possibly have their job affected in such a way to not favor it?

Rules

Rules are generalizations; they are made by the interviewee about what is right or wrong for everybody and are frequently judgmental. In fact, they are usually what interviewees believe to be true for themselves and to be true, in general, for everyone. The intervention is to ask "For whom?" Here are examples:

Q: How do you feel about the proposed new process?

R: We do it the right way now.

Q: Right for whom?

Q: How does having marketing quote delivery dates affect scheduling?

R: It is wrong for them to quote the dates.

Q: Wrong for whom?

Q: What is your reaction to the new employee recognition system?

R: It is wrong to recognize employees for doing their jobs.

Q: Wrong for whom?

Nominalizations

Words that have been transformed from verbs into nouns are called *nominalizations*. Changing a verb to a noun causes something that is ongoing to become something that is fixed. For example, the word *relationship* is a nominalization. The verb is *to relate*. It is much easier to think of changing the way we relate to a person, another department, or a union than it is to change a thing called a *relationship*.

Identifying a nominalization is easy to do. The first test is, "Can you put it in a box?" You can easily put a hat, a pencil, a computer, or even a car in a box if the box is big enough. It is difficult to put a relationship, a process, a projection, or a failure in a box.

The second test is to put the word in the phrase *an ongoing,* and if it fits, it is a nominalization. For example, *an ongoing house* does not fit, but *an ongoing process* does. Here are some examples of how nominalizations come up in normal business discussions and how to reframe them as verbs:

Q: What was the result of your quality circle work?
R: I didn't get any recognition.
Q: How would you like to be recognized?

Q: What prevents you from implementing the new inventory system?
R: We have a very poor relationship with the union.
Q: How can you improve the way you relate to the union?

Q: How are the employees reacting to the new system?
R: There is a great deal of confusion about their part in the implementation program.
Q: How can the announcement material be changed so that they will not be confused?

Cause and Effect

Interview subjects sometimes infer that something done by someone else—another group of people, another department, or customers—causes them to act in a certain way or to experience some inner feeling. The question to clarify the situation is simply to ask, "How does X cause Y?" Here are some examples:

Q: What is the primary reason for the excessive error rates?
R: The union workers cause most of the quality problems here.
Q: Specifically, how do the union workers cause the problems?

Q: What causes the high absentee rate in the department?
R: The management here makes us sick.
Q: How does management make you sick?

Q: The employee opinion survey indicates very low morale in this department. What seems to be the problem?

R: The salespeople keep everyone upset here.
Q: How do they keep things in turmoil?

One more NLP skill is needed to tie together all these techniques. In NLP terminology, it is called *sensory acuity*. Sensory acuity refers to a high level of awareness of what is going on in the interview process.

Pay close attention to the physical posture and breathing patterns of the interviewee in order to match and mirror. Be sensitive to words and sentences in order to use the meta model questions. Notice what part of the information is supplied by the interviewee and what part is implied by the interviewer. These are the NLP meta model techniques that can obtain the high-quality information needed from interviews with task-level employees, managers, customers, and suppliers. They require practice and a high level of awareness.

Many readers may already use these communication techniques, some very effectively. It is hard to imagine an executive, a manager, or a professional being effective without using most of these skills.

Our objective in describing them here is to heighten awareness, to encourage practicing them formally, and to observe the results. Coupled with the rapport-building skills, they will aid in becoming more effective in quality improvement efforts.

AFTER THE INTERVIEW

One of the key activities in improving your business processes is to observe the activity being performed. Immediately after the interview, the interviewer and the interviewee should go to the work area to observe the activity discussed in the interview. Observing the individual tasks being performed will stimulate additional questions. As one of us (H.J.H.) puts it, "You never really understand the activity until you do it yourself. If that isn't possible, the next best alternative is to observe the activity while it is being performed, and ask a lot of questions."

Documenting the information that was collected is the key part of the interview process. Do not put it off, no matter how good your notes are. Schedule some quiet time immediately after the interview to document the data collected and your impressions. Putting it off can distort the results.

It is too easy to forget an important point that can change your impression if you do not summarize them right after the interview.

SUMMARY

The interview process is a critical part of every manager's and every professional's assignment. Too many people do not prepare for the interview. A good interviewee can lead the interviewer away from the weak points if the interview is not well designed. Think of it as a final exam. Both the professor and the student need to be prepared if the individual's skills are to be evaluated fairly. We believe that interviewing an individual for a new work assignment presents a major challenge to the interviewer. Making an error in selecting an individual to perform a specific job activity can be extremely detrimental to both the individual and the organization.

A good interview question results in conversation not a short, quick response.

—H. James Harrington

REFERENCE

1. Camp, Robert C. (1989). *Benchmarking: The Search for Industry Best Practices The Lead to Superior Performance.* ASQC Quality Press, Milwaukee, WI.

Index